GROUNDED GLOBALISM

JAMES L. PEACOCK

Grounded Globalism

How the U.S. South Embraces the World

The University of Georgia Press | Athens and London

Set in Sabon by Bookcomp, Inc.
Printed and bound by Maple-Vail
The paper in this book meets the guidelines for
permanence and durability of the Committee on
Production Guidelines for Book Longevity of the
Council on Library Resources.

Printed in the United States of America
11 10 09 08 07 C 5 4 3 2 1

Library of Congress Cataloging-in-Publication Data

Peacock, James L.
Grounded globalism : how the U.S. South embraces
the world / James L. Peacock.
p. cm. — (The new Southern studies)
Includes bibliographical references and index.
ISBN-13: 978-0-8203-2868-3 (hardcover : alk. paper)
ISBN-10: 0-8203-2868-5 (hardcover : alk. paper)
1. Southern States—Civilization—21st century.
2. Southern States—Civilization.
3. Cosmopolitanism—Southern States.
4. Globalization—Social aspects—Southern States.
5. Group identity—Southern States.
6. Pluralism (Social sciences)—Civilization.
7. Regionalism—Southern States.
8. Southern States—Religion.
9. Political culture—Southern States.
10. Arts and society—Southern States.
I. Title. II. Series.
F216.2 .P425 2007
306.0975'090511—dc22   2007015453

British Library Cataloging-in-Publication Data available

To James L. Peacock Jr. (1912–2005)
and Sara Claire Peacock

Contents

Preface

In *Grounded Globalism: How the U.S. South Embraces the World,* I reflect on the U.S. South and southerners as they experience global forces today. I focus on attitudes, values, beliefs, and, ultimately, identities and meanings, asking how these are being shaped, how they are changing and abiding. The southern United States was not always the South: it formed its regional identity as our nation formed its national identity. Forged in the early nineteenth century, southern identity was hardened—for certain groups—by secession and war into a defiantly resistant sense of who we are and are not. Is this changing? Has the recent influx of immigrants and global forces strongly affected the deeply rooted sense of southern-ness? Has this impact been felt not only externally, in demographics and economics, but also internally, in identity?

The old question for the South and for southerners was, "How do I re-late to the nation?" The new question is, "How do I relate to the world? How do I respond to immigrants, the loss of jobs to foreign countries, to international terrorism? What shall I do about other cultures, new foods, new cars, new religions, new markets, new business opportunities or threats, new travel opportunities or dangers?"

My thesis is this. Globalization has the capacity to fundamentally trans-form the South—not only economically, demographically, and, perhaps, politically, but also culturally and psychologically—to create an identity at once global and regional. Among other things, grounding openness and global outreach in human-scale traditions and other regional norms can transform a crippling oppositional identity that has led the South or, at least, some southerners, to feel different from, opposed to, even scorned by the rest of the nation. Why does globalization transform this identity? Because the rest of the nation is no longer the dominant framework; the world is. The nation no longer dictates who you are and are not, who you should be and should not be, what matters and does not. One orients not only toward the nation but toward the world. To the extent that this is true, this is a major turning point for the South, perhaps equal to the point when, as its slave-based plantation economy spread westward in the nineteenth century, the South became the South.

When Sukarno was president of Indonesia in the late 1950s, he called for a *Konsepsi*, or "concept," to guide that new nation and make sense of its varied struggles. The one he came up with, "guided democracy" (*Demokrasi Terpimpin*), was flawed—more guided than democratic, crit-ics charged—but it served. My *Konsepsi* is "grounded globalism." Like guided democracy, grounded globalism is not tied to any grand social theory. It is a *Konsepsi*, a simple, workable perspective and also a guide to organizing a range of activities that has already helped link academic and broader work, bringing global and theoretical trends and scholar-ship into contact with local and grounded thought and action. Grounded globalism describes and prescribes syntheses of international connections and local traditions that are fueled by energies from both. With respect to the South, to ground globalism is to fuse a transformative global identity to a sustaining regional identity—a fusion that potentially enhances the strength of both identities and their potential for energizing action.

I acknowledge the assistance of certain foundations and organizations, including the Center for the Study of the American South, the University Center for International Studies, the Sonja Haynes Stone Center, and the Institute for the Arts and Humanities, all at the University of North Carolina at Chapel Hill, also the Mellon Foundation and especially the Rockefeller Foundation, all of which supported work pursuant to this book. The National Humanities Center in Research Triangle Park, North Carolina, directed by Geoffrey Harpham, afforded me the opportunity to spend eight months during 2003–4 drafting this book. I thank my wife, Florence; my daughters, Claire, Louly, and Natalie; and my mother and father. Other relatives, friends, colleagues, and students, including Vernon Burton, David Moltke-Hansen, Lothar Hönighaussen, Charles Joyner, Michael O'Brien, John Reed, Merle Black, Peter Coclanis, Robert Anthony, Bill Ferris, Harry Watson, and Jon Smith, informed this project with insight and wisdom, as did Ruel Tyson, with whom I have shared years of companionship in fieldwork and other collaborations. Especially, I thank Fred Appel, Derek Krisoff, Julius Raper, John Bagget, Michael Curtis, David Davis, Carie Little Hersh, Jon Smith, and David Perry for reading drafts or portions. Carie Little Hersh, Anil Bhattarai, Chen Zhu, and Sarah O'Callaghan provided assistance in checking references and other information. Throughout the preparation of this work, the collaboration of Carrie Matthews has been absolutely essential, and I am also in debt to Karen Carroll at the National Humanities Center and to Patrick Inman, Ruth Homrighaus, and Madelaine Cooke for their excellent editorial help. I thank the University of Georgia Press, especially Nancy Grayson, John McLeod, Derek Krissoff, and Jennifer Reichlin, for expert and enthusiastic support.

PART ONE

Orientation

Softly, do you not hear behind that the gallop of Jeb Stuart's cavalryman? Do you not recognize it for the native gesture of an incurably romantic people, enamoured before all else of the magnificent and the spectacular?
WILBUR J. CASH, *The Mind of the South*

CHAPTER ONE

A Model

ON MEMORIAL DAY 2006, I take a taxi from Raleigh-Durham airport after flying in from Dothan, in South Alabama. The driver has a trainee with him. "Where are you guys from?" I ask. "Guess," answers the trainee. "Eritrea," I suggest, succeeding after two wrong tries. "Where's he from?" the trainee asks, referring to the driver. "Ethiopia," I guess immediately. I then ask, "How can this be? You are supposed to be enemies!" (In 1998 I had flown out of the Eritrea airport just before it was bombed by Ethiopia.) They explain that they are friends, that it's only the politicians who make the two countries enemies, that they are the same in culture. As we pass Barbee Chapel Road, I say, "Look at that sign when you return." The sign says, "Adopted by the Sons of Confederate Veterans." We discuss the parallels between the U.S Civil War and Eritrea's secession from Ethiopia and the resulting war until we arrive at my house.

Such parallels are so frequent that patterns are easy to identify. The focus of my study is the U.S. South, but I begin by describing a model of movement from regional to global identity; it applies in the U.S. South but also elsewhere.

This model features seven steps:

1. regional identity,
2. opposition to national identity,
3. rebellion,
4. defeat,
5. resentment and oppression,
6. transmutation by global identity, and
7. grounding of that identity in sustained regional identity.

Consider each element.

The first step, *regional identity*, is the development of an identity with a locale within a nation or with a region spanning national boundaries. The Committee on Regions of the European Union formally recognizes such identities: Scottish, Bavarian, Irish, Basque, and so forth. These are identities with distinct languages and customs, with ethnicities associated with a locale. Such identities can be poignant. "Will he ne'er come back again," sing Scots or would-be Scots about Bonnie Prince Charlie and the Battle of Culloden. Just before the airport bombing in Asmara, Eritrea, in 1998, following Eritrea's secession from Ethiopia, thousands of Eritreans danced in the streets, celebrating independent nationhood. The Kurds are another ethnic group with a strong independent identity, as we discover in Iraq.

Regional identity can become *actively oppositional to national identity*—not just different from but opposed to and, at least in the region's own perception, oppressed by the rest of the nation and the central government. This is step two. The Uigur, a large Muslim population in West China who are culturally and linguistically different from the Han majority, provide an example. The Uigur experience prejudice from the majority Han Chinese, who are colonizing them by sending Han officials to the Uiger region and pressuring the Uiger to learn Chinese and forsake their own culture. The Chinese justify these actions by deeming Muslims terrorists.

This sense of opposition can lead to step three, *rebellion*. The Irish, the Basques, and the U.S. South have all rebelled, as have the outer islands of Indonesia against the central government on Java. Rebellion may be peaceful, expressed as calls for political clout or autonomy or independence in literature, songs, sermons, and the mass media, or it may be violent, expressed as guerilla activity, bombings, or extortion. Rebellion in the form of secession is a drastic step that may lead to war. The U.S. Civil War is one example, but hundreds of others have occurred. As in the Civil War, the seceding region fights for independence, while the nation strives to preserve the union.

The next step, *defeat*, is a likely though not inevitable outcome, likely because the nation is larger than the seceding element and boasts a standing army. Defeat and its aftermath breed *resentment* (step five). The Lost Cause of the South is an example. The North's military victory and subsequent occupation of the South was countered by the South's claims to a kind of moral victory; the South had fought heroically against great odds, and their pride was transmuted into nigh-religious glorification of the Confederate leaders. Germans felt somewhat that way about their defeat in World War I and the outcome of the Versailles Treaty, sentiments that nurtured Nazism. Palestinians resent Israeli occupation of their territory; Iraqis resent U.S. occupation of theirs. Occupation, oppression, and resentment can persist for decades, for centuries. A group may come to cherish these injuries, anchor its sense of identity to them, and keep their memory alive in many ways.[1] Loss, resentment, and a sense of destiny can motivate almost any endeavor. For example, on the eve of World War I, many small southern towns built out-of-place skyscrapers even though they "had little more use for them than a hog has for a morning coat"; W. J. Cash compared the construction of these buildings to a cavalry charge, a "native gesture of an incurably romantic people."[2]

The ignominy of defeat, together with occupation, slavery, and other bitter legacies of the U.S. South, is what C. Vann Woodward famously called the "burden of history."[3] Racism, and the resultant oppression of African Americans within the South, is a correlate to that burden, in the sense that the colonized region, oppressed, then colonizes internally, oppresses. Oppositionality within the nation (the United States) is correlated with dualism within the region (the South).

How do you lift that burden and get past that blockage? Direct reconciliation was attempted to heal the wounds of conflict. In one effort, Fitzgerald, Georgia, was founded as a colony in the South. P. H. Fitzgerald, a veteran's pension attorney, led the creation of a new community in South Georgia, near where the capture of Jefferson Davis ended the war. Streets were named for Northern and Southern generals: Grant, Lee, Jackson, and others. Though settled by Union veterans, Fitzgerald is now indistinguishable from neighboring towns except that it does proclaim itself, quietly, a community of reconciliation.

Pickett's Charge was restaged decades after the war was over and resulted in the reconciliation of former enemies, by then aged veterans. The reenactment began with the Confederates' charge across the meadow and up the hill toward Northern guns, but ended with the old soldiers embracing. The Camp David negotiations attempted to resolve differences between Israelis and Palestinians but without such a reconciliation. Irish Catholics and Protestants in Ulster achieved, with the help of mediation by priests and others, a remarkable truce and a certain reunification despite divisions still signaled by geographic separations.

Unfortunately, reunion does not erase resentments. Resentments persist. David Davis depicts the deep ambivalence some southerners felt about fighting for the U.S. military in World War I. One man who won a medal for valor was ashamed to show it to his father, who would have dismissed it as a Yankee medal. The burden of history is still heavy.[4]

A further possibility, which may enhance reconciliation within the nation, is to transcend the framework that produced the conflict in the first place. For the South and for other regions this framework was national.

A substitute framework may be global, or at least transnational (partially global), as in the European Union. When the national framework is replaced, relations within the nation, including long-standing intranational conflicts, become less central in one's cognitive map. On a global cognitive map, regions such as the South and the North appear smaller—no longer *the* elements of a dualistic division but *some* elements among many within a much wider horizon.

This broadening of framework would seem to be common sense, akin to the saying that travel broadens, allowing one to see the forest rather than just the trees, but the effect is powerful, deep, and profound. A favorite anecdote I have used in teaching anthropology illustrates the shift. A worker in a wheelbarrow factory pushes his wheelbarrow through the gate each evening. The guards inspect the wheelbarrow; finding nothing, they let him pass. After months, they discover he is stealing wheelbarrows. Their mistake was to look too narrowly, to see the contents but not the container, the parts but not the whole. The truth is discovered when they broaden their field of awareness. Such cognitive transformation is potentially profound; it is basic to religious insight, to Buddha's enlightenment under the Bodhi tree, to Saul's revelation on the road to Damascus, and to the conversions and mysticisms of many traditions: particulars matter less when attention shifts to a broader, deeper, more ultimate or universal framework. Here the transformation pertains to place-based identity. When one thinks in global terms and identifies with the world, divisions within a national framework matter less. This cognitive transformation, I argue, can lighten the burden of history that results from step five.

A *global perspective* (step six) can emancipate at various levels, not only mentally, the way one thinks and views the world, but also in more embodied modes, such as in social relationships and in one's sense of place, how space is experienced, and how that experience is embodied. "He's not heavy, he's my brother," declared one character to another in the film *Boys Town* as he carried his crippled younger brother. Can a burden be lightened by a heightened meaning it acquires? Of course, as anyone knows who has carried a backpack as part of a hike; I remember walking some forty miles in twenty-four hours through the Luangwa Valley in Zambia, not noticing the pack in the excitement of striding through the wilderness in the company of noble human beings such as Kwonga, an old friend of my friend Stuart Marks, encountering such wondrous sights as hippopotami and crocodiles on the river and a politician in a purple suit. Frail persons can lift automobiles off injured passengers when emotions are heightened. The Javanese express a metaphysical dimension to this lightening of burdens in a belief about the leather puppet that represents the clown-god Semar; they say that when the puppeteer adds Semar to his box of puppets, the box grows lighter. Semar represents a transcendental reality: higher than our heads, lower than our feet, he is the highest god but also the lowliest, most earthy servant-clown, fat, short, grotesque, and androgynous, wise and powerful, comprehending all dualisms. It makes sense that he lightens burdens, for he comprehends, frames, and subsumes them in broader, deeper, more ultimately meaningful realities than the mere physical force of a felt weight. The logic and the experience of lightening, or even banishing, a burden of history by entering a broader, deeper, global reality is analogous.

Our local public radio station tells the story of Michelle and Thomas Nikundiwe. When they were in the Peace Corps in Uganda, Michelle worked in a hospital where she met a small boy, Ishmael. He was so weak and undernourished that he was confined to his bed. She "fell in love with him" and determined to adopt him. Against enormous obstacles—legal, medical, and social—she, now with the support of Thomas, finally succeeded in winning a ruling by the supreme court of Uganda that permitted them to do so. This experience joins a global and a personal relationship. She fell in love with a person, which drew her into a cross-cultural global relationship, thence, one can infer, into an expanded cross-cultural identity as a mother bridging nations. Her description of the process, while matter-of-fact, is passionate and even spiritual, suggesting a kind of transcendence of a narrower identity.[5]

This story moves, however, from a romantic, passionate transcendence to realities with which Michelle must cope: first, the obstacles concerning adoption, next, the work required by motherhood itself. Adoption across cultures, and the commitments, adjustments, and personal growth it entails, illustrates several points. A global identity is transformative, drawing a person into a deeper, broader experience. Such an experience is empowered and mediated by concrete situations, in this case, by immersion in a foreign culture and the entry into a new relationship as a result of falling in love, whether with a child or another adult. And, finally, that transformative identification is sustainable only by integrating it into one's life, into a family and a community that are localized somewhere, including home regions. This last step illustrates one kind of grounding.

A global perspective can be inspiring, transformative, and energizing, but alone it is insufficient, unbalanced, and insubstantial. Sometimes termed cosmopolitanism or internationalism, a purely global identity may be observed at jet-set cocktail parties, at scholarly conferences, and in airports among those few who spend more time in transit than at home anywhere. Rootless globalism lives in cyberspace and in the air, alongside messages and persons transported around the world by electronic technology and by airplanes. It surfaces in our thoughts as we wrap our minds around faraway news stories, conflicts, disasters, and celebrations we cannot see up close, cannot touch or hear or smell. It is difficult to embody so vast and abstract a perspective, to weave it into our experience. As the example of adoption illustrates, to integrate into one's life a global relationship, even one that is deeply personal, demands work and struggle.

While an abstracted global world may excite and emancipate us, most of us seek also to come down to earth. We treasure having a home or at least a locale; we want territorial attachment of some kind. If you doubt this, ask those who do not have it, such as the estimated 20.8 million refugees, asylum seekers, and others, expelled from their homes by various wars and natural disasters, currently aided by the United Nations High Commission for Refugees.[6] When our attachment to our home territories is threatened or challenged, we feel it sharply. Both drastic threats—of terrorism, invasion, or natural disaster, for example—and gradual changes—alterations in the landscape or the density of human settlement—remind us of what we stand to lose if we lose our place on earth. Even peaceful invasions, by immigrants or new ways of life, elicit reactions that are defensive and protective of one's locale. In this so-called global era, people still seek and find a place to call home. The model must acknowledge this, for an abiding desire for home affects how we understand global processes and attempt to shape them. This is the final step in the model: some kind of *grounding* in locale is necessary to human beings. Once we achieve global identities, we must ground them, integrating the global and the local in some way that energizes and sustains both.

There is a further possible dimension of this model. Not simply historical or chronological, this model is also psychological. That is what the psychoanalyst Erik Erikson meant by psychohistory: a certain pattern of oppression and rebellion not only is enacted in each life history but is then reenacted again and again in the psyches of individuals and in the cultures and histories of societies. In the mid-twentieth century, he examined the once well-known life stories of a German dictator (Hitler) and of a Russian poet (Gorky) and explained that these stories revealed what paths people from each nation expected their lives to take. German families, he said, were ruled by authoritarian fathers whose sons rebel then mature into authoritarian fathers themselves, retaining a certain rebelliousness internally, in their psyches, that found external expression in Nazism. A film version of Gorky's life juxtaposed love for a primordial motherland, the *mir*, with oppression by father figures, culminating in a kind of crucifixion of a young hero who is crushed by the weight of a cross. German psychohistory fueled sadism, while Russians expected to suffer cruelty at the hands of their fathers and leaders. Although these particular analyses can be criticized as simplistic, a strength of these and later psychoanalytical approaches is to suggest the power of historical experience—individual and collective—in shaping psychological complexes and cultural symbols.[7]

We can tell a broadly similar story about the U.S. South. Historical experiences of regional identity, defeat, and resentment were elaborated into "the myth of the Lost Cause" and replayed again and again in individual psyches, in popular culture, in historical mythologies such as *Birth of a Nation* and *Gone with the Wind*, and in the stories told about Sherman's march. These historically seared and culturally elaborated memories and myths helped keep resentments fresh and left southerners with a chip on their collective shoulder. Insults or slights, seemingly trivial but tapping into what Freud termed "the narcissism of minor differences," can prompt quick reactions. At the extreme, one could speak of a regional neurosis that mixes pride with shame and can paralyze, blocking and sapping creative energy. Such a neurosis is the real burden of history.[8]

What can cure such neuroses and free us from reactivity and obsession? What I think I have observed in process throughout the South is an engagement with the world that serves as a sort of therapy and bears a slight resemblance to the classic model of psychoanalysis. Freud sought freedom through "making the unconscious conscious," exploring life history to lay bare traumas of the past that inflict repressions in the present. Our model is somewhat analogous to such therapy, but where Freud worked with individuals, our model refers to a group, the region, and it adds sixth and seventh steps that extend globally. Step six entails the broadening of identity, subsuming and absorbing earlier steps and blockages into a global identity that can embody, crystallize, and integrate earlier steps. In step seven, however, the psyche must reintegrate the new identity into older ones and into older and less transcendent contexts; neosoutherners must integrate global identities with our region and its history and realities, both psychologically and culturally.

One could envision this model as a dance (think of Pilobolus, Paul Taylor, Alvin Ailey, or many others whose choreography is more subtle than this but akin). Steps one to five end with the dancer bent under a burden. In step six, the dancer throws it off, or perhaps is joined by others who share it, shrinking its weight on any single back: this is the global step. In step seven, all the dancers must land safely and anchor their feet again, each shouldering in his or her own space that new global burden, now shared but still the responsibility of each and embodied by each: this is grounding.

Steps one to five are well known, whether in the U.S. South or elsewhere. This is background for the main thesis, step six, which asserts that globalism transmutes the patterns set in the first five steps and energizes the changes. Step seven describes whether and how such globalism is grounded within a localized context. Steps six and seven are at once the most debatable and the most important parts of my argument.

Significance

The model is potentially significant because it describes and prescribes a way past the paralyzing and dangerous aspects of regionalism, a way to move beyond the burden of history. That way is through globalism. The useful possibilities of globalism are plumbed and prescribed, while I reject ungrounded globalism as untenable and risky.

With respect specifically to the U.S. South, this approach is significant because it offers a distinctive perspective from which to understand the South and through which southerners can understand themselves. Southerners and the South have been seen for two centuries largely within a national framework. The South is labeled, by both nonsoutherners and southerners, as different from, lesser than (poorer, lazier, dumber than) the North; hence the South resents the North, and the North decries the South. Seeing the South as part of a global world potentially emancipates both South and North because sectional opposition—diminishing, perhaps, but still latent and salient—is dwarfed by larger world issues and patterns.

Thinking beyond this South to other Souths and Norths, two major dangers are apparent. One is a too-narrow particularism, the other, a too-broad globalism. Particularism, whether regional, ethnic, or religious, has generated the most pervasive conflicts since the Cold War period, namely terrorism and locally based wars, of which an estimated forty are currently being fought. Globalism, if unanchored, threatens every dimension of life, economic, political, and cultural: outsourcing, disengagement from government, and lack of identity can all flow from ungrounded globalism and globalization.

The solution to these problems lies in recognizing the strength of both forces, global and local, and in clearing paths that productively and creatively unite them; grounded globalism is one effort at mapping such a path. The U.S. South is one example.

Format

Our task now is to explore this model empirically.[9] We proceed as follows. First, we sketch our context, the South, as a regional identity that is globalizing. Second, we describe how this process is evidenced in thinking: how are southerners thinking globally? Third, we illustrate the effects of globalization in two particular domains, race and place. Fourth, we ask what challenges this process poses for meaning in religion, especially, and in less formal kinds of subjectivities, such as dreams and the arts. Fifth, we reflect on how it plays out in politics. Finally, we assess the model in light of the evidence and illustrations. How viable is that model, what do we learn, and what is implied for action and for future study?

While all seven steps of the model frame our analysis, emphasis is on the last two: creating and then grounding a global identity.

I'm a black Japanese, wee-o

I'm a black German, wee-o!

REVEREND H. D. DENNIS, Vicksburg, Miss.

CHAPTER TWO

The South as/in the World

JAMES MCBRIDE DABBS once wrote: "Of all the Americans, the Southerner is the most at home in the world. Or at least in the South, which, because of his very at-homeness, he is apt to confuse with the world."[1] Dabbs used the word "world" in the first sentence to refer to the southerner's immediate surroundings, as in "worldly," "of this world," "the world around us," what German philosophers, with whom Dabbs was familiar, term *Umwelt*. Dabbs's southerner is "at home" where he is and is not driven to change it. Dabbs contrasts this southerner with the Puritan New Englander, who saw the world as inadequate, even evil, not a place in which to feel at home but, instead, a space to change to match a vision of some superior, ideal other world.[2] (Dabbs characterized himself as someone who came to feel at home in the South Carolina Low Country by imbibing its spirits.)

In the second sentence, "the world" is distinguished from "the South" by Dabbs, though presumably not by the southerner, who confuses the two. The confusion has two dimensions: "South" as a cultural identity with "world" as reality, and "South" as a regional identity with "world" in its physical entirety. Dabbs's southerner projects his southernness not only onto immediate surroundings but also onto the globe, experiencing the wider world in terms of his own immediate and regional one, rendering the global as local. He does this because of the South's "at-homeness," a quality of coziness, familiarity, and welcoming intimacy.

Why start with Dabbs? Because Dabbs evokes a certain South, once upon a time, somewhere, yet he implies possibilities for other Souths, at other times, elsewhere. Who is this southerner, where is he (if it is Dabbs), what is he, ethnically, racially, and, more important, philosophically? Dabbs was writing a half-century ago; he was an elderly white male, living in Low Country South Carolina. I heard him speak around that time, in company with another, younger, white male, Donald Shriver, a North Carolinian who was an activist in civil rights and, later, president of Union Theological Seminary in New York City. Shriver spoke from the standpoint of social gospel, espousing civic change; Dabbs characterized his own theology as combining Presbyterian and Low Country pantheism. He did not, as I recall, emphasize change but instead depicted a psychology of southerners—of at least some of them, one presumes white males, perhaps elderly, low country, like himself or his friends and kinfolk. His evocation may be limited, but it is grounded, and in its grounded construction of experience, it opens the possibility of globalism. Dabbs captures an insularity of the South (of at least a certain South, once upon a time, somewhere), yet he presciently hints at an encounter between this insularity and the world. Might Dabbs's southerner extend that feeling of intimacy to the wider world, and even welcome the wider world as part of the South?

Starting with Dabbs, we start with a certain kind of southerner and a certain kind of South, or at least a depiction of it. One could also start with others—younger, older, black, Native American, immigrant, female, more conservative, liberal, or radical, less intellectual, more so.

W. E. B. DuBois, for example, is historically and intellectually seminal. He is often compared with Booker T. Washington, who represented a pragmatic approach in contrast to DuBois's critical and intellectual perspective. DuBois was not born a southerner, yet he lived in the South. He was also global. He saw parallels and unions between Gandhi's independence movement in India and moves toward the emancipation of blacks nationally and regionally in the United States. He wrote a novel pairing an Indian heroine and an African American hero that expressed such a parallel. Among his confidants was the German-born anthropologist Franz Boas, whose student Zora Neale Hurston wrote brilliantly about her own African American milieu in Florida as an ethnographic counterpoint to Boas's European background. Heiress to DuBois and Hurston is Johnnetta Cole, also African American (though with a German grandfather) and likewise a globalist (see chapter 4). Moving into a localist–popular cultural stream, one could evoke southern hip-hop, as does Riché Richardson, where a regional emphasis within the black musical world parallels white regionalism. There are many Souths within the South, and many kinds of southerners.

Reverend Dennis, who provides the epigraph for this section, is a black preacher in his nineties who has built, in Vicksburg, Mississippi, a cathedral, a work of art assembled from found objects, reminiscent to me of Gaudí's Sagrada Familia in Barcelona; his professed identity rejects racial stereotype. Born in Mississippi, he left home at age twelve, riding on the cow catcher of a train for several miles, and began to pick cotton to support himself. He was so hungry that he stole pecans from an orchard and was caught by the white farmer, who adopted him. Much later he had contact with Japanese immigrants and learned bricklaying from German prisoners of war in Alabama; they inspired the epigraph. He is married to Margaret, of Native American Mississippi background. She, too, is in her nineties.[3] They exhibit global openness.

I start with Dabbs because his book portrays an ur-southerner, an archetypal southerner. That southerner, one suspects, is implicitly white male, upper class of lowland, perhaps even Low Country, vintage of a

certain period. He may also speak for a spectrum of other southerners—
Cajun, African American, poor white, mountain, bayou, western, border-
state, historic, contemporary, old, young—who share some, if not all, of
the perspective Dabbs evokes, but it is useful to start with this purer, sim-
pler type, the "real" southerner—constructed but not reconstructed. Such
a one inherits, creates, and sustains an image, an identity, a myth, and a
reality. He may be oppositional, refusing to cave in to liberal, national,
northern, so-called rational, progressive, modern, or postmodern virtues.
Nonetheless, he is, Dabbs claims, at home in the world, comfortable with
a certain regional identity. These ur-southerners are still a majority, perhaps, though diminishing. Genteel and polite, some are hard core, stub-
born, last ditch, the ones who are the test cases: they have the most to lose,
in a way, by globalizing or otherwise transforming their regional identity.
Yet, I argue, they are changing through connections with a wider world
and, in doing so, press toward consequences that affect all southerners.
My thesis then entails the "education of James McBride Dabbs," after
the model of Henry Adams—an evolution of a type of regional identity
as part of a larger movement toward a global southern identity.

Before proceeding, let us remind ourselves of this larger movement.

My model holds that identifying with the world as a whole, rather than
with just the region, nation, or some other smaller unit, transforms identity. Since the southern United States became the South, which is to say
a region within a nation, it has defined itself oppositionally within a national frame of reference against the North and the rest of the country.
I argue that the South is shifting its frame of reference from nation to
world, causing its oppositional identity to diminish.

The questions, then, are these: First, what evidence indicates such a shift
from opposition within the nation to identity with the world? Second,
what are the effects or implications of this shift, to the extent it occurs?
Third, why is it important?

Concerning the shift from opposition, I explore a range of evidence,
from individual opinions to events and institutions. Concerning the effects of the shift, I focus on three pillars of southern identity: race, place,

and religion. Race and ethnicity are no longer dualistic in the South; immigration and cultural influences that express global forces have made the pattern of southern race and ethnicity more pluralistic. Place itself—a sense of the region as a special space—is perceived increasingly as affected by global forces. And, in deconstructing the pillars of an older identity, one constructs new identities, which require new frames of meaning. Such frames inform and are informed by religion.

Why is the shift to globalism important? For the South itself, these transformations are fundamental. Deeply rooted identities are uprooted and new ones are planted. The region is potentially emancipated from crippling resentments based in sectional division yet is set loose in a dangerous and confusing global galaxy. Whatever understanding we achieve of this paradigm shift can inform other Souths everywhere that undergo similar processes.

Connections by Experience: The U.S. South and Other Souths

A Philippine/Indonesian couple left Southeast Asia forty years ago and settled in North Carolina. They lived for several years in Kentucky but have moved back to North Carolina, where they hold a house blessing for their new home. A hundred or so of their fellow Catholics, primarily Filipinos, join them in a ceremony led by a priest who comes annually from the Philippines for this purpose. They chant Hail Marys and other sayings in a printed English-language liturgy in this house in a neighborhood called Historic Hillsborough.

How might Dabbs's concept apply to them? They are southern. Their son is actually "Tar Heel born and Tar Heel bred." They are not Tar Heel born and bred but may be "Tar Heel until they are dead." Do they feel about the South as Dabbs suggests southerners do? Perhaps even more so, since the world really is their universe: they have relatives in Indonesia and in other countries as well as in Texas, so they can feel at home, to a degree, around the world as well as in the South.

There is another dimension to their identity. My wife and I lived with the man's family forty years ago in Surabaya, Indonesia. His mother and father we called *ibu* ("mother") and *bapak* ("father"), as is the custom. We share family bonds. What does this do to our identity as southerners? Do we feel the at-homeness, the sense of the world as part of our universe, as a result of our experience? Do they? That is, does the shared experience—our having lived in his country, in fact in his hometown, and their having lived in ours—give us all a sense of connection between our respective Souths?

A few miles away from the couple's house, people gather in a backyard for a performance of Lillian Hellman's *The Little Foxes*. The play is set in the Deep South a century ago. It portrays a family in conflict over change stimulated by Mr. Marshall from Chicago, whom some of the family's members lure south to open a cotton mill. One of them, the wise but dying Horace, knows what is coming and opposes it. His wife, Regina, embraces it and yearns to go to Chicago. The characters represent the preglobal racially dualistic South: blacks, whites, and a Yankee; by and large, so do the cast and the audience. The Indonesians are not present, though they are represented, once removed, by the set designer, who happens to import antiquities from Indonesia. Were they present, they would be amused to consider that they are now the Yankees, the newcomers.

I am a further example. Two formative experiences for me are these: growing up in the South (minus three years spent moving around the country when my father was in the army) and doing research while living in a *kampong* in Indonesia. The first was long and still endures; the second, followed by other stints, was intense. I was born in Montgomery, Alabama, but moved quickly to South Georgia, where my father, an electrical engineer, worked for the Georgia Power Company until he was called into the army, eventually to take part in D-Day. During the war, my mother, sister, and I moved everywhere my father did, from Massachusetts to Oklahoma and points in between, until he went overseas and I went to a country school in Alabama, the fourth school I had attended for the first grade. After the war, we returned to South Georgia, where my father joined a partner to start an electrical contracting business; I worked as a laborer for it, beginning at age thirteen, as did the partner's son. My most vivid memory of those years are what we thought of as brilliant tricks, such as jumping off a truck as it went down the highway.

This was the postwar and pre–civil rights South. Schools were segregated racially, as were churches and just about everything else; when I got on a bus as a teenager and moved toward the back seats, the driver called me to the front. (Contrast this with Julius Chambers' recollection [see chap. 8] of being forced not only to the back of the bus but out of it when too many whites got on to fit in the available seats.)

That South was also preglobalization. Cars and trucks were not Toyotas, Hondas, and Mercedes, but Chevrolets, Buicks, and Studebakers. Foods were not Chinese or Mexican, but ice tea, cornbread, and fried chicken. Religion was Protestant, primarily. Foreigners and foreignness were the occasional immigrant and often connected to the military: war brides and stories of foreign wars. Karl Von Ebenstein was allegedly a German refugee with a degree from the University of Heidelberg. He was a celebrated newcomer in the small Georgia town where I lived, invited to speak to civic clubs about his German experience. He became engaged to a local English teacher. He turned out to be an imposter, however, an escaped convict from Tennessee. Later he was inserted as a character in an epic told by the "boys" about a Don Juan who is recognized by a woman in a morgue who sees not his face but his phallus and intones, "Karl Von Ebenstein is dead." My point is that a foreigner, even a fake one, made an impression.

Study abroad was rare, and I did not do it in college, but I did study German language for three years (perhaps inspired by Karl Von Ebenstein) and seized an opportunity to go to Germany for five weeks before graduate school. After three years of graduate courses, including Indonesian language classes, I passed my doctoral oral exams, won a research grant, got married, and went to Indonesia for a year of fieldwork; wrote a dissertation, got a doctorate at Harvard University, and got a job. After years of teaching, research, and administration, I began various organizational initiatives, some of which helped connect my two formative experiences—the South and other Souths, including Indonesia, in a global or transnational perspective and project.

My first fieldwork was in Surabaya, Indonesia, in 1962, on the eve of what President Sukarno called "the year of living dangerously." My wife and I lived in a *kampong*—a settlement, partly of squatters—with the family mentioned above, at a time when the Indonesian Communist party was the third largest in the world—after China and the Soviet Union—and living conditions were desperate. In 1965 came Gestapu, the massacre of approximately a million alleged Communists by the army and some Muslims. In 1970 I went back to Indonesia to live and work with Muhammadiya, a reform-oriented, somewhat fundamentalist Islamic movement that now claims some thirty-five million members. I maintain connections to Indonesia and neighboring Singapore.

After working with Muhammadiya, I returned to UNC–Chapel Hill, where I met Ruel Tyson, later to be chair of the Religious Studies department in the years I chaired the Anthropology department there. We began fieldwork together on Christian groups in the U.S. South. From 1975 to 1979 we worked with white, black, and Native American Pentecostals in the Piedmont, followed later by some students: Kim Diehl, for example, brought a diverse ethnic background and a woman's perspective to that of two white males, and Marsha Michie became deeply engaged with one congregation, rising to be a worship leader. In the eighties, we worked with Primitive Baptists in the Blue Ridge Mountains, teaming with Daniel and Beverly Patterson. In 1989, in conjunction with the Institute for Arts and Humanities, which Ruel founded, we convened a conference, "The Multicultural South," exploring the then emerging influx of immigrants to the South, several of whom chaired discussion groups. This led to a series of Rockefeller Foundation seminars and conferences on global, comparative, and multicultural aspects of the U.S. South, held from 1990 to 2006, initially in cooperation with the Institute and then with the Center for the Study of the American South, the Sonja Haynes Stone Center for Black Culture and History, and the University Center for International Studies. These gatherings brought together students, faculty, and laity to explore aspects of the changing South. These efforts joined others by colleagues at UNC and elsewhere, such as studies of the African diaspora by Colin Palmer, Karla Slocum, and others.

Michael Jordan, a geography major, was my research assistant for a study of the 1984 Olympics, when he played on the U.S. basketball team; he had thought-provoking insights about that global experience. Traveling in Curacao, Aruba, Jamaica, Puerto Rico, and Haiti with my late colleague Julia Crane, I became aware of Caribbean connections to the U.S. South and of Latin American connections, especially through my son-in-law Emiliano Corral, who is writing a dissertation comparing steel production in Birmingham, Alabama, and Monterrey, Mexico.

Aside from my research, I was exposed to issues of diversity and multiculturalism through certain quasi-administrative engagements. Most intense was the issue of the Sonja Hanes Stone Center. Sonja was a professor of African American studies who died suddenly in 1991. Her close friend Margo Crawford was director of the black culture center at UNC and proposed, with fervent support from Sonja's students and others, to honor Sonja by creating a building to house the center. Distilling grief at Sonja's death and other passions, this idea inspired a movement that envisioned the building as free standing, symbolizing independence in contrast to a history of enslaved or servile dependence on white rule. Chancellor Paul Hardin espoused a liberal view. He was influenced by a letter Martin Luther King wrote to Hardin's father, a Methodist bishop, when King was in the Birmingham jail. Hardin called for "a forum not a fortress," thus favoring dialogue and integration between black and white rather than a separated black culture center seen as a return to segregation. Advocates of a separated center saw his view differently, as refusing to honor their independent and equal status. Various actions were undertaken: a march on the chancellor's house, a rally led by Spike Lee at the basketball arena, and a student camp out in shacks labeled "Hardin's plantation." Various faculty and administrators, black and white, who favored the forum position received death threats. At that time I was chair of the university's faculty senate, and I came forward to support the independent center, with the proviso that it be "inclusive," that is, connected to diverse groups. A panel was created that included Dolores Jordan, Michael Jordan's mother; Harvey Gantt, the architect who in 1990 nearly defeated

Senator Jesse Helms; Richard "Stick" Williams, later chair of the university's board of trustees; and me. Eventually I chaired a committee to draft
a proposal for the center, and a slightly revised version that changed the
proposed location—an issue that itself evoked passionate debate, including suicide pacts—was approved by the trustees. The center was built. It
is chaired by Joseph Jordan, who does link it to various groups, cultures,
and issues in an inclusive fashion. The process distilled and revealed to me
crucial issues about diversity in today's South. During that same period,
I was helping to create a center for study of the South. Later, for seven
years, I directed a center for international studies. These efforts merged
academic and administrative goals and connected regional, global, and
ethnic domains.

Statistics and Snapshots

Population growth in the South and in the bordering states of Kentucky,
Oklahoma, Texas, and West Virginia has led the nation for nearly four
decades; one-third of all Americans now live in the region.[4] In 1970 the
demographics of these fourteen states were 1.4 percent Hispanic, 27.5
percent black, and 72.5 percent white and other. (The last group combines non-Hispanic whites and all other non–African American ethnic
groups; roughly 3 percent of this group falls into the Asian census category, 2 percent are mixed race, and 1 percent are Native American.) By
2003 the proportions had shifted to 13.6 percent Hispanic, 17.8 percent
black, and 64.6 percent white and other, the result of migrations and
of differences in fertility and age pyramids. Between the censuses of 1990
and 2000, 75 percent of the 1.6 million increase in the region's population
age sixty-five and older was in the white and other category, as was 70
percent of the 5.8 million increase between ages forty-five and sixty-five.
By contrast, 62 percent of the 3.5 million increase between ages twenty
and forty-four was in the Hispanic category, as was 50 percent of the
3.3 million increase in the population under twenty. Although the large
populations of Texas and Florida and their high percentages of Hispanics
skew the figures somewhat, rapid increases in Hispanic populations char-

acterize most southern states: growth between 1990 and 2000 equaled or exceeded 300 percent in North Carolina, Arkansas, and Georgia, topped 200 percent in Tennessee and South Carolina, and fell to less than 50 percent only in West Virginia and Louisiana. African Americans are seeing their proportion of the population decrease, despite their having migrated to the South since the mid-1980s in greater numbers than to any other region of the country. [5]

Led by its younger, more evangelical denominations, Protestant Christianity still dominates religion in the South; however, although the number of mainline Protestants increased slightly, at least among whites, between 1970 and 2002, there are now more Catholics in the South than mainstream Protestants. A large part of Catholicism's rapid growth is due to Hispanic immigration: by 2003, the South was home to 32 percent of the country's Hispanic Catholics.

The economy of the South is characterized less and less by basic manufacturing (although the construction industry is expanding) and more and more by services and advanced industries. The number of employees in the service sector has increased 45 percent in the last twenty years, both in high-paying professions and in low-wage jobs. The South produces less tobacco, textiles, and furniture, and more electronic equipment, industrial machinery, and pharmaceuticals. Although its poverty rate is still high relative to the rest of the nation—and Appalachia, the Black Belt, the Mississippi Delta, and the Rio Grande Valley remain particularly poor—a smaller proportion of the population lives in poverty than previously. One engine of the transformed economy are several sprawling, cosmopolitan megacities whose economic and population growth far exceed that of the rest of the region, such centers for commerce, biotechnology, banking, and entertainment as Atlanta, the Research Triangle, Charlotte, and Orlando.

The migration of retirees and job seekers to the region has increased its political power as well as its economic weight. Between the early 1970s and the present, the South gained twenty additional seats in the House of Representatives. At the same time, the region became truly bipartisan:

seventeen of twenty-eight state legislative bodies are led by Democrats, while a majority of the fourteen governors are Republicans.

In short, the region has changed notably in the past quarter century while retaining some key features. The economy has grown, and its emphasis has shifted from manufacturing to service and high-tech; more and more southerners live or work in cities; the polity has become more Republican; and religion remains predominantly Protestant, especially evangelical Protestant, although Catholicism, especially Latino Catholicism, has surged. The South is no longer divided ethnically into black and white: immigrants, especially Hispanics, have made a predominantly biracial population an obviously multiethnic one. C. Vann Woodward wrote of the "bulldozer revolution" that followed World War II, bringing most southerners within a county's width of a superhighway and changing the typical landscape from farms to suburbs.[6] That revolution has continued. As the barriers to travel fell, and as economic opportunities grew, southerners became less rural, less likely to be poor, and more likely to have been born outside the South.

A few scenes suggest the ways new diversities and global influences are entering southern life. In the parking lot of the Carolina Inn in Chapel Hill, North Carolina, an American man in a wedding costume mounts a white horse (in India, it would be an elephant, people say) and, to a driving drumbeat, leads a procession toward his in-laws-to-be, who are from India but have lived in Fayetteville, North Carolina, for many years. After they receive him, he sits on a throne in a structure outside the inn, separated from his bride by a white cloth. His father- and mother-in-law-to-be pay homage to him. Then the bride arrives, followed by her entourage of family and friends, including sorority sisters from the University of North Carolina, where she and the groom met in medical school. The music is Indian and European; the drummer and instrumentalists and singers are from Houston. Pachelbel is played by a cellist, violist, violinist, and clarinetist from among the groom's family and friends. The priest, from Fayetteville, chants in Sanskrit while explaining—in English—traditions of twenty-five hundred years involving Rama,

Sita, and Ganesh. The groom's forebears on his father's side are Mormon, his great-grandmother having moved from Denmark to Utah; his mother is from Colorado. He has grown up in Chapel Hill, his bride, in Fayetteville. Such events occur often now in the South, reflecting the influx of migrants from Asia and Latin America or elsewhere.

As the world comes to the South, the South goes out to the world by many means. CNN, Bank of America, Coca-Cola, and the like connect the South to international markets. SAS, a North Carolina business intelligence company, provided the software for the 2000 census of China. The military departs from Fort Bragg, Fort Benning, or Camp Lejeune for Iraq or Afghanistan. Fulbright scholars (William Fulbright was a senator from Arkansas) go everywhere, as do missionaries. The comings and goings connect, of course. "Why are you here?" the native asks the immigrant. "Because you were there," replies the immigrant, referring to our global intrusions—colonial, commercial, and cultural.

Even business transactions reflect odd couplings of southern and immigrant cultures. William B. Harrison Jr., CEO of JP Morgan Chase and Company, is described in a *New York Times* article as "the last gentleman on Wall Street," speaking with a "soft southern accent" like a character from the work of Walker Percy. James Dimon, Harrison's new business partner courtesy of a recent merger, is described as descended from Greek immigrants. He bounds past Harrison's outstretched hand without shaking it, "a clumsy prank" suggesting to the reporter a clash between southern gentleman and brash immigrant. The awkward juncture is intriguing. [7]

Assimilation is apparent in many spheres. The Order of the Golden Fleece, an honorary society at UNC–Chapel Hill, holds a commemorative celebration to mark its first century. The contrast between the oldest alumni and the newest initiates is striking. The older ones are white males; the younger ones (some of them women) include African Americans, East Asians, South Asians, and even minorities within these, such as the creator of the Hmong Student Organization. (Hmong have settled in the mountains near Marion, North Carolina). Thinking of a fraternity—less esteemed than the Golden Fleece—that I joined in college, I had this experience in Mississippi. I met a family from Lebanon. The grandfather, small and bent, had migrated and was most "ethnic," the father had a southern accent, and the son turned out to belong to an Ole Miss chapter of my fraternity. We gave each other the secret grip.

The private sphere, too, seems to point to signs of assimilation. Kindnesses often arrive with immigrants, it seems, or remain with minorities (a pattern Jesus noted in the parable of the Good Samaritan). Why, in recent years, have those who come to help when our car breaks down on the road almost always been immigrants? An African gave my wife and me a jump start in Georgia, another African (from Liberia) helped out in North Carolina, and a Korean in Georgia gave us a place to sleep in her trailer. In South Carolina recently, an elderly black man offered us a ride in his truck full of cabbages, which we did not need to accept because a white couple finally stopped and provided a cell phone to call AAA. These are all accidental globalisms.

Various organizations—for example, the University Center for International Studies at the University of North Carolina at Chapel Hill, the International Visitors Bureau, and Sister Cities—have sprung up to foster global connections to the South. Huge enterprises reach out from the South to connect globally. In Asmara, Eritrea, where our international center aids the national university, I watched an interview on Atlanta-based CNN. The interviewee was Phil Knight, the CEO of Nike, commenting on Nike's decision to enforce labor standards for subcontractor factories.[8] This decision resulted from a UNC student protest of unfair labor practices; the protests led to the creation of a committee that recommended solutions Knight accepted. UNC, reportedly the largest university licensor, permits use of its insignia by more than five hundred corporations, most of which subcontract with factories abroad. A state university, allied strongly with local communities, alumni, and citizens, is strongly global in connection. A Georgian, Rutledge "Rut" Tufts, began the initiative at UNC and then led the formation of national consortia that monitored thousands of factories globally. Rut was managing the Fair Labor Association based in Washington, D.C., when he died in 2006.

Other globalisms are by-products of sports-related initiatives, as well.

Trevor Graham, from Jamaica, has created a track and field center in Raleigh, North Carolina. Justin Gatlin, who is tied for the world record in the hundred meters, trains in the Triangle with Graham. Olympic champions Marion Jones and Tim Montgomery reside in North Carolina. Attack 81, a high school soccer team in Alabama, wins national championships and fields a player, Catherine Reddick, on the U.S. Olympic soccer team. The top American javelin thrower is from Monroe, Louisiana, and trains in Athens, Georgia; the top miler is from Virginia. Carly Patterson, the first U.S. woman gymnast to win the Olympic gold medal in two decades, is from Texas. The Carolina Hurricanes won the Stanley Cup in 2006 by defeating the hockey team from Edmonton, Canada. The South, known for football, a largely U.S. pastime, takes a lead in international sports. A regional and national focus in sports expands to a global one.

Globalization also pervades technology. As the world comes to the South, the South goes to the world. In an article in the *Georgia Engineer*, the editor emphasizes the link between technology and international relations: alluding to the Olympics in Atlanta and the G-8 summit on St. Simons Island, he writes, "Our world has grown considerably smaller, as foreign ownership, subsidiary relationships, and strategic alliances have helped bridge the once formidable gap between Georgia and the rest of the world."[9]

Civil War and Civil Rights

When Malcolm X made his pilgrimage to Mecca, he experienced brotherhood among Muslims of many ethnicities and nationalities. He found acceptance that he had not experienced as an African American in the United States. Islam integrates ethnicities and nationalities not only in Mecca but at local mosques in the South as elsewhere. African Americans join Egyptians, Pakistanis, Malaysians, and others in a global religion that harkens back to African forebears for some and bypasses Christian traditions still seen by some as the religion of the white majority.

African Americans at mosques in the South experience a special dimension of globalism. Not only do they join a global community—in this instance, the *umma*, the world community of Islam—they are welcomed as brothers, as fellow Muslims. As Muslims, global citizens, they are emancipated from the second-class citizenship often imposed on them by racism. (Here, for the moment, we disregard the discrimination and hierarchy within the world of Islam; for example, Arabs in general and those of Arab descent in particular who are termed Syed, signifying descent from the Prophet Muhammad, sometimes claim a higher status than other ethnicities including Africans.)

Wearing a hat that says "Guatemala," Chuck Stone, an eminent journalist and teacher, claims his African American heritage as one aspect of a multicultural identity. Norris Johnson, an anthropologist, has a passionate research interest in Japanese gardens. Alice Walker, whose book *The Color Purple* was derived from her Georgia hometown, has moved to California, traveled to South America, and taken a shamanistic turn. Senator Howard Lee, from Lithonia, Georgia, is a leader in internationalizing K–12 schools in North Carolina. Each of these persons of African American descent has embraced an international or global interest or identity. So doing, they resemble Malcolm X and other African American Muslims who go beyond a minority identity or minority issues to connect globally. The point is not that such persons compensate for a minority status at home by gaining a global status abroad or at home, though such a motive may be relevant sometimes, but rather that a minority background may infuse a global identity with special meanings.

Such meanings are not necessarily restricted to African Americans. John, a poor white from the Blue Ridge Mountains, was determined to go to Japan. He told me he had saved a thousand dollars, and I told him that a thousand dollars would last only a few days and that he should not go unless he had a job assured. He went anyway, supported himself for a year, and had a fine time. Southerners marked as minorities within the region by their ties to the region's most isolated or poorest parts—the Appalachians in this example—plausibly respond strongly to the global pull and are able to leapfrog over their marginal standing within the regional society to embrace a global connection or experience.

This brings us to the Civil War. Minority status, a sense of being treated as inferior, different from, lesser than a majority, can derive not only from ethnicity or location but also from history, as in military defeat; thus we encounter again the question of identities derived from the Civil War. While visiting a cosmopolitan Charlotte lawyer in his seventies, head of several international organizations and widely traveled, I notice two pictures of Robert E. Lee. I ask him about them, and he explains that he was a member of Kappa Alpha, the college fraternity which explicitly professes a southern, Confederate identity. On some campuses KA men dress in Confederate uniforms and ride horses, imitating cavalry while women don period gowns. My oldest daughter was born in Boston but had southern ancestry and moved to the South when she was about four years old. She asked me, plaintively, "Am I a Confederate?" Her sister, my youngest, however, seemingly couldn't care less. She asked, when she was about eight, "Who won that war anyway?" As we explore various ages, genders, ethnicities, locales, and economic statuses, we find much variation in extent of interest in the Civil War; we even find variation within a given individual, depending on circumstance. But one overall impression is that this ghost still haunts—sometimes, here and there, at some levels of identity.

Two streams of history, then, can lead to or feed into a southern global identity: civil rights and the Civil War. Civil rights derive from a history of slavery and oppression based on race, and its subjects are notably African American (though some parallels can be drawn to other disadvantaged groups, such as Appalachians). Civil War defeat has instilled a sense of Lost Cause primarily among whites (especially lowland). This dichotomy of Civil War/civil rights oversimplifies southern history, obviously, but it serves to distinguish two possible lines of argument that we can follow. The civil rights line will pertain especially to blacks, the Civil War line primarily to whites. Either can intersect with the global process, and I shall explore both. However, emphasis is on the Civil War line because my argument is primarily geographical or geopsychological; that is, it pertains to region more than race. My primary question concerns whether the southern region can overcome its oppositional stance toward the rest of the nation and how globalization, which is also a spatial movement, can neutralize or overcome that spatially located stance.

Racial dualism and civil rights issues enter this process, to be sure. The Civil War was indeed about states' rights, among other issues, but the Confederacy stood for white supremacy and slavery. Whatever the particular position held by leaders in the Confederacy, such as Robert E. Lee or Jefferson Davis or Nathan Bedford Forrest, the historical legacy of the Lost Cause has a racist dimension that is undeniable. For example, the Ku Klux Klan flew the flag of the Confederacy. Accordingly, while some justifiably honor the valor of Confederate heroes, others, including African Americans, justifiably question or condemn the connection of the Confederacy and its symbols to slavery, segregation, and racism. Civil War does intersect civil rights. However, to quote an African proverb I once heard from Zulu anthropologist Absolom Vilakazi: to say that one has a mother is not to deny that one has a father. That is, an entity has many aspects; hence, do not reduce all to one. To acknowledge the civil rights aspect of the Civil War heritage is not to reduce the Civil War heritage to civil rights nor should one deny its civil rights aspect. For example, to acknowledge Robert E. Lee as an icon is not to praise or affirm him or what he stood for—to some—in every way, but to note his image within an important segment of southern identity—that segment that focuses on territory, regional identity, and the South as a region. Race is an important but not dominant concern; our model focuses on regionalism not race.

Historical Context: Global to Regional to Global

Viewed from certain angles—geographically—the South is at its most important turning point since becoming the South. The most crucial change in the history of this region was its becoming a region—when it began to define its identity as a region, as the South. If this had not happened in the early nineteenth century, there would be no South. The history of the South might be divided into three phases: first, the sixteenth to eighteenth centuries—early globalism—when the South did not yet exist as a region but was a node in a network of commerce (including the slave trade), agriculture, and colonization by Europe. This was a global and cosmopolitan period for the South, when fifty languages were spoken in Charleston, southern ports and plantations were part of a commercial and cultural network extending through the Caribbean, and immigrants came from across Europe. Second, in the nineteenth to twentieth centuries, the South was characterized by regionalism and oppositionality; as America became a nation, the South became a region often opposed to the nation. Before this time, there was no South as we know it: Thomas Jefferson and John Adams, close friends who died on the same day, would not have thought of themselves as southern and northern in the sense that developed after their deaths. Around 1830, the South began crystallizing a regional identity that gave its diverse populations a sense of unity founded on a black-white dualism and an agrarian economy. The South then cemented this regional identity by means of secession, civil war, and reconstruction, continuing a certain oppositionality through the twentieth century. What is the third phase, the next crucial change? It is for the region to unmake itself in a sense, to open itself up, to free itself for relations to the outside—to the rest of the nation, of course, but even more comprehensively to the world.

Thus, globalization is a momentous force for the South because it reverses a trend that made the South in the first place. It had to turn inward to define a distinctive identity. Now one sees it turning outward, influenced, to be sure, by many factors, but most radically by globalization.

Definitions

To describe how global forces are shaping the identity of the American South requires, first, understanding two key terms, "global" and "the identity of the American South" and then investigating the relationship between the two. Of definitions, John Stuart Mill once said, "As few as you can, as many as you must." A working definition, or at least a characterization, can get us started.

"Global" simply refers to the globe, the world. "Globalization" is a process composed of many aspects (commerce, cyberspace, migration, and cultural exchange, for example) and many entities (the media, the military, and, ultimately, everybody and everything around the world) moving toward worldwide connectivity. In a word, globalization is "connectivities" on a worldwide scale. Other terms, such as "international" or "transnational," denote some of those connectivities. Globalism is a perspective emphasizing, perhaps favoring, global connections; in contrast, such words as "provincial" or "local" (as in local yokel), emphasize, perhaps even denigrate, connections to a locale.

Arguments over globalization and the related ideas and phenomena are many. Is it bad, is it good, is it new, or is it old? Is it primarily economic (dollars go round the world and make the world go round, oil is the reason for the war in Iraq, and governments don't matter anymore in an age of world capitalism), or is it political, military, and cultural too? The answer is yes: globalization is bad and good, new and old, and it is all of these connectivities. These and other questions pertain to discussions wider than ours. One issue, however, is relevant to us: how does global relate to local?

Global can oppose local, even endanger it, as when jobs go abroad or terrorists attack, but we can conceive synergies as well, where global and local interact and enhance each other: why else would Dothan, Alabama, sponsor a tennis tournament bringing world-class players from Ukraine and Australia? Perhaps the foreign stars intensify local interest in tennis. (After we watch them play one night, we run into them at the Atlanta Bread Company, drinking coffee, sending emails home, but also mingling; they enthuse about Dothan's hospitality. My mother, in her nineties, enjoys these young global athletes visiting her native Alabama just as she does her granddaughters who publish books about Ukrainian feminist artists, lead symposia on cosmopolitan feminism, and pursue international fashion design.) A friend watches Al Gore's movie about global warming; I go to Hog Day in Hillsborough, North Carolina. Al's roots are in Tennessee, and Hog Day includes organizations supporting the environment, and a spectrum of foods, music, and participants—including the hogs—who are diverse and global as well as local. Our aim is to characterize those synergies, to explore global connectivities to the U.S. South, and to ask how such connectivities shape regional identity.

What is the South?

The South

Here are fragments overheard from the seat behind me on a recent flight from Atlanta to Dothan:

"We moved to the Panhandle [of Florida, I think, not Texas], would've thought we was moving to Antarctica. . . . [The] whole South end of Florida is Hispanic. . . . Got a hundred acres, as red as my jacket. Get down deep, it's like digging in concrete. . . . Granddaddy worked for the city, for the prison . . . bet somewhere along the line they're kin to you." ("Probably," she says.) "Old boy down the road from us . . . me and my daddy fixed his barn. . . . I like to observe things, notice that first they check our seat belts then get up there and show us how to fasten it. . . . People up there where I come from . . . go to the doctor's office, ten people sitting there, five of them got the same appointment you do, figure you'll have to wait. I was coming here from Jackson, Miss, crew done left, gave me a five-dollar meal voucher. . . . Have a granddaughter, she's in the seventh grade, give her five years and see." ("I'll be gone by then.") "Don't say that. My daddy was a sharp old bird, fell down, flipped around, hit that guard rail. . . . [I didn't hear whether he survived.] Went to a commencement. Sitting there, I saw him [a student, apparently wearing "low rider" trousers]. . . . You could see his underwear. Wants a job, he'll have to change his attire." (She: "Times have changed.")

The pilot breaks in, with a cheery Midwestern accent: "85 degrees, nice warm day down there, you folks have a great day."

The attendant, African American, tall, and formal: "Keep your seat belt fastened until the captain turns off the seat belt sign. . . . Ladies and gentlemen, the captain has turned on the seat belt sign, so please check the security of your seat belt. Thank you."

Man resumes: "Got to fill up the car, three dollars a gallon. Got stuck in traffic, gone about a hundred miles, a little faster than I can walk. Last time, this flight was thirty-eight minutes."

"Can I get anything for you?" asks a short, stout, white attendant with glasses.

"Here we go!" says the man, as the plane takes off.

The speakers are a man, perhaps in his fifties, and an older woman sitting behind me on a Delta flight—one scheduled in cooperation with Korean and Mexican airlines. The Atlanta-based crew has a black female head attendant; her assistant is white. The man lives off route 231 near Dothan.

The conversations I overheard, in fragments, illustrate two or three of millions of "discourses" heard around the South. The man, someone Faulkner might have claimed as one of his Snopses, "poor white trash," uses expressions and an accent straight out of country and western music, though I suspected he was "putting on" a bit for the elderly woman, probably tuning in to what he suspected was her own background. Varieties of speech represent even wider variations in ecology, society, and culture within the region.

Who or what is the South? Already we have discussed the South as part of a historical process, including globalization, and this discussion presumed some sense of what it is we are discussing—as a territory, an identity—but also that this identity is in flux. We will never nail the South down like a butterfly collected, but must pursue it as a butterfly in flight—so much better, for the thing is alive! And as many argue, the South is not only a place but a "construction," an idea, a myth whose valence depends on viewpoint. Nonetheless it is possible to define some of the region's dimensions and boundaries. The South can be delimited geographically as stretching from the Potomac to the Rio Grande, as including the states of the Confederacy and some border states. Within these, of course, great variation must be noted—ecological variation, from Appalachia to the Low Country; ethnic variation, including blacks, whites, Native Americans, and other minorities, new immigrants among them; and urban to rural variation. John Reed suggests another kind of variation, arguing that there are three Souths: Dixie, the Southeast, and the after-hours South. "Dixie" is the Confederate historical heritage; "the Southeast" is the New South, industrializing and integrating; and "the after-hours South" concerns food, music, and folk, or popular, culture. Obviously there are variations in what the South means from one class or occupation to another: the job loser in Henderson, North Carolina, lives in a South different from that of the CEO in Atlanta or Miami. Reed also explores numerous indices of boundaries of the South, including the growing places of the plant kudzu. Sorting out the South, both within the region and between itself and other areas, can be vexing.[10]

"Southern identity" implies that there are limits to variation, that one can identify a bounded core that is "southern." In referring to southern identity, I follow most scholars or commentators on the South in recognizing a kind of ideal, typical core identity and some boundaries to that identity while also acknowledging the existence of complex levels, variations, and flux. No one is a southerner pure and simple. Everyone possesses many identities, of which southern may be one. One's occupational, ethnic, gender, class, and religious identity or one's interest in music, science, or crime can override one's identity as a southerner, yet outsiders may ignore these other identities and stereotype one simply as southern. Context influences whether regional identity is accentuated. Southerners realize they are southern when they go to the North, some say, and the same person who rebels against the South while in it may defend it when outside it.

Defining identity entails both setting boundaries and tracing networks, what Mary Douglas termed "group" and "grid." "Group" refers to boundaries between in-group and out-group, "grid," to networks that fan out and overlap. An identity links a person to both kinds of social entities. Boundaries get drawn around a given issue or in a given context.[11] A Californian told me that his great-great-grandfather fought for the Confederacy, and, were there a war today, "I know which side I would be on." I must confess that even today, sometimes when in the North I sense that I am "behind enemy lines." On the other hand, I identify with nonsoutherners much more than with southerners in many contexts—on some political or academic questions, for example. But still I feel strongly loyal to family and kin, regardless of their political or academic leanings.

Boundaries get fuzzy, too, as grids come into play. An Iranian immigrant married to a Kentuckian mentions having gone to the three-hundredth-year reunion of her relatives in Boston; such a network connects a so-called southerner to both New England and Iran. Gay country and western music, which seems to carry southern values in some way yet is found in northern and western locales and violates traditional family values, is another example of boundary crossing. Yet another is the shared kinship (and DNA) of descendants of former masters and slaves. Boundaries are crossed, and family resemblances (both in the colloquial sense and in Wittgenstein's formal sense) come into play: A is like B, B is like C in some other way, so A claims kin to C. A New England friend's family name is the same as mine, both several generations back, so we sense kinship between us. Perhaps southerners are especially prone to seek such kinship and recognize it, so the connection may mean more to me than to him, reminding me of how we are alike but also different. So boundaries are drawn, yet networks cross boundaries, and we recognize huge variations along many dimensions—gender, race, class, region, and life histories.

So far, we have thought of identity as individual. What about collective identity, not the southerner but the South? The South has manifested itself as a government, the Confederacy; as a political force, the Solid South; and, most enduring, perhaps, as a sensed community encompassing manifestations from "The South will rise again!" to the Southern Growth Policies Board. With globalization, both individual and collective identities expand to link region to world. Governor James Hunt of North Carolina sets up a trade center in Tokyo. Mayor Michael Dow of Mobile, Alabama, forges a connection with Indonesia. Professor Yoshumitsu Ide of Japan and Professor Djuhertati Imam Muhni of Indonesia, who head programs in American studies in their countries, focus on the U.S. South. Connections seem endless.

Defining boundaries of southern identity is difficult, yet without at least provisional boundaries, southern identity disappears as experience and concept. Immersion in variations is a trap, a tar baby, yet stereotypes of a simple and clearly bounded southern identity mislead. Clearly, to be southern means something, as does the South, but neither of these identities is simple: the South is not merely the South, and a southerner is not merely a southerner, so it is problematic to reduce the place or the person to a stereotype. My solution is to recognize a kind of purified or simplified type, a configuration of features that compose a clear enough identity to allow us to proceed with our inquiry yet to keep in mind variation and complexity as we go. I strive to be inclusive and to treat variations. After all, that is what globalization is about, in part. Hence, whatever is going on in the South is of interest, and the interplay between global forces and anybody or anywhere in the South is of concern.

It would seem reasonable, however, to take particular note of those to whom southern identity matters most, those who have most visibly created and sustained the identity. In many contexts these are white males, starting at the extreme with the Ku Klux Klan or, more mildly, the Sons of Confederate Veterans (locally, the former burn crosses, while the latter adopt a highway). Yet even among white males, the strength of identity varies. Southern identity would seem to matter more in the lowland than in the upland. I recall the man from Ash County, North Carolina, who told me he identified himself first as a Primitive Baptist, then as an Appalachian, and then a southerner. The first two identities may lead elsewhere than the South: that man was more likely to follow the route of Primitive Baptist churches up the spine of the mountains to Pennsylvania than to travel down to Raleigh or Richmond. And remember that some mountain counties did not secede and join the Confederacy, so certain white lowland males are arguably the leading carriers of southern identity traditionally, while it may mean less to others or take on a different shape. Black southerners may identify with many features of the place but reject the allegiance to slavery, to the flag, or to Dixie. A black dancer on the NPR radio program "Fresh Air" was asked by Terry Gross about food; "I like to eat; I'm a southern girl," she replied, affirming one kind of regional identity.

For some, southern identity is formalized by membership in an organization, most notoriously the Ku Klux Klan, more peacefully, the Sons or Daughters of the Confederacy or Kappa Alpha. For most, regional identity is much less sharply marked than membership in such an organization, and for many who live in the South some other identity, such as class or ethnic identity, is primary. But even those who put first priority on an identity other than their southernness may include it, sometimes unexpectedly, in their repertoire. "Shalom, y'all" puts the Hebrew word first, but the southern expression follows; stories like "Driving Miss Daisy" depict a southern Jewish lifestyle and attitude about race that mirrors that of the southern majority. Immigrants who identify primarily with their homeland or ethnic group yet come to include southerner as an aspect of their identity range from Scots to Vietnamese. There is a special reason to attend to these new minorities: they represent important ties to the world. Immigrants are not the only ones, however; globalization is many kinds of connectivity.

Region, Nation, and World: Intersecting Cycles

The South is not only in the world; it is, ambivalently, in the nation. The story of South-in-nation is the dominant one; South-in-world is an emerging one. The two narratives can be seen as parallel. South-in-world has three phases, as I noted above, spanning four centuries: a formative quasi-global period through the 1600s and 1700s, when the South was just a southern part of a New World colony, a node in a trading network; a regional period through the 1800s and 1900s, when the South crystallized its regional identity, as opposed to a national identity; and an emerging global period beginning in 2000. Likewise South-in-nation has three phases within its two centuries. The first phase, late 1700s and early 1800s, saw the South as a nation builder. The second phase, mid-1800s through the Civil War and Reconstruction, saw the South as a nation destroyer. The third phase, beginning during Reconstruction and

proceeding steadily, though with conflicts and reversals, gradually rein-
tegrated South and nation. The two cycles converge in a reintegration of
South with both nation and world as we enter the twenty-first century.

Key points in the South's move toward integration with the nation have
long been noted. The Spanish-American War and the world wars that
followed brought southerners into a national force against a foreign enemy. The Civil Rights Act of 1964 and the Voting Rights Act of 1965
spurred racial integration and undercut Jim Crow, liberalizing southern
society and making the South a more livable place for outsiders as well as
for blacks, and facilitating economic and educational development that
attracted outsiders and encouraged blacks who had left to return. Leaders such as Martin Luther King and Jesse Jackson were addressing not
only the region but the entire nation, demonstrating that racism was a
national, rather than merely regional, issue. These developments led to
greater political integration of South with nation, eventuating in the election of presidents from the South, beginning with Jimmy Carter and continuing through Bill Clinton and the second George Bush.

In the twenty-first century, then, regional, national, and global identities are all in play, often in the same individual, although one can note
differentiation. See, for example, American and Confederate decals on
American-made trucks alongside "Think globally, act locally" bumper
stickers on foreign-made cars. Whether in such incidental yet suggestive emblems or in policies and pronouncements, contemporary culture
displays a dynamic interplay among all three levels, region, nation, and
world. The South joins that dynamic, with important consequences. The
opposition-to-nation paradigm that has dominated the South for over a
century diminishes in salience as it is replaced by an integration-with-the-
world model, a globalized identity that subsumes regional and national
identities.

A Perspective: Grounded Globalism

Globalization is grounded, rooted in locale. The point is obvious, but
consider briefly an alternative viewpoint. Globalism has been asserted as

overriding all localisms: nation, state, community. Dipesh Chakrabarty, for example, described "Cosmopolitanism" as a cultural globalism, as do Arjun Appadurai and Ulf Hannerz. In this vision, cosmopolitans move freely across national boundaries, wedded not to any nation or locale but to a global culture. Thomas Friedman depicts an economic and electronic globalism. He asserts that "the world is flat," meaning global markets and global communication flatten out differences and distinctions among nations or other territorial entities. Manuel Castells discusses the same more voluminously. In all these cases, local boundaries and identities are dissolved as global systems and identities conquer. Emphasis is on the global phenomenon, global networks, markets, the Internet, media, and culture.[12]

The slogan "Think globally, act locally," on the other hand, emphasizes globalism, but it grounds this globalism in the local, asserting that action happens somewhere. Disembodied globalism is not sufficient as either a concept or a theory to explain what is happening or as a policy or practice to make things happen. Charles Taylor reminds us that globalism does not offer an institutional basis for democracy, which seems to work only in a local setting, the nation. Patriotism is the basis for the democratic state: without loyalty to the nation, the nation falls, and so falls the institutional basis for democratic government. Craig Calhoun and Robert Putnam argue for the importance of local communities. Similarly, the "Battle in Seattle" and the riots in Milan and elsewhere protest policy by the World Bank, the World Trade Organization, multinational corporations, and others that insufficiently take account of localized needs. Locally, workers decry the loss of jobs to global outsourcing, ecologists decry pollution, and social critics lambaste a neocolonialism in which wealth and power concentrate in multinational corporations dominated by the citizens of wealthy nations whose armies perpetuate military occupation.[13]

In short, abstracted globalization cut loose from locales is problematic in both theory and practice. We need a more holistic framework embracing global and local, taking account of the interpenetration of the two. I use the term "grounded globalism" in an attempt to capture the interplay between global and local. Other terms, including "glocal," have made the same attempt, but "grounded globalism" carries more information. It speaks not just of merging local and global but of grounding, building a groundwork in which global meanings and issues enter our life-worlds. "Grounded globalism" refers to an organic conception of globalism, rooting globalism in the ground rather than relying overmuch on cyberspace or other abstracted systems.

The Silesian representative in the Polish parliament practices grounded globalism. She is a folklorist as well as a senator. She represents a region of Poland—Silesia—and builds on Silesian culture as a base for her political constituency. This base then leads her into a parliament that sets national and international policy.[14] Jimmy Carter has engaged in grounded globalism by building the Carter Center and doing international work in human rights, health, and the environment and at the same time affirming his own roots in Georgia. The European Union exemplifies grounded globalism in its Committee on Regions. The committee uses regions—locales such as Scotland, Bavaria, and Friesland that have linguistic and cultural unities—rather than nations as units for economic, social, and cultural development. A commencement address, "Carolina in a Global World," was covered by two North Carolina newspapers, one from Raleigh, the other from Charlotte. The *Charlotte Observer* described it as touting the local: the South, the region, and the state; the *Raleigh News and Observer* described the address as highlighting the global. Neither got the obvious point that both local and global—and the combination of the two—were being promoted. When this address was given by me at the UNC–Chapel Hill 1998 mid-winter commencement ceremony, globalization was seen primarily as economics and positively, while since 9/11 it is also seen militarily and negatively, associated with terrorism, outsourcing, and job loss. In either case, globalism has come home, to where we live and work.[15]

Globalism gets grounded in ways less extreme than terrorism, less traumatic than outsourcing and job loss. The automatic teller machine asks if you want to conduct your transaction in English or in Spanish. My daughter marries a man from Mexico. When I call an American airline based in the South, I speak to someone in India. A student in class announces that she wants to do a paper about the Hmong. "I am Hmong," replies another student, explaining that she is a member of that Southeast Asian mountain group but now resides near Marion, North Carolina. Vignettes given earlier offer further illustrations. In simple ways, the world enters local contexts.

"Grounded globalism," then, is suggested as a general orientation that guides our inquiry and suggests implications for other places. Obvious as it may be, thinkers and actors often attend to only one emphasis, either global or local, while grounded globalism presses us to seek a relationship. Our model sees grounding globalism as completing a process of moving from regional to global and back to a globalized regionalism, a cycle of feedback loops that can reverberate in new patterns.

Theory into Method

The seven-step model of regional estrangement from the nation and reintegration into the world is applied here to a single place, the U.S. South. I proceed deductively (spinning out logical implications of the model) and inductively (exploring evidences—facts and data). This exploration is "interdisciplinary" in the sense of deploying history, demography, literature, geography, anthropology, and psychology; however, it is especially based on observation: looking and listening to what is going on. I report anecdotes or experiences, many of them involving people I live with and work with. In the course of such activities many domains and many locales are examined, but many are not. Each reader's experience and interpretation of them may vary from mine and, hence, can usefully enrich our query; however, the point of considering any experience is to address our larger argument. I offer, again, an essay, illustrative not exhaustive, suggesting not confirming a perspective, a model in terms of which we can both perceive and shape what is happening in our region and beyond.[16]

To explore this thesis, we proceed as follows. First, we ask about global identity in the South, contrasting it with an oppositional identity. What clues suggest that a global identity is emerging in the South? What can we find in surveying opinions? What projects are being pursued? What relationships are being engaged that suggest global connectivity? These are the questions for chapter 3. Second, how is such identity expressed "on the ground," in such key domains as race and our sense of place? Race and space are the focus of chapters 4 and 5. Third, how do all these changes challenge frameworks of meaning, as in religion; call forth subjective expression, as in the arts and in dreams; and expression in action, as in politics? These are the foci of chapters 6, 7, and 8. Finally, we conclude by summing up what we have learned as a way of assessing our model: examining how useful it is as a perspective on what is happening and can happen. Although the seven steps of the model are considered, the emphasis is on the last two, the creation and grounding of global identity.

We try, then, to fathom interactive energy converging in this spot, the South, and to attend to that energy, which is our true object of study.

PART TWO

Trends

It's five o'clock somewhere.

ALAN JACKSON, in song by Jim "Moose" Brown and Don Rollins

CHAPTER THREE

From Oppositionality to Integration

DABBS, WE RECALL, characterized southerners as at home in the world, which they think of as the South. It seems that southerners are now broadening their awareness of the world while retaining an identity with the region, and in so doing they are burying their sense of opposing the nation, especially the North. More frequent relations with the world away from home (which then becomes part of home by extension) create a notion in southerners of being world citizens, global human beings, in contrast to a regional and oppositional identity. Far away penetrates deep within. Such a shift entails change—economic and political, to be sure, but also cultural and psychological—a shift in southerners' conceptual framework. Indeed, Dabbs's world becomes a new world or at least a new worldview, necessitating a new sense of identity, of who I am or who we are.

So pervasive and powerful is this shift of identity that we must approach an understanding of its potential in stages, by examining analogous experiences. We begin with the experience of losing one's native identity by taking on a foreign identity, losing the self—culturally and perhaps psychologically—to become the other. Pat Noone, a British anthropologist, became Noone of the Ulu, a westerner who went native, marrying into and apparently becoming a member of the Ulu tribe of Borneo. Doing so, he disappeared from the Western world; he was never found by the brother who went to search for him. Most anthropologists do not give up their identities in order to "go native," but they do attempt participant observation, which requires that they learn a society's language and culture so as to participate in and learn about it. John Walker Lindh became a participant in the Taliban by taking part in training camps and schools. I once lived and worked for eight months in such camps and schools run by an Indonesian Muslim organization, Muhammadiya, but I remained an observer. I did not become a Muhammadiyan in the way Lindh allegedly became a member of the Taliban, though the experience deeply affected me nonetheless. A photograph shows me in their training camp, doing calisthenics with the Muhammadiyans—a white man a head taller than my companions—yet I don't remember that I thought of myself as different at that time. During the weeks in the training camps I spoke only Indonesian, yet I don't recall noticing that I was speaking any language at all. On one occasion I thought I might never go home; home seemed so far away. The far away (which had become close to home) did affect the deep within, though within limits. I never did convert to Islam or join Muhammadiya, though a standing joke was that I was "*kenak da'wa*"—hit by evangelizing—in the camp. Because I was living with the Muhammadiyans twenty-four hours a day but was neither a member nor a Muslim, they confronted my distinctiveness by occasionally expressing hope that I would convert, as an *imam* voiced in a prayer at a certain mosque. Later a headline in their magazine, *Suara Muhammadiya*, stated that I was about to do so. This sort of experience is standard in anthropological fieldwork; rare but telling is the conversion to the other, as in the case of Noone or Lindh.

Better-known shifts in identity include milder cross-cultural exposures and identifications, from study abroad to tourism or merely by reading, looking at museum exhibits, and communicating electronically. Reactions to other cultures range from casual interest to some degree of culture shock but rarely, if ever, to conversion. Certainly all of these reactions entail shifts of identity, and more radical shifts can be traumatic. Post-traumatic stress disorder (PTSD) often arises when soldiers move from combat to home or from home to a foreign place and then back to home. PTSD is caused not only by combat but also by dislocation into a foreign context. Likewise, dislocation can be stressful to immigrants, whether or not they experience violence, because they too change orientation and identity, often forever.

Global Identity

Global identity does not necessitate shifts of identity as particularized as that of Noone. One does not abandon a particular identity to become a particular other, such as an Ulu; rather, one identifies with many others, who compose the world. As a world citizen, one identifies with some kind of entity that claims global scope. One shares a sense of community and identity beyond national, geographic, or other restrictive boundaries. In so doing, one edges toward empathy, necessarily identifying somewhat with the other without becoming the other.

The global entity with which one identifies can be vague—the human species, all humanity, or the world at large, but it may also pertain to a certain sphere or aspect that has global scope. Examples are religious (ecumenical Christianity, the Muslim *umma*) or governmental (the United Nations or, to a lesser extent, the European Union), the one based on a unity of belief, the other on shared citizenship. The global entity can also be functionally oriented, for example, the North Atlantic Treaty Organization, the U.S. Agency for International Development, the World Bank, or the International Monetary Fund, which involve not identity so much as a mission of defense or transformation. Terrorism can be a global entity with a mission to destroy or radically transform; even if terrorism is more oppositional than integrative, terrorists may still evoke a concept of world community (for example, the Islamic *umma*) as justification. Global identity, especially in a religious or ideological context, can replace a particularized identity with a more transcendent one; Saul became Paul on the road to Damascus, thereby forsaking his particularized Judaism for a more universalistic Christianity. Recognizing the power of such conversions, we speak of "brainwashing"—a term applied both to politics and to religion, as when prisoners of war and converts to so-called cults are psychologically manipulated. Christ pulled no punches in explaining such impacts—one loses one life in order to save it, one is reborn, and earthly parents are replaced by the heavenly Father. Moving into a new world, one loses particularistic and localized identities and relationships, including relations with family and the locales with which they are associated. Even if a global identity does not erase regional ties and markers, it transforms one's localized identities, subsuming them in a larger entity. Even if we assume that global identities do not necessarily require brainwashing, or religious or quasi-religious rebirth, they still transform one's world and worldview.

Oppositionality

Oppositional identities emphasize difference from instead of unity with. It is said that Martin Luther asserted "Here I stand! I can do no other" against the Catholic hierarchy. Martin Luther King more inclusively proclaimed "I have a dream" and envisioned an egalitarian and just social order, one which stood in opposition to the prevailing one. Gay pride marches further illustrate a stance indicating refusal to bend to the status quo. Jimmy Creech, a heterosexual Methodist preacher from North Carolina, tells of his moment of conversion to that movement, when he felt called to step off the sidewalk into the street, joining a march in Raleigh, a step that led to a stormy career of opposition, resulting in his being excluded from the ministry at the church he took in Kansas.

Regional opposition to national dominance is, then, a particular kind of oppositional stance, resulting in rebellion, perhaps secession, war, defeat, and resentment, as outlined in steps one through five of our model.

"Forget, hell," grumbles the Confederate soldier in a cartoon seen at "redneck" hangouts, expressing a lingering resentment of the Yankee invasion of the South. Other examples include Quebecois, Scottish, and Irish Catholic separatism. Oppositional identities can exist at many levels, from tribe to region to nation. Two seemingly opposed features are common to oppositional identities: first, commitment to an "imagined" community intense enough to inspire a willingness to make sacrifices and to use violence on the communitity's behalf; second, a membership of real persons as well as of persons known only symbolically. Benedict Anderson's argument about imagined communities pertains to nations, but it would also hold for the Confederacy, a "nation" of sorts.[1]

Such an oppositional entity may be imagined, but it is also localized as a territory, a place, and this place assumes images alluding to emotionally evocative experiences. Internally the home territory is idealized and sentimentalized as motherland, fatherland, or *Heimat* (homeland), or as Dixie or Dixieland in the South. Externally the opposed territory is demonized, especially if it invades or colonizes the homeland. In the South, as is well known, the historical events of secession, war, and reconstruction were mythologized as the cult of the Lost Cause. Even today, more than a century after "the war," reenactments at battlefields sustain the cult, as do organizations such as the Sons of Confederate Veterans. Memories constructed from stories and symbols, not from witnessing events, remain salient for some. I share much with a close friend from New England, but I doubt whether he feels the same as I do about Pickett's charge, since I would identify with the troops charging to their deaths on the meadow, while his forebears were more likely manning guns on the ridge above. As president of the American Anthropological Association, I was informed by a regional unit of the association representing the northeastern United States that they wished to secede (largely for economic reasons: their regional interests, they felt, would be better served by autonomy than by remaining in the "union"). I responded by saying, "Fine, and you can keep your horses and sidearms"—alluding to General Grant's generosity toward the Confederates at Appomattox—an allusion that they probably thought weird but which would be apparent to many southerners who grew up with that history.[2]

Beyond historical references, a generalized, somewhat vague sense of opposition is a strong part of southern identity. In fact, as experimental psychology documents, an inchoate sentiment may tend to endure more than a sharper one; the sharper one is easier to refute or erase by negative reinforcement.

Oppositionality comes from outside as well as inside. That is, southerners' oppositional attitudes derive in part from the way southerners are perceived and in part from the way they perceive. The examples that follow may seem trivial compared with the more brutal and overt conflicts and oppressions. We are not describing torture or war; the genocide of Jews, homosexuals, and East Europeans during the Holocaust; or mass murder in Rwanda or Darfur. Closer to home the treatment of African Americans under slavery and Jim Crow was obviously more overt than the treatment of white southerners by nonsoutherners within the United States, even including the Civil War, whose six hundred thousand casualties fell on both sides. Still, though they may seem insignificant, the attitudes outsiders hold and express about the South partially explain southern oppositionality.

Memorial Hall at Harvard, noted Mary Steedly, a colleague on the faculty there (who was raised in Charleston, South Carolina, and is sensitive to such things), records the names of alumni who were killed in wars, even those who fought for Germany against the Allies, but it omits the names of alumni who fought for the Confederacy.[3] This particular symbolism may be the residue of abolitionist times, and one should keep in mind Harvard's occasional, somewhat positive nod to the South, such as the plaque showing where Faulkner's character Quentin Compson jumped off a bridge. Nevertheless one still hears of incidents such as negative reactions to a southern student at Harvard who hung a Confederate flag in her window. Some say the reactions were occasioned by the student's racism, not by the flag; however, other students equated the flag with the swastika.[4] I neither owned nor unfurled a Confederate flag, but a milder equivalent during my student days at Harvard was a car with a Georgia license plate. I recall finding obscenities referring to its Georgia tag written on my car when it was parked downtown in Boston. A psychoanalyst from North Carolina who was practicing in Boston at the same time I was studying there mentioned that one of his patients, a native Bostonian, worried about his being southern. "Why?" I asked. "She assumed I was backward and prejudiced," he replied. A similar view is expressed explicitly by a distinguished literary scholar of European Jewish background—a holocaust survivor—who states that she despises southern literature, music, and much else, even though she has spent much of her career in the South. Interestingly, however, she trusts deeply another psychiatrist who happens to be from the South. She assesses much of southern culture as simply dumb. (My weak reply is to recall another time when my car, a Model A Ford, broke down, and a hydrocephalic man, considered to be "retarded," fixed it—he wasn't so dumb after all.)

Without exaggerating or ignoring the many kindnesses granted the Quentins at Harvard or the complexities of attitude (positive sometimes), the point is that a certain sectionalism has been present and perhaps endures; these examples do not clinch the argument, but they at least suggest the kinds of reactions southerners experience sometimes and how they receive them—defensively, no doubt, but both the stimulus and the response play into the sectionalist attitudes and fuel the South's and the southerner's sense of being stigmatized by nonsoutherners.

Sectionalism is not confined to white males of the Dabbs ur-type, though it may be strongest there. Riché Richardson depicts southern hip-hop in opposition to northern hip-hop. Southern hip-hop taunts northerners as claiming to be more urban and sophisticated, therefore less manly, and threatens that northerners better watch out if they come south. In this instance, among African Americans one sees a conflict between regional categories and stereotyping that parallels attitudes held by whites and, perhaps, generally.[5] While the following comments pertain primarily to whites, they can apply to other groups as well and perhaps generalize to some extent across ethnic lines, for example, to southern and northern

Jews and to newer groups such as Vietnamese immigrants and their descendents, who live in the southern and the northern United States. My son-in-law, who is from Mexico but who grew up in Chicago, mentions Hispanic characterization of the Florida panhandle as the Redneck Riviera, taking over a disparaging view from the wider Chicago perspective. A student who migrated from Vietnam to a small North Carolina town at age twelve describes with some wonderment his best friend, a fundamentalist southern Baptist who had very high SAT scores yet asserted that "slavery was a good thing."

As any stigmatized group or person will recount, discrimination is not only overt but also informal or subtle; African Americans speak of being "dissed," or disrespected. While imitating black speech is unacceptable in most public contexts, imitating southern white speech remains common. "He speaks English as a second language," quipped a Californian about a southerner. Mangled grammar, such as "you all" imagined as a second person singular, is common in imitations. At a gathering commemorating his colleague's retirement, a certain nationally known columnist and critic was recently heard imitating a southerner's accent reciting Shakespeare. Klaus Schneider and Meghan P. L. McKinnie at the Rheinische Friedrich-Wilhelms-Universität in Bonn, Germany, and Dennis Preston at Michigan State University, research "perceived dialects." Schneider has cited several phrases that were identified as southern speech by Michiganders but in fact are not spoken by southerners; that is, dialects are perceived, imagined in terms of stereotypes. In Preston's study, Michigan students drew a map of the United States showing zones of ideal and denigrated dialects. The South was most denigrated, with Alabama at the bottom, while Michigan (specifically East Lansing) was identified as ideal. These studies map, then, a geography of perceived dialects, showing dialects attributed to southerners by U.S. nonsoutherners, where they locate those dialects geographically, and how they evaluate them.[6]

More nuanced or intangible, yet still emotionally powerful, are attributions of character or intelligence in association with accent. Competence is attributed to the dominant accent, and incompetence or stupidity, along with perhaps a certain "charm," to the nonstandard accent. Playing into this kind of stereotyping, Teresa Heinz Kerry, the wife of presidential candidate John Kerry, remarked, I recall, that his running mate from North Carolina, John Edwards, had the beauty, while her husband had the brains. A Mississippi Catholic complained that fellow Catholics from the North did not listen to what she was saying but instead just commented on how she talked. An Ohioan who moved south told of waking up at night to realize with horror how her grandchild sounded: "You know what they say, that your I.Q. drops a hundred points if you open your mouth and speak with a southern accent."

Such comments reflect an attitude by nonsoutherners—often internalized by southerners themselves—about the South and southerners. Such attitudes, often covert, are expressed in seemingly silly ways; take the sweet tea debate. Robert Seymour, a Baptist minister, wrote an op-ed for the Chapel Hill newspaper several years ago in which he fondly and nostalgically discussed how sweetened iced tea is a signature southern drink. That piece reportedly evoked the largest number of responses of any piece that paper ever published. Many of the responses angrily condemned or defended the South: northerners saw southern sweet tea a sign of degeneracy, and southerners defended their region and their beverage.[7] Anecdotes such as this one illustrate oppositionalities between South and North, or non-South, within a national context. To be sure, the North/South divide is often dormant and irrelevant, yet neither southerners nor northerners quite forget it. The old wound is reopened surprisingly often, perhaps by a slighting remark. (A new arrival from the north complains about benefits, saying to fellow workers primarily from the South, "Of course, what do you expect? We're in the South.") Expectations about southern work habits remain a force in decisions about hiring ("He talks northern but works southern"), elections, marriage, and many other relationships. (An admissions committee rejects a southern applicant with a perfect GRE score on the grounds that her essay does not fit their preferred model; she did not elaborate claims of future achievement, offering instead a terse and reticent plan.) Although analogous in many ways to race, gender, ethnicity, class, and religion, regional identity in the contemporary United States is not accorded equivalent legal status, as in affirmative action or equal opportunity hiring. Perceptions of regional identity and possible resulting discrimination are more covert but, perhaps partly for that reason, remain salient.[8] Recalling our seven-step model, then, we meet our southerner as a personality and a culture still nursing—in some quarters, in some aspects—a psychology distilling the first five steps—regional identity, oppositionality, memories and feelings of rebellion and defeat, and resulting resentments buttressed by stigmatization on occasion. Furthermore, while this complex is arguably most readily observed among white males, especially of a certain generation, elements sometimes surface among others raised in or residing in the South as well.

From Oppositionality to Integration

The question is, When, then, do southerners (not to mention northerners) transcend this oppositionality? Sometimes they do so as part of a nation, as in the reunification following the Civil War. In myriad ways and in every moment, individuals do so; after all, humanity is not the monopoly of any region. Our focus here, however, is on when southerners do so by thinking globally.

LEADERS

One could cite many examples of high-profile southerners who have made this shift: transcending oppositional identity by espousing an international or global identity. Presidents Woodrow Wilson and Jimmy Carter, Senator Fulbright, and U.N. Ambassador Andrew Young (notable for his work in Africa) are just a few. Think also of Bill Clinton (assisted by his chief of staff, North Carolinian Erskine Bowles) working with the elder George Bush after the December 2005 tsunami. Condoleezza Rice's Birmingham, Alabama, childhood led her to the world stage. Outside of government, Georgia businessman Millard Fuller founded and led Habitat for Humanity, Billy Graham is the world's best-known Evangelist, George Washington Carver invented agronomy. Helen Keller, the

Alabamian who was blind and deaf, became an inspiration for women internationally, and Juliette Gordon Low, the Georgian who created the Girl Scouts long ago, and Mississippian Oprah Winfrey today are remarkable female leaders. The recent president of Rotary International, Glenn E. Estess Sr., an Alabamian, is a less well-known example, as is Robert Phay, the founder and head of World View. Phay, a Mississippi native with a Yale law degree, has created in World View a network of K–12 schools in nearly all one hundred counties of North Carolina, working together to infuse education with international ideas. Rotary International combines community leadership and service in virtually every nation. Should one include the Southwest, Texas has nurtured other styles of global leadership. LBJ is, of course, an example, as is the younger Bush. Less famous but nevertheless remarkable is Walter Davis. He dropped out of school in Kitty Hawk, North Carolina, made a fortune in oil in Texas, and transported fertilizer to China during the Mao period. Sonny Brown, a large man in the LBJ image, is a Rotary International leader who, among other things, has built connections between the United States and Mexican groups across the border at El Paso. There are many other international leaders with southern backgrounds. In life stories such as these, one can trace movement from regional identities and outlooks to global ones with impacts on national and world affairs. While these stories are familiar, this particular point is not usually made but becomes self-evident if the various accounts are viewed together; these biographies trace diverse paths through southern contexts toward global ones.

While world leaders demonstrate the theme, we shall find it in a myriad of other contexts. We pursue it in a range of ways. A poll illustrates a general attitude. Specific projects show it. Exchanges and relationships hint at it. Southern symbols express it.

As we explore the theme in these contexts, paradoxes are apparent: how can southerners signify global outlooks when they are defined by fellow nationals as regional, as provincial? And how can globalism penetrate the provinces (as compared with the national identities)? A certain national identity is taken by some as necessary to connect globally. This would impair the leapfrog process postulated, that regional identities can bypass blockages imposed nationally by making direct transnational connections.

While I do not cite cataclysmic eruptions signifying transformation of a regional identity in one fell swoop, bits and pieces of evidence reveal emerging changes in outlook.

THE SOUTHERN FOCUS POLL

Turning from leaders to ordinary people, consider the results of a recent poll. In spring 2001, the Southern Focus Poll, a joint project of the Odum Institute at the University of North Carolina and the *Atlanta Journal-Constitution,* was administered to 800 persons who were interviewed by telephone across the South. Of the 800, 601 identified themselves as "southerners." A number of questions were asked of these self-identified southerners, one of which I formulated. Interviewees were asked to choose one of two emphases that they felt best characterized their sense of being southern. Option one was "As a southerner, I am different from other Americans"; option two was "As a southerner, I am connected to others around the world." While some interviewees responded that the two options were not mutually exclusive and chose both, they were encouraged to go ahead and choose the one they felt best reflected their attitude. Seventy-eight percent did so, and the greater number of them chose option two (49 percent). Twenty-eight percent chose option one, and the rest chose both or declined to choose either.

The poll was administered annually for many years using a procedure that meets the highest standards of survey research. It was carefully designed to include a full complement of representative subjects from throughout the South across a spectrum of race, class, gender, occupation, educational level, locale, and age, including those born in the South, relative newcomers, and recent transplants. In fact, the results were broken down into such subcategories, and the overall statistics given held for each subcategory. That is, whether one was black, white, old, young, highly educated or less so, urban or rural, and regardless of occupation or where one lived in the South, the strong tendency was to emphasize less that one was different from other Americans and to emphasize more one's connections to others around the world. This poll result suggested that southern identity inclines less in an oppositional direction and more in an integrative global direction.

The poll question provided only two options, which boil down to "think globally" or "think locally." It did not offer an in-between option, namely, "think nationally." While this omission was intentional, designed to accentuate the local/global distinction, it does leave open the possibility that some respondents would have preferred national identity to either regional or global identity. More likely, if permitted to do so, many respondents might have chosen all three.

On numerous occasions—at civic clubs and in classes—I have asked people to predict which of the two options the southern respondents would choose. More predict the "different from" than the "linked to" option, whereas the findings are the reverse. An undergraduate student suggested a reason for this discrepancy: the result reflects the difference between how we perceive others and how others perceive themselves. She suggested that we perceive southerners as being regional and oppositional rather than global, so we predict that they will see themselves the same way. The individual respondent, however, expresses his or her own feeling, and this turns out to be global more often than we predict. Another person predicted that only a "very small educated elite" among the respondents would think of themselves as global citizens. This suspicion was not confirmed by the survey, for individuals from all levels of education and employment, both blacks and whites and males and females, chose the global alternative more often than the other.

One feature of the survey is that it was constructed so that a respondent merely chose and did not have to compose. Recognition, not generation, was measured. Such a survey may, then, pick up subliminal, not-yet-articulated attitudes. The poll is no longer administered, so this question could not be retested. The results we have, however, are highly suggestive. The results of the poll, whatever interpretations one makes, indicate the existence of a global sense among southerners, which would confirm the presence of a trend away from oppositionality toward a global identity. What other kinds of evidence do we see of such a trend?

ANGLICAN RECENTERING

An intriguing and significant example of a shift toward global identity is taking place in the Anglican/Episcopal church. It is divided between liberal and conservative wings, with the liberal being located primarily in the American and European North—the U.S. Northeast and Britain. The larger, more conservative population is located in the global South, notably Africa and parts of Asia. The point of interest for this study is that within the United States the leading impetus for affiliation with the global South comes from the U.S. South, including Texas. On certain issues, such as the ordination of a gay bishop, but also in pervasive values, such as the strength of spirituality as a total guide to living, the U.S. South tends to find common ground with the global South and to split with the liberal U.S. North. This common ground seems to trump racism, at least on some level. Thus, a Low Country Anglican church on Pawleys Island, South Carolina, has subordinated itself to the bishop of Rwanda. Parishioners from South Carolina have visited and established relationships with congregations in Rwanda, despite entrenched racial hierarchies.[9]

While one may view such relationships with skepticism, they do require depths of change and commitment that are not trivial, and they work on levels different from—perhaps deeper than—the institutional, secular programs of liberalism, such as the promotion of human rights or attempts at poverty reduction. They require shifts in identity from regional and racial to global and spiritual. One step is acceptance of South-to-North missions: the bishops of Singapore and Rwanda deputized missionaries from the global South to the United States, including the American South. The next step is to dispel the South/North distinction and to think of global missions.

Consider, on the other hand, the case of Peter Lee. Lee is bishop of the Episcopal Diocese of Virginia, the largest Episcopal unit in the United States. He was born in Mississippi, grew up in Pensacola, Florida, and graduated from the Virginia Theological Seminary. Described as a centrist, he edited a newsletter, "Center Aisle," but he deviated toward the liberal side by voting for the ordination of Gene Robinson, an openly gay priest, as bishop of the Diocese of New Hampshire. This action evoked strenuous protest from some of Lee's Virginia parishioners. One, Rector Minnus, professed to have "more relation with global Anglicanism than with the Bishop of Virginia." Lee, then, is a southerner who, in this instance at least, moved toward his liberal northern counterparts. Speaking geographically, he located himself within the northern American and European sphere rather than within the global South. In this sense, he exemplifies an older but still recent journey by southerners toward the liberal North and perhaps Northern Europe, while Minnus, who happens to be a one-eighth Jewish Englishman residing in Virginia, takes a global journey that is conservative from a liberal perspective.[10] Another wrinkle has been added now that the Episcopalians have elected a woman as bishop. Global Anglicans look askance at this too.

Religious, gender, and sexual issues aside, the Anglicans illustrate a remarkable geographical decentering and recentering. The previous center, the northeastern United States and Northern Europe, is replaced by a new center, the global South. Among those who identify with this global South are some congregations and leaders from the American South. From the standpoint of the American South, this is quite remarkable in several regards. Anglicans from the American South who are joining the global South are allying themselves with African colleagues who would previously have been regarded as subordinate or alien: they are black, they were colonized, and they are citizens of a continent that provided slaves. And in this allegiance, the U.S. southerners bypass the northeastern United States, which was formerly the source of liberal thinking about race relations and civil rights, and go straight to the global sphere. In so doing, the southern U.S. Anglicans repeat a certain pattern of the past:

they secede from a northern union. This time, however, their international linkages are not to Britain and France, as during the Civil War, but to Africa and Asia: they reach out globally to other souths.

Granted, this argument is counterintuitive or paradoxical: it shows that globally reaching out—a certain kind of global identity—violates common expectations in this instance. Shouldn't the liberals be the globalists? Is it a good thing or a bad thing when global connections are built at the expense of liberal values, including a more open view of sexual orientation or of gender in relation to leadership? My point is not to praise the conservative Anglicans for all they do but to acknowledge their accomplishment in moving toward global community and identity.

GLOBAL PROJECTS

Consider, next, five southern global projects.

Exploris

Three decades ago, Gordon Smith was in India in the Peace Corps. A native of Raleigh, North Carolina, he returned there to prosper in an investment business, but his calling is internationalism, globalism. Drawing on corporate, state, city, and private funding, including much of his own money, he built Exploris. Exploris is a global interactive museum on twenty-two acres that includes an IMAX theater, a global charter school, housing for international visitors, and a converted church to host international events and organizations from the surrounding area, all owned by Smith. Exploris is gradually being transformed into a global locale.

International studies

The University of North Carolina at Chapel Hill vies with the University of Georgia in claiming that it is the oldest public university in the United States. During its first hundred years, the University of North Carolina was largely regional: its first international student, from Japan, arrived in 1893. During its second hundred years, it remained regional and state based while attaining a national stature. In the university's bicentennial celebration and campaign—its first major development campaign—in 1993, international interests were hardly noted. The symbolism was national and state oriented: President Clinton spoke, bands came from each of North Carolina's one hundred counties, and sprigs of Davie poplar— the ancestral campus tree—were planted by children in the counties. That same year, however, a University Center for International Studies was created, and it became one of the catalysts for the university to make a global and international orientation a universitywide priority and to link myriad international efforts. Subsequent programs have included the creation of one of seven Rotary Center for International Studies in Peace and Conflict Resolution. This kind of activity is not unique to the University of North Carolina. What has happened with international studies at Chapel Hill is happening throughout the South. At Louisiana State University, for example, international studies is the fastest growing major in the College of Arts and Sciences.

Mobile, Alabama

Mobile, Alabama, has a history as a cosmopolitan city on the Gulf Coast, boasting a small Catholic and European facet although its physical facade is more antebellum and Gulf Coast Deep South than international. In the late 1990s, Mike Dow, a dynamic mayor, met the president-to-be of Indonesia, Bacharuddin Jusuf Habibie, at an air show in Paris. The two hit it off, and Mobile competed with several other cities to attract an industry from Indonesia. Habibie, a German-trained engineer, had developed an airplane designed to make two- and three-hundred-mile trips in commercial service, and he wanted to build it in the United States and sell it in the U.S. market. Mobile already had a Singapore-based delivery company using its Brookings Field. Dow explained to me how the city of Mobile related to Habibie. Whereas one competing town picked him up in a SUV and had a barbecue—for a Muslim who does not eat pork—Mobile accorded him a limousine and the courtesy due a head of state. Also, Mobile named a street named after Ghatotkacha, a mythological figure from the Hindu epic poem *Mahabharata*, popular in Java, who can fly.[11] Though the enterprise was postponed because of economic and political shifts, the effort of Mobile to court Indonesian industry nonetheless formed a remarkable partnership between a city and a nation from two different "Souths."

Columbus, Georgia

Columbus, on the Chattahoochee River across from Alabama, is perhaps best known as the site of Fort Benning, but it has also been a southern industrial city since before the Civil War; it boasts Georgia's longest-operating school, Whynton; it was a birthplace of Coca-Cola and of the author Carson McCullers; and it is the home of AFLAC, a renowned insurance company. Shortly after the Civil War ended, Columbus instituted Confederate Memorial Day, which is still celebrated throughout the South.

Acknowledging the approach of the millennium, the Columbus Chamber of Commerce and the Commission on International Relations and Cultural Liaison Encounters (CIRCLE) sponsored the publication of *Columbus Celebrating the Millennium: An International Quest*, a large photography book written by Pam Baker. The last chapter, "The Millennium Milieux: 1990s and Beyond," depicts the period as global, featuring CIRCLE endeavors to promote Columbus's relations with the wider world, including the establishment of relations to Kiryu, Japan, a sister city of Columbus for twenty years, and, more recently, Zugdidi, Georgia, in the former USSR. The book notes that in the 1800s, cotton was shipped down the Chattahoochee abroad. In the early 1900s, Lummus Industries sold cotton gins in Russia. And today, AFLAC insures millions of people in Japan. Fort Benning was founded in 1920 and ever since "has sent soldiers to fight on foreign soils, exposing them to cultures unlike their own." Some of these soldiers "brought home spouses from across the ocean."[12] Kiryu has named a street Columbus Street, and Columbus State University has created a Kiryu Garden honoring the sister city relationship. Columbus also hosted an Olympic event (women's fast-pitch softball) in 1996, the same year in which CIRCLE was created by city ordinance.

History's undersides are, of course, hardly mentioned in such a book. "Indian civilization" eulogizes Indian mound cultures that flourished for centuries and were exterminated by settlers in decades; plantations, slavery, cotton mills, and poor whites are also glossed over, though they are part of the context of Columbus. Remarkably creative individuals, such as Carson McCullers, are omitted, as are less-known people, such as Minerva Peacock, my father's mother. Minerva was born in a rustic house on a farm in Stewart County in the late nineteenth century and was orphaned as a young girl. She became a schoolteacher and at age sixty matriculated at Auburn University in the 1940s, majoring in mathematics and graduating at the top of her class four years later. Dorothy Madding, Minerva's daughter and a native of Columbus who lived in Okinawa and Guam because of her husband's military career, today teaches children to make origami to honor victims of Hiroshima and in other ways has an international outlook; at the same time, she steadfastly maintains the family farm where her mother was born.

At Houlihan's Restaurant in the Marriott Hotel in Columbus, where I found Baker's book, a black hostess seats numerous black families who are served by white waiters and waitresses, one of whom was seen squatting below the eye level of seated customers—in this case black customers—to take orders. Columbus has many layers of history and society interwoven with its announced internationalism.

The University of North Carolina, like most universities, contracts with companies that subcontract with factories around the world that make apparel with the university's insignia. In fact, the university has more than five hundred such licensees. One is Nike. UNC signed a contract with Nike in the late nineties, and students protested, saying Nike has sweatshops. To inform the process, three of us offered a course, the Nike course. Twenty students, from freshman to graduate level, took it. At the last class, the students offered recommendations to Nike to reform. The Nike CEO, Phil Knight, paid a surprise visit to the class. A few days later, he held a press conference at the National Press Club in Washington, D.C., and announced that Nike would implement the reforms. This step helped stimulate a coalition of many universities and corporations to reform sweatshops. It is called FLA, the Fair Labor Association, and is based in Washington but works globally with licensees and factories. It is led by Arret van Heerden, a South African in Geneva, and was managed by Rut Tufts, a Georgian at UNC. FLA and Nike illustrate a supply chain reaching from global factories to a southern state university—issues and methods in grounding globalism.

Interpenetration of the World and the South

Deliberate projects are one way of connecting South and world; another way to foster connection is through imports and exports, to the South from other parts of the world, from other parts of the world to the South.

The South increasingly embraces diverse peoples and cultures from around the world. How receptive are southerners to new immigrants, to imports? to exports? Circumstances vary, of course. At one extreme is the poor treatment of migrant workers in farms and factories, as Sandy Smith-Nonini and Steve Striffler document for North Carolina and Arkansas in essays in *The American South in a Global World*. Rachel Willis's study in the same volume argues that the picture for the Hmong is more positive, as does Ajantha Subramanian's discussion of professionals from India.[13]

Sometimes southerners show more receptivity to migrants from abroad than to migrants from elsewhere in the United States; foreigners seem more appreciative of where they have come to, some southerners feel, and are less critical and less rude. At a church in North Carolina, a "bossy" migrant from Ohio was less welcome than a "polite" migrant from Thailand. Southerners may be less familiar with the languages and cultures of immigrants from abroad, but they also do not have the same history of oppositional relations with foreigners as they do with migrants from the non-South United States. Native southerners and immigrants from the North and elsewhere in the nation often find common cause, however, in relations with global immigrants. Such is apparent in our local International Affairs Council, for example, which is directed by a southerner and staffed by immigrants from abroad and other parts of the United States.

The inverse of people coming here is people going there. Note, then, the growth of many practices and relationships that, by exporting the South, link southerners and the South to the world : sister cities, study abroad, work camps, Rotary teams, and so on. These link local groups and individuals from the U.S. South to local groups and individuals elsewhere. Rotary clubs are one of the most remarkable examples of integration at the community level; Fulbright scholarships do the same at the academic level. The World Affairs Council, based in Washington, D.C., is currently directed by someone who grew up in Alabama and Virginia and studied and worked in England and on the Trobriand Islands.

Not only nonprofits spread from the South. Wal-Mart and Coca-Cola, Bank of America and CNN, Delta Airlines and Kentucky Fried Chicken are examples of for-profit global southern entities that are best considered as spreading globalization rather than as instilling globalism. But as well as spreading products globally, these companies convey a sense of the South as being in the world, the global world.[14]

EXPORTING PROVINCIALISM GLOBALLY

Within this global/local gestalt, nuances and issues are many: consider one dilemma emerging in such global/local interactions, that of the southerner who attempts to reach out globally yet is still identified as a provincial by fellow Americans. A zero-sum theory would assert that the less regional identity you have, the more easily you can move into a world culture sphere. Cosmopolitans do better than provincials, it is presumed. A variant is that those who conform more closely to national norms will do better internationally than those who are more regional. Carried to an extreme, however, this premise seems false, for "opposites attract," and exchange is based on X bringing something to Y that Y does not have; otherwise, one "carries coals to Newcastle," bringing nothing more than what is already there. This truth explains why regional or other particularized differences frequently interest foreigners. The British watched *Dallas*, while Americans watch *Masterpiece Theatre*; *Gone with the Wind* played well globally, as do bagpipes, mariachi, and "local color," a staple of tourists—an obvious point in support of the thesis that provincialism appeals to other provincials, which all of us are.

A further consideration is that regional, national, and international are different perspectives; therefore, what is regional from a national perspective may not be perceived the same way internationally. Provincials in American eyes (Jimmy Carter and Bill Clinton, for example) may or may not be so perceived internationally. "They didn't want me to teach English phonetics because I have a southern accent," reported a southerner living in the Ukraine. Who were "they"? Was it Ukrainians or Americans who discouraged this fluent Russian- and Ukrainian-speaking southerner from teaching English in the Ukraine because southern-accented English was a liability, while a midwestern accent was an asset? Of course, preferred accents change, as do stereotypes. Globalization throws into contact and conversation global, regional, national, and other locales, and it shifts emphasis from national to global frameworks. As the gestalt shifts from national frames of reference to global ones, who is southern and who is northern diminishes in importance, so national integration coincides with global integration, at least to a degree. More generally, this shift should dissolve or diminish oppositional attitudes within a national perspective while encouraging an integrative move globally.

IMPORTING GLOBALISM PROVINCIALLY

How open is a closed identity? Posed starkly, the question prompts a negative answer: closed means closed. The answer is not that simple, however. Compare the provincial and the cosmopolitan as extreme types. Which has more to lose by openness to outside influences? If the provincial has more to lose, then that process of losing inside identity by opening to outside identities may arguably be more complicated, more difficult, and perhaps more consequential—at least to that individual or that culture—than it would be for the cosmopolitan. The South and the southerner, we surely realize by now, are complex identities, neither closed nor open. But at least since the Civil War, a certain resistance to the outside, to change, has been discernable, and while we argue that this resistance may be bypassed somewhat when the change comes globally rather than nationally or from the North, one must acknowledge postures of seeming resistance to globalism.

The Korean bride of a soldier who brought her back from Korea to Wrightsville, Georgia, felt ostracized by his working-class family. A Jewish immigrant to Strasburg, Virginia, was beaten on Christmas Day. In education, fields that stress openness to diverse cultures—such as anthropology, area studies, and international studies—came late to the South as compared with the rest of the nation. So, too, have most of the other expressions of globalism, ranging from foreign consulates to sister cities and publishing houses that offer international perspectives institutionally.

Globalism penetrates most markedly in the South at the level of the individual and of relations between individuals—the domains the South characteristically celebrates. A particular person joins the diplomatic corps or becomes an anthropologist or a journalist, a traveler or an artist, or in some other way forges particular friendships across cultures. Yet while these maneuverings and seismic shifts occur as part of personal and international relationships, reconceptualizations and realignments proceed in summative institutions—museums, programs, missions, centers—and through summative symbols as illustrated below.

GLOBAL SYMBOLS AND CONTEXTS

Names reflect globalism: one sees not only regional names (Dixie, Carolina, and Southern everything—even Southern Bodies, the name of a fitness center in Tifton, Georgia) but also global ones (for example, the World Congress Center in Atlanta). An intriguing example is the World Motel in McCrae, Georgia, created by a Pakistani immigrant. In naming his business, he identified himself not as a mere immigrant, marginal to natives, but as a citizen of the world. "World Citizen of the Year" and similar designations are similarly symbols of globalism. Less exalted and more nuanced is Alan Jackson's affirmation of globalism: "It's five o'clock somewhere." In the slightly degenerate world Jackson creates, the good ol' boys inhabit the whole world—as Dabbs would say, feel at home there—because it's always happy hour somewhere, wherever they are. The song contrasts with those that romanticize locale ("Oh I wish I was in the land of cotton") or foreign destinations ("Slow boat to China" or "Off we go, into the wild blue yonder" or "From the halls of Montezuma to the shores of Tripoli"): Jackson domesticates the world, just as Dabbs suggests southerners do, while globalizing domesticity, casual comfort, and pleasure. Balancing locals thinking globally, globals think (or symbolize) locally: a Chinese woman, crossing the street near my office, speaking Chinese, carries a bag with the slogan "Tar Heel bred."[15]

The argument is not that regional identity or national identity is lost, replaced by global identity; such was the assertion, it seems, of earlier notions about globalization and globalism by Chakrabarty, Appadurai, and Friedman, essayists who emphasize how globalization is erasing national boundaries and creating a seamless global or cosmopolitan world culture in which locale shrinks in importance.[16] Rather, regional, national, and global identities connect in new ways; both regional and national identity are reconfigured as part of that connection and the enhanced global identity. The connections and reconfiguring occur at many levels, and may fail to occur at some, but the gestalt favors globalism.

What, if anything, is distinctly southern about the South's efforts at globalism? Context more than content, I would say. Of course, some features of global content have southern content, including Cajun zydeco, jambalaya, and blues, Kentucky Fried Chicken, and the manners and style of Texan or Arkansan presidents or other southerners abroad who are sometimes described with clichés about friendliness or hospitality. Yet context is important, for the globalism of the South emerges from an earlier history, especially nineteenth century. Some special features of that historic southern society may have encouraged certain kinds of attitudes and behaviors that southerners extended into international settings. The nineteenth- and twentieth-century South was a dualistic society, dividing higher and lower classes along racial lines. Especially among wealthier families, slaves and then servants had an accepted, if subordinate, role reflected in certain manners, for example use of terms of respect such as "sir" or "ma'am" and combining "Mr." and "Miss" with first names to create terms of address such as "Mr. Robert" and "Miss Frances." Blacks were involved in intimate aspects of the lives of whites. Sometimes they mated; at other times they were caretakers for each other—blacks as nurses, whites as masters, employers, and sometimes mentors. This portrait is too often idealized, to be sure, suppressing the realities of oppression, but the combination of formality and intimacy was also a reality in the South as in many similar colonial situations and, for that matter, in many societies where an upstairs/downstairs master/servant pattern obtained. Here one should recall the particular variety of cross-cultural and cross-racial relations in the South, including the Creole experiences in New Orleans, free black slaveholders in Charleston, and the sort of genealogies exemplified by Strom Thurmond, the South Carolina senator who finally acknowledged his partially black daughter, who then applied to join the Daughters of the Confederacy in order to "acknowledge her heritage." Dualism atop diversity is a feature of the historic South just as it is a feature of many similar colonial agrarian societies where planters and workers, either slaves or natives, combined intimacy with hierarchy and all that hierarchy implies, including, of course, sometimes, cruelty and oppression.

Such a context lends a distinctive meaning to southerners' conceptions and overall experiences of globalism, even if the overt and explicit words and programs are the same as those of nonsouthern globalists with, say, urban middle class northern backgrounds. When Jimmy Carter champions human rights and works toward curing blindness in Africa, his globalist values reflect universalist vision and, perhaps, obliquely reflect southern experiences in countless ways, including, perhaps, special affection for African linkages, guilt and noblesse oblige derived from past black-white relations, a mix of intimacy and taboo, and Protestant values concerning service and mission, all topped, of course, by the American can-do activist's search for solutions to problems. When George Bush the younger and his compatriots Rice, Rumsfeld, and Cheney champion their particular kind of foreign policy, each brings a distinctive background—

Connecticut-originating family and Texas oil-country upbringing for Bush; Birmingham, Alabama, African American background for Rice; and midwestern and western backgrounds, respectively, for Rumsfeld and Cheney—despite converging in seeming agreement on policy. When I go to Guatemala with William Peck, a friend and colleague, we carry out the same activities guided by quite similar values, but his background is New England, with missionary parents who went to Wellesley and Williams, while mine is "southern." (We shared a similar graduate school education, however, meeting in a certain seminar.)

Lest one get bogged down in assessing the impact of cultural heritage, note a counterprinciple: differences that are strong at home may diminish in a global context. An Alabamian of Christian background who converted to Judaism marries a Jewish northerner in Indonesia, and a North Carolinian joins a Chinese-dominated church in Singapore. The marriage reflects a similar national background and somewhat similar religious background, the church membership, a similar religious background, and in each case these commonalities override cultural or ethnic difference. A similar trend is observed among migrants whose homeland differences diminish when they come to the new land, such as Indians of different castes or Chinese from Beijing or Shanghai who emphasize their commonalities within the context of a foreign land.

The southerner moves toward overcoming the opposition between South and nation, then, as a by-product of the trend toward world integration. Within a world context, one ceases to be a southerner, but is an American; thus, one "joins the nation." One's concern about one's national identity diminishes, and one's oppositional status ceases to matter as much. Or, finally, one's regional identity may find a legitimacy and meaning within a world context that it lacked in a national context. A southerner abroad becomes, on the whole, just an American, as perceived by others who distinguish the national, not the regional, difference. Pakistanis burn an effigy of Colonel Sanders, for example, not because he symbolizes Kentucky or the U.S. South but because he and his fried chicken franchise represent the United States.

The dynamics of region, nation, and world are complex. The overall trend may be one of diminished oppositionality by southerners within the nation, coupled with greater integration of southerners in the world. The nation's relation to the world is also a factor, however. The world-integration movement of the region is countered by the nation's becoming more oppositional to the world, even as the South becomes less oppositional within the nation. That is, southerners as southerners may diminish their oppositionality to the nation and increase their integration with the world while as Americans they increase their oppositionality to the world. Southerners may welcome diversity at home yet join other Americans in opposing terrorism abroad. Opposition to enemies and threats is balanced by alliance with supporters, however, so that the overall move toward global integration continues.

Evidence of global identity in the South is abundant and multileveled. What is the relationship to oppositionality within a national framework? Here, too, we have evidence on multiple levels. One level concerns individual choice about whether to emphasize global, national, or regional identities. The Southern Focus Poll forced a choice by the individual, and more chose the global identity over the regional one. Choices are evident in less artificial settings as well. Few, if any, vehicles display both "Think globally, act locally" stickers and American flags or, for that matter, Confederate ones. Anglicans choose, too, when an individual or a church secedes from the national or northern liberal wing and identifies with the global southern one.

These examples consider individual choice, but our larger emphasis is on the collective level, on how the culture frames identity. The Exploris museum in Raleigh, Gatokaca Street in Mobile, the World Motel in McCrae, and various Atlanta-based global endeavors—the World Congress Center, CNN, Delta, the Carter Center, the Olympics—are all collective expressions of global identity located or based in the region. So are military bases, though with more defensive connotations—keeping us safe from terrorism or foreign threats generally; so are immigrants and the myriad evidence of global cultural influence in religion, food, and music, not to mention manufactured goods ranging from cars to clothing, which may at once signal globalization and the threat of job loss for local workers. The culture pervading the region displays aspects that are strongly global at the same time that it maintains many regional dimensions.

In this culture, because the national frame becomes less important for the regional culture as the global identity becomes stronger, oppositionality becomes less dominant as a cultural value. Such a change is collective, a shift in worldview, in cultural conceptualization. Expressions of it vary in scope and intensity, in context and form. The change pervades the culture, affecting millions of people but is most easily illustrated in the lives of particular individuals. Take Jimmy Carter. He affirms southern roots, even sectional sentiments (for example, when he stated that his book on the American Revolution corrected an underestimate of the importance of southern battles), yet his predominant orientation is global, as illustrated by his presidency and his founding of the Carter Center. Whatever oppositionality Carter may feel—and he doubtless felt plenty when he was caricatured as a provincial peanut farmer—it is subsumed and subordinated to a global frame; his energies are channeled into global needs, creating a global/regional endeavor and identity. In Carter's life, one can trace a dialectic between global, national, and local: he left Plains to go to the naval academy and become a career officer in the U.S. Navy, he left the navy to return to Plains when his father died, he left Plains again to become governor, then president, and he left the presidency to create the Carter Center, which, while located in Atlanta, is global in scope and outlook.

A less idealistic symbolism is illustrated by Alan Jackson in his statement that "it's five o'clock somewhere," and Jimmy Buffett's adding, "It's always on five in Margaritaville, come to think of it," which evokes a good ol' boy corollary to Carter's moral world—an immoral one, but one that is also global. A grimmer redneck message is conveyed by the Confederate flag that reads "Made in China" that is on sale at the demolition derby. Even regional identity is now owned by the global market, specifically China, which is where our jobs go. Blacks on the Delta felt global competition long ago when Italian and Chinese immigrants came to do their jobs, and they feel it again presently, when Latin Americans do so. Global/local impacts run a gamut between good and bad and are experienced in many ways.

Whatever the valence, the point is that regional identity, including oppositionality, changes meaning when it is subsumed in a global identity framework or gestalt. The dynamic is illustrated by an Indonesian joke. Vehicles crash at an intersection. Whose fault is it? Answer: the Dutch (or some other foreign villain—this joke was told when the Dutch were blamed as neocolonial oppressors). The shift is from the expected local framework to a global one, which changes levels of discourse and identification. The logic behind this joke is that oppositionality in a local context diminishes when framed globally. That logic is manifested by individuals in varying contexts, but most important, it is manifested culturally in the larger gestalt that shapes the experiences of millions of individuals.

With respect to the South, the argument is not only that individual southerners frequently lift their sights to a global level, thus consciously and deliberately eschewing regional oppositionality—that can happen and does. My emphasis is on what is happening culturally—that multiple levels of global identity pervade the culture, and this impacts regional attitudes, including regional oppositionality, whether intentionally or not.

At this point, then, we have considered some evidence for the sixth step in our model—that a culturally embedded oppositionality is being replaced or supplemented by a global identity.

CHAPTER FOUR

Dualism to Pluralism

Global Diversity on Southern Ground

GLOBAL IDENTITY is expressed locally by diversity, or pluralism. In the American South, the impact of globally derived immigration and cultural influences has a special character. The South's complex
history of diverse peoples and cultures—ranging from Native American
groups of great variety and complexity to ethnically diverse migrants
from Europe, Africa, Latin America, and Asia—has been overlaid by one
dominant theme: dualism, stereotyped as black against white. While the
range and complexity of the early South remained, evolved, and differed
by locale, an overriding black-white dualism became pervasive during
slavery and segregation continuing through the twentieth century. New
immigrants and cultures complicate this dualism, however, as we enter
the twenty-first century and the South experiences a large influx from

Latin America and elsewhere, especially Asia. As the South continues to move from dualism to pluralism, multiple scenarios of diversity emerge. Pluralism does not guarantee globalism, nor do some globalisms embrace pluralism. On the whole, however, the new pluralism, or diversity, reflects globalization and global identity, constituting the global in local contexts. In this chapter we examine the transition from dualism to pluralism in light of its opportunities and pitfalls for a southern globalism.

The import of diversity for the South is made clear in a joke told locally by Hispanics. Jesse Helms and Jesse Jackson argue about whether God is white or black. Both die and go to heaven. God greets them: "Buenos días." As the joke aptly illustrates, diversity has changed the terms of conversation—not only the language but the variables and actors involved.

New diversities result not only from the arrival of immigrants but also from new cultural exchange and the practice of religions new to the South—Islam, Hinduism, Buddhism, Baha'i, Taoism, and alternative religions such as shamanism—as well as from ethnic diversity within old ones, as evidenced in Korean Christian churches, for example. Mainline churches still dominate the centers of southern towns, but now one sees Spanish-language churches, mosques, and Hindu temples. Mexican, Indian, and Chinese restaurants and grocery or video stores dot streets and neighborhoods, workers constructing roads and buildings are Latinos, and Indian names appear on the signs of medical clinics. Obviously the landscape is changed and changing. But how deep is that change? At what levels does it occur? What is happening, not only in economic and political arenas but also in culture, in minds and attitudes? How does its impact vary according to ethnicity, class, or gender? Most important, we pursue our argument; we do not survey the variety and complexity of diversities in the South but, instead, focus on issues and examples that show relations between diversity and emerging global identity. We begin with an occasion, the recent commemoration of Martin Luther King Jr., the towering symbol of change in relations between blacks and whites. Beginning with current celebrations of such a figure, we investigate whether the symbolization of southern dualism now encompasses the presence of new immigrants and cultures.

Gatherings

MARTIN LUTHER KING JR. COMMEMORATIONS

At the annual Martin Luther King Jr. banquet in Chapel Hill held Sunday night, January 18, 2004, the attendees are predominantly black, with a large representation of whites and many leaders from both groups. Among those present are one state representative, two state senators, the local congressman, the chancellor and the provost of the University of North Carolina, white ministers of Methodist and Presbyterian churches, black and white Baptist ministers, the mayor, the school superintendent, and a rabbi, all of whom are invited to stand. Missing are Asians. Latinos are in evidence mainly as waiters and waitresses except for one, the leader of El Pueblo (a nonprofit state organization that advocates for Latinos), who gives an opening statement. The names of the Martin Luther King Jr. scholarship recipients are called out; they are said to be eligible regardless of race or creed, and one is a white student at Harvard. The keynote speaker, Trudier Harris, is African American, as are the singer and the pianist. They perform an African American gospel song, "Precious Lord, Take My Hand." The rabbi gives the invocation. The speech outlines a "Martin Luther King report card" detailing various assignments for the next twelve months to be graded by the "one you see in the mirror," that is, by oneself. These entail efforts at race relations, mainly black-white, largely ignoring other ethnicities. (The speaker does not note, for example, the irony of the Latino waiters.) The banquet ends with the singing of "Lift Every Voice and Sing" (the "Negro National Anthem") and a benediction.

What grade would this gathering receive on a "diversity," or "pluralism," report card? A solid B, I would say. Despite the absence of Latinos and Asians, diversity was apparent in the rabbi (who, the following year, brought a Muslim friend to share the invocation), the El Pueblo head, and the scholarships. Understandably and appropriately, given the occasion, the main concern of the evening was black and white relationships.

Other contemporaneous celebrations of King, however, pressed further toward pluralism. On Tuesday, January 20, 2004, at the University of North Carolina at Chapel Hill, the third annual Dr. Martin Luther King Jr. lecture was delivered by Johnnetta Cole, president of Bennett College, formerly of Spelman College in Atlanta, both historically black institutions for women. Cole spoke cogently and compassionately about equality and inclusiveness regardless of race, gender, class, or sexual orientation and identity (she specifically mentioned transgendered persons).[1] While her audience was predominantly black, her framework was humanity writ large. She discussed Latinos in detail, distinguishing their various countries and cultures of origin and chastising her audience (predominantly blacks and whites) for thinking "they are all alike." She also referred specifically to Muslims, Jews, and Hindus as well as Christians, and she dwelt on the Holocaust and quoted Elie Wiesel, explaining that she worried about anti-Semitism and Nazism. Identifying herself as an anthropologist, she asserted that all cultural differences were learned, and that "if they are learned, they can be unlearned." She wove in colloquial sayings and allusions to her background in Jacksonville, Florida, with a more universal, elevated rhetoric. She connected pasts and futures in figures such as Rosa Parks, whom she called a "shero" who "sat down so that we can stand up." To judge from Dr. Cole's analysis, standing up entails reaching out past dualisms and toward pluralism and globalism. Cole's care in distinguishing the nationalities of Latin America and in making links to the Holocaust performed a similar function. She endeavored to extend the King legacy past dualism toward pluralism.

Martin Luther King Jr. is an icon of the struggle for equality, justice, and freedom, perhaps the single greatest such icon in America and in the South. Accordingly, patterns expressed in regard to King are suggestive of trends in the wider society. King himself had global resonance and reference: after all, Gandhi was an inspiration to him. And in his "I Have a Dream" speech, he called for unity not only between blacks and whites but also between "Jews and Gentiles, Protestants and Catholics." Still, at the time of his death, King was seen predominantly as addressing the division between black and white, especially in the South. Modern events that commemorate King illustrate how this figure who initially focused on overcoming inequalities of a dualistic society—the divide between black and white—moved toward pluralism.

The point is illustrated further by a feature story on racism that appeared the week of King's birthday in 2004 in the *Raleigh News and Observer*.[2] Depicted and interviewed were an African American, an Asian, and a Hispanic. In this article, a Hispanic woman describes telephoning a doctor's office. The receptionist, hearing the caller's slight accent, asked if she would like to be referred to a less expensive physician. The woman interpreted this question as being based on the assumption that she, as a Hispanic, was too poor to afford the doctor. Her response, which was about class and ethnicity, was included in this article about racism, conflating the three categories—which of course happens in our daily thinking and acting. The point here is that Hispanics, Asians, and African Americans were included in the article as part of a complex of "diversity" linked to the symbol of King.

Robert E. Lee's birthday is a few days after Martin Luther King's. Conspicuous by its absence in our area of North Carolina in January was any public recognition of Lee's birthday, with the exception of a single letter to the newspaper from a reader in New Bern. Editorials commemorated King, not Lee, and no attempt was made to link the two. Can this be taken as a sign of the passing of the Old South? Is it politically incorrect to praise Lee in relation to King? Perhaps this shift obtains only in the Triangle area, since elsewhere in the South, including Virginia, Lee was commemorated.

Chapel Hill, while billing itself "the southern part of heaven," shares the region's history of racial dualism.[3] Slaves are buried in unmarked graves at one end of the Old Chapel Hill, the oldest town cemetery. African Americans remain somewhat segregated from whites residentially. Cornelia Spencer, an early feminist who reopened the university after the Civil War by ringing its bell, reportedly expressed racist sentiments. Airport Road, so named because of the Horace Williams airport (whose name comes from an esteemed philosopher at the university a century ago), was recently renamed for Martin Luther King Jr., an act resisted by those who defended the preservation of history. Yet Chapel Hill did elect a black mayor, Howard Lee, who now, as state chair of the board of education, champions global education.

Let us continue to follow, for a bit, Martin Luther King's trail to Birmingham, Alabama. Recall images and events of civil rights—Eugene "Bull" Connor and the photograph of him with the police dogs threatening a young black man. That image contrasts with a smiling young woman on a recent cover of *Newsweek*. The magazine has selected the top one hundred high schools in America. Number one is hers, Jefferson County International Baccalaureate School near Birmingham, Alabama. The contrast seems to announce a change from the old dualistic South to the new pluralistic—indeed international—South.[4]

Also in Birmingham, the last in a set of discussions sponsored by UNC's Center for the Study of the American South and titled "Unfinished Business" was held; Birmingham was chosen as the location for the final meeting as a way of revisiting a summit conference held there before World War II to assess prospects for race relations in the South. Touch points, then, were the late thirties and the violent times of the sixties, culminating in the reflective and prospective discussions of the nineties. We met there, in Birmingham, at the church that was bombed. John Lewis, who had marched with King, spoke, as did Governor Winter of Mississippi, the journalist John Egerton, and many others. Next to the church is a civil rights museum, and next to that is a human rights annex, recognizing a global dimension—rights of all peoples. Here, then, is a hint of the well-known stream of southern history exemplified by Birmingham and civil rights but with global allusions at the edge. The dualist stream, focusing especially on inequality and the black struggle for civil rights, is now enriched by a nascent but promising pluralist and globalist stream.

FAMILY GATHERINGS

If we move away from public domains into family spheres but stick to the famous sites of civil rights history in Alabama, we come to Selma and Montgomery, the latter the first capital of the Confederacy, before it moved to Richmond, Virginia. Here are three quick sketches, the recent weddings of two young white couples, both held in Episcopal churches, and one family gathering. The first wedding took place in Selma, a small town, and included a traditional stream of international culture: classical music (Pachelbel and Handel played on an organ and a piano in the church and later by a harpist at the reception at a country club). Guests were largely from Alabama, and allusions ranged from formal to folksy (the couple would be "at home" at Speigner, a crossroads out in the country in the vicinity of Montgomery, but the groom "had to wait until deer season was over to get married") within a basically southern white universe. The second wedding, in a more urban Birmingham setting, united a pair who were natives of Birmingham, though the groom graduated from NYU, and guests included several ethnicities. The groom's sister is at Harvard majoring in anthropology. Her grandmother, who was raised in and lives in Tuscaloosa, went to Radcliffe. The third gathering was held in a backyard in Montgomery. It was an annual family gathering, including some of the same people who were at the weddings. No blacks were present, though mention was made of Ula, a servant and nurse to several of the families, who lived to be nearly one hundred and had attended previous gatherings where she reminisced about persons present whom she had known since they were children and their ancestors whom she had also known. (Ula had recently died, occasioning a large funeral in the small town ancestral to this family.) One foreign person was present at the gathering, the German wife of a cousin, and a certain international dimension entered through my father, who was asked by my brother-in-law to describe how he invaded Normandy on D-Day. Another relative turned out to be recipient of a Silver Star and a Purple Heart, also in World War II.

Should one inquire about genealogies and histories, which are the topic of such gatherings, suggestive intersections with diversity appear. A grandfather was treasurer of the Methodist Protestant denomination and present in Kansas City in 1939 when northern and southern branches, divided since the Civil War, reunited, forming a union of the Methodist Episcopal, Methodist Episcopal South, and Methodist Protestant churches. That union nationally did not accomplish a union of black Methodist churches, so the African Methodist Episcopal Zion Church, for example, remains separate from the United Methodist Church, which partially explains the issue of integration discussed by the committee below. When that grandfather died, shortly after the Kansas City meeting, a large number of African Americans reportedly attended his funeral in rural Alabama, some coming from far away. Does that signify that he was sympathetic to inclusion of African American churches in the union? That he was diplomatic while supporting the somewhat exclusive union that resulted? That as a landowner he was paternalistically humane? His daughter is not certain about the answers. Nor are his grandchildren, including a surgeon now residing in Seattle who is certain only that his grandfather was overcharged by a doctor in New York City, where the grandfather spent months under treatment for cancer. That surgeon's son has married a Japanese woman and moved to Japan, illustrating a global step that moves past the regional and racial setting in which his great-grandfather was embedded.

What should we make of this jumble of encounters? The historic dualism is evident, as one compares the civil rights dimension for blacks and "life as normal" for whites. Blacks commemorate Birmingham, Selma, and Montgomery, and Alabama as sites of the struggle for civil rights; whites associated with the same sites hold weddings and reunions, pursue science, or serve in the army, activities not associated with civil rights. Yet both blacks and whites are diversifying and globalizing. A rhetoric of globalization and diversity is apparent especially in the Martin Luther King speech of Johnnetta Cole; diversity is perhaps less evident among the whites, on the occasion noted, and globalism, likewise, is present but unstated or understated. And it is worth noting that Montgomery is historically significant for both streams of history, civil rights and the Civil War; it was at once the site of Rosa Parks and of Jefferson Davis. She occupied a seat at the front of a bus, and he occupied the Confederate White House, which still stands near the capital building.

In terms of the civil rights report card mentioned by the banquet speaker, grades might be only passing, but currents are apparent that flow toward diversity. Those currents flow past localized diversity toward global identities and associations that arguably may transform local relations, but not necessarily or immediately.

A CHURCH RETREAT

For evidence of southerners' intentional engagement with pluralism, let us consider a discussion among a minister and his largely white congregants in Chapel Hill's largest Methodist church, which is in its second retreat, envisioning the next decade. "Diversity and inclusion" were identified as priorities at the first retreat, and the group of a hundred or so is asked to self-select that topic or others mentioned in the first retreat for small group discussion. Those who gather to discuss the diversity and inclusion topic are some ten, including the lay leader, Robert; the minister, Bill; and me. Others are also leaders in the church and community. All of the ten are white, as are all of the larger retreat group of one hundred, and most of the ten are of southern background. Except for Jeff, probably in his twenties, all are in their fifties or sixties. The task is to build on the overarching goal by defining more-specific goals and actions and then specifying who will perform them and with what resources. We begin in the late morning and work until nearly 5 p.m. on a chilly Saturday. The site is the Sunday School classroom where English as a second language is taught. On the wall are photos and brief biographies and self-statements by ESL students, all Asian.

A first point of interest is the interplay between global and local and the understandable emphasis of the small group's discussion, which was almost entirely on local diversity (albeit local diversity achieved in part through a global process, immigration). Obvious is the lack of diversity in the congregation and a felt need to add diversity, so discussion focuses on how to do that. A crucial point, made by the minister, underlines the need and desire to transform individual outlooks through experience and relationships. This would necessarily utterly "transform the congregation" collectively. The global perspective that is, to some degree, behind the emphasis on diversity is mentioned but not developed except implicitly. This is partly because the diversity issue is perceived as more than a global issue: diversity is seen as pertaining to sexual orientation, class, gender, and race, as well as to diversities of cultures coming from varied places in the world. Discussion tends to focus on the need to include blacks and Hispanics, while the other features are brought in at the edges and later.

Beverly, who had written a narrative report on the first retreat, mentions the "global" perspective there, noting that Ann and I had alluded to that. I suggest framing this discussion from a global viewpoint, noting the schism within the Episcopal/Anglican Church that entails a global church's contesting a largely northeastern constituency (Canada, England, and parts of the northeastern United States). I do not go into the radical position in which the global majority sees itself as missionary to the northeastern minority, turning the tables on the customary direction of missionary work from West to rest, and the further possibility of missions seen not as from West to rest or from south to north but as global— from all to all. Such a perspective would seem to frame the more localized need to diversify in order to reflect and engage the wider local society, but also to reflect and engage the wider world, of which local diversity is a result and reflection.

Nick brings us quickly back home, stating that the world is here, in our local diversity. Discussion then shifts to goals, several of which are agreed upon. The first, rather overarching, is that of moving self and congregation toward diversity and inclusivity. A second, seen as counterpoint to the first and the others, is to preserve what we have, our own identity, while diversifying: to "sustain and leverage the heritage of our church and share gifts with the community." Other goals flow from the first. Suggested actions, consensually selected and ranked, include the following: declare the church an open church, work toward revision of denominational platforms to invite diversity (perhaps especially pertaining to sexual orientation), develop relationships both collectively (with other congregations, such as African American ones) and individually (personal friendships across cultures), continue ESL classes, diversify hiring, create

Spanish-language literature, hold forums to explore global and diversity perspectives and issues, engage gay and lesbian church members, support an Interfaith Council, and diversify forms of worship. After brainstorming about the actions needed to move toward our goals, we check our list of areas in which diversification is needed, and add actions tied to sexual orientation and class and gender, which had not been emphasized in discussion. An especially telling goal, discussion, and set of actions focus on creating a "safe harbor" for diverse spiritual journeys. That might entail providing meeting space for various religious groups and practices, creating opportunities to meet with these groups to discuss their diverse perspectives, and offering hospitality and support to transient internationals.

The next day, Sunday, Nick presents the vision—goals, actions, and resources needed—to the large retreat group, the one hundred, which is invited to respond, first by indicating "resistance," then by asking questions for clarification. Tom, one of the oldest members of the congregation, indicates some resistance to having varied faiths meet in the church, asking whether this privilege should be restricted to those of Christian faiths. He seems concerned about changing the church's symbols to fit other, non-Christian, faiths. Later, after Jeff explains that the idea is just to provide an empty room for non-Methodists or non-Christians to use for their own worship, Tom accepts, or at least ceases to "resist." Whereas the primary topic in the small group was intercultural diversity—the items about sexual orientation were added after the main discussion—most of the discussion on Sunday is about sexual orientation, and in particular about what kind of resolution would be presented to the annual Methodist conference on this matter. Nick responds delicately, declining to state a substantive position or to specify what such a resolution might state.

What do we learn from this encounter? The setting was different from those of the Martin Luther King celebrations in that it was a focused discussion rather than a celebratory occasion; also, the participants were mainly white, while the Martin Luther King organizers and the majority of the participants were black. Despite these differences in people and circumstances, however, the concerns and perspectives were similar: both groups value diversity, both are moving out of a dualistic history, and both are reaching out—blacks toward whites, whites toward blacks—beyond black-white dualism toward pluralism. For both groups, the focus is primarily local, but the goals of both suggest global connections to local manifestations. Both are alert to the kinds of diversity that are not globally derived but that relate more to gender identities and sexual orientation than to national, racial, or ethnic identities, but these are secondary concerns. The groups are alike, in contrast to the weddings and reunions, in that the groups focus explicitly on issues of diversity (and globalism), while the other gatherings exhibit such patterns incidentally—hinting at ways diversity exists in daily life in comparison to in speeches and discussions.

Having considered illustrative occasions, we must now explore more broadly and systematically (1) what kinds of patterns of distribution of diversities are apparent, to what extent, and to what degree; (2) how profound or superficial the impact of diversities is and where diversities are found; and, finally, (3) what diversities' linkages are to global identities.

Terminology

Let us pause briefly for an alert. Above, I have used and quoted others using such terms as "black," "Hispanic," and "Asian," which are always questionable and often changing. Race and ethnicity are problematic yet essential categories for analysis. One issue is how much of identity—whether termed "race" or "ethnicity"—is genetic and how much environmental. The American Association of Physical Anthropologists has issued a statement that essentially denies the scientific value of "race" for a variety of reasons that can be found in any introductory anthropology textbook. The basic reason is that commonly used terms for race, such as "black," do not correlate well with genetic or other biological features that researchers measure. While genetic research progresses rapidly, as, for example, the Human Genome Project, this point presumably remains true. A second resolution, from the American Anthropological Association (responding to *The Bell Curve*, a study that claims racial bases for intelligence), argued the same, as have other statements.[5] Yet race as an identifier is widely used in society, in census definitions, for example, though this usage has been vigorously critiqued by certain physical anthropologists. It is the social reality of race, regardless of one's scientific conclusions, that led Michael Dyson to insist on including the term in the mission statement of a newly formed Institute of African American Research at the University of North Carolina, which he chaired and on whose committee I served, though I dutifully noted the anthropological view of the spurious status of "race" as a word. Unless one recognizes that others affirm race, one cannot combat racism, much as provisionally accepting essentialist definitions of "woman" or "female" enables one to be feminist. This is strategic essentialism.

Less vexing but somewhat similar is the term "ethnic." Ethnicity is less problematic because it does not carry as much presumption about genes and biology; ethnicity refers to cultural features such as language, way of life, religion, and foods. Still, like race, one is commonly thought to inherit rather than choose or acquire one's ethnic identity: one is born Hispanic, Scottish, or Chinese. One is normally Jewish by birth, also, although Judaism is a religion which one can convert to or abandon, and particular physical features are associated with Jews, even though Judaism encompasses a wide spectrum of physical features. Judaism is ethnic as well as religious because it encompasses distinctive foods, language, and customs that have a religious base as well as cultural and social significance.

Thus, "race" and "ethnicity" are complex, somewhat tricky terms. Several features characterize them, however: they define identities, and the identities they define tend to be particularistic and ascribed rather than universalistic and achieved, to use some still-useful sociological jargon. That is, a particular racial or ethnic identity is imputed to some but not all of a given population, and it is commonly assumed to be inherited, born into, and difficult to rid oneself of. The first feature, the particularism rather than universalism of an ethnic designation, separates race and ethnicity from gender (because if you are male or female you are part of a rather universal category—roughly half the human population), although race and ethnicity resemble gender in their inherited feature. The second feature, ascription, distinguishes race and ethnicity from class, which one can change, within limits.

Having offered this cautionary reminder about the difficulties of using racial and ethnic terminologies, I will go right ahead and follow common usage, because the biological or genetic difficulties with the terms do not prevent their prominence in the social and cultural arenas that are my focus. The globalization perspective, furthermore, shifts discussion away from ethnic or racial categories toward processes of social, cultural, and economic history. Race and ethnicity are aspects of world processes, entailing colonialism and immigration, markets and cultural exchange, all of which lie behind the diversities experienced in locales.

Distributions of Diversity: Eight Scenarios

In exploring to what extent diversities are present in the South and in what patterns, we consider pluralism, dualism, and globalism as our variables. Many scenarios are apparent, running the gamut from the old dualism, to overcoming dualism, to emergent pluralism, to pluralism as part of global identity.

In the first scenario, dualism remains. Jim Crow segregation ends or diminishes, but de facto segregation continues. Pluralism does not yet overcome dualism, and immigrants are just a third group, still on the edges. Examples are schools and churches: schools are resegregating as whites move to the suburbs and blacks stay in inner cities; churches are divided between predominantly white ones, such as United Methodist, and black ones, such as African Methodist Episcopal Zion or Christian Methodist Episcopal Zion.

In the second scenario, dualism is overcome, but pluralism is denied. Blacks and whites move toward integration, excluding new minorities. In Clinton, North Carolina, for example, the town celebrates the selection of leadership award recipients. One is a white man (a recently deceased doctor), the other a black man (a legislator). At the banquet, each honoree has a constituency, more than a hundred blacks and whites, relatives and friends. But the new immigrants, notably the numerous Hispanics now residing and working in this county, are missing. They have not yet moved up in the leadership hierarchy. This is also true at the state level: several blacks but only one Hispanic and one part-Hispanic person have been elected to the North Carolina state legislature. It is noteworthy, however, that one Hispanic, one black, and several whites in the legislature support the internationalization of education, linking pluralism and globalism.

In the third scenario, dualism is overturned, and pluralism is nascent. Julius Chambers, the esteemed NAACP lawyer and recently retired chancellor of North Carolina Central University, heads the Center for Civil Rights at the University of North Carolina. Younger members of the institute spoke in favor of broadening the center's concerns to include the "new diversity," addressing global human rights issues, but Chambers and others consider black-white relations to be "unfinished business" to the extent that they should remain the center's central focus. A similar debate, mentioned earlier, was apparent in the vigorous controversy of the 1990s about constructing a new building to house the black culture center (BCC) at the University of North Carolina and to name the new building after the recently deceased Sonja Haynes Stone. Early in the debate, a black student proposed that a multicultural center be built instead, but this idea was rejected. BCC proponents wished to have a free-standing center, symbolizing an autonomous validity of black identity.

In the center that the university built, however—constructed largely with funds contributed by a white alumnus from Alabama—inclusiveness is a key theme, and cross-cultural communication a major program. This inclusiveness theme offers a mediating position between a single ethnic identity and plural ethnic identities (multiculturalism). Exactly how the relationship will evolve with respect to new pluralisms remains to be seen, but cross-cultural activities (including speakers from Asia and Europe) suggest a move from dualism to pluralism.

In the fourth scenario, pluralism has been partially achieved by means of immigrant-led integration. At the Raleigh, North Carolina, fairgrounds, the annual Fiesta del Pueblo attracts approximately a hundred thousand people. The attendees are largely Hispanic, but the crowd includes a few non-Spanish-speaking blacks and a few non-Spanish-speaking whites, as well as some of each who speak Spanish.

In the fifth scenario, pluralism has been partially achieved by means of a limited degree of class-based integration. Whites and new minorities move toward integration, but older minorities are excluded. This scenario is evident especially among the highly educated and economically successful population: class as well as culture is key. Asians and other internationals (including Africans) share jobs with professionals from throughout the United States and educational niches in the Research Triangle area of North Carolina, in local universities and technical multinational business, and in hospitals or medical clinics.

In the sixth scenario, pluralism has been partially achieved by means of the integration of old and new minorities. An Indian in a South Georgia town marries a black man; a Japanese woman in a high-tech area marries a black man. The new minority is global, the old one provincial. These particular instances cause conflict: the Japanese woman feels that her family will not accept her new husband, for example.

In the seventh scenario, globalism has been achieved without pluralism. A white southerner wants to import teak coffins from Indonesia to sell at Wal-Mart, thus undercutting the monopolies of U.S. funeral homes. His commercial interests are global but do not necessarily imply local pluralism: he does not associate with Indonesian immigrants, for example. CEOs of multinational companies who live in gated communities may likewise segregate global interests from pluralistic associations locally.

In the eighth, and final, scenario, pluralism and globalism are both achieved. Logically, this should be the case, especially if the principle of grounded globalism is applied so that globalism includes local diversities. Embracing the world logically includes embracing diversity locally. Take, for example, two intelligent, vibrant students at Louisiana State University—a young black woman from Texas and young white woman from Louisiana. Both studied in France, and both seek international careers; their diversities at home seem subordinated to global integration. Such an example is unusual, since U.S. minorities so far tend not to enter international studies, and some mistrust international foci as diverting attention from the plight of local minorities. They may opt to focus on civil rights as opposed to human rights. However, I see evidence that minorities see minority issues as part of diversity issues within global frameworks or that they simply shift emphasis to global issues as a concern for all groups, minority or majority. Consider several African American North Carolinians: Senator Howard Lee, chair of the state board of education, asserts this view; he has declared global concerns a top priority for K–12 education. Less publicly, Narvis Green is, and has been for years, the financial officer for the University Center for International Studies at the University of North Carolina at Chapel Hill. She handles finances and much else for the foreign fellows and global projects of the center. Suphronia Cheek has a somewhat similar job in the university's anthropology department. These are quieter examples of global work that happens to involve minority personnel. (The inverse would be an African American college in Mississippi that employs Russians, who originally came as exchange students—again, merging pluralism and dualism or formerly dualistic statuses.)

The Penetration of Pluralism

How deeply and widely does integrative pluralism penetrate? Looking at depth, I consider what "layers" of society and culture are engaged. Is pluralism reflected in legal regulations, official pronouncements, and public commemorations only, or is it showing up in less formal and more private contexts—in dreams, in profound discussions, in the body, or in emotions? Looking at breadth, I consider social and cultural scope. Do we see pluralism in the wider society or only in restricted spheres such as academic discussions or workplaces? Does pluralism/globalism penetrate private parties, churches, retirement homes, families, and neighborhoods? Here are some impressions, and a few examples.

Externally, in formal statements and the practice of law, policy, or vision, pluralism is noticeable, as we see in the Martin Luther King Day speeches and rituals. Salient, too, is considerable attention to migration, visas, and citizenship. This includes debates about issues such as the Patriot Act that temporarily curtail or limit pluralism but, by engendering discussion, may eventually enhance it. External examples also include automated bank machines programmed to operate in several languages, and curricula (from K–12 to universities) that require students to take a course in global perspectives or cultural differences.

In the marketplace, bookstores increasingly have a section of Spanish-language children's books. A greatly increased variety of foods is found in grocery stores and restaurants. Videos are available in languages ranging from Spanish to Urdu. And there is a Spanish channel on television and an Indian program on an Atlanta radio station.

Or consider the workplace: the University Center for International Studies at the University of North Carolina has a Swiss American associate director, an African American manager, a Russian accountant, a Polish outreach director, and southern and northern American staff, as well as delegations and projects involving many countries and continents. Offices, laboratories, clinics, and other workplaces throughout the South show similar pluralistic diversity, though minority ethnic groups continue to dominate some workplaces—Mexican workers in a chicken factory or Hmong sock makers, for example.

So far I have asked how the dualistic South ingests the new pluralism. But it is also important to ask how the new pluralism ingests the South. That is, how do immigrants view the South? What is their experience with the society? From their standpoint, how do they relate to southern identity?

An Indian couple from Lynchburg, Virginia, has lived in the South for thirty-two years, ever since the husband came from India to work for a U.S. company. One of their daughters is about to graduate from the University of Virginia with a major in economics. She is feeling very sad about leaving Virginia, says her mother. "Where does she want to work?" I ask. Lynchburg is too small, but she will remain in the South, looking toward the Triangle area or Charlotte, North Carolina. "Will she stay in America?" Yes, she identifies as an American, the mother tells me: "She doesn't have an accent like we do." Another daughter is getting her MBA at Harvard Business School, but the Triangle might be a possibility for her too. "Do you think of yourselves as Virginians?" I ask. The mother smiles, saying yes, but chuckling a bit. I was reminded of the Tennessean who lived in Virginia and grew tired of Virginians asking him if he was from Virginia. He would reply, "No, but my dog is." Virginia is perhaps the extreme in the general southern tendency to treasure ancestry as a feature of belonging, and an Indian (who of course has an even longer cultural pedigree but from elsewhere) has to be even more wary than a Tennessean about claiming the heritage of Mr. Jefferson.[6]

I saw another Indian standing in line for hours to get Jimmy Carter to sign his book about growing up in Georgia. This person served as president of the student body of the University of North Carolina and is active in alumni affairs and, to a degree, in state affairs, though he now lives in Boston. Other immigrants are active in campaigns around the state and region, and some whose families can claim several generations of residence (like Nick Galifianakis, a North Carolina congressman of Greek descent) have been elected to office.

New immigrants appear to identify first with family and friends and then enlarge their identities to include both the ethnic and the native community. A few, such as Assad Meymandi, an Iranian psychiatrist, broaden to sponsor major community projects—in Meymandi's case, Meymandi Concert Hall and the North Carolina opera. Immigrants' regional identity, if they have one, is grounded in these local groupings and cut through with national and global networks less evident among natives but not necessarily absent. The convergence between an international ethnic identity and a localized southern/regional one is well shown for southerners with Scots ancestry by Celeste Ray, but such a convergence is not yet evident among newer immigrants. Some of those who attend the Grandfather Mountain Highland Games, held in North Carolina each year, also reenact Civil War battles.

More-recent immigrants do not usually join regional celebrations such as Civil War reenactments, though I have seen Vietnamese watching a reenactment. Vietnamese and others are developing attachments to the region, however. Consider Long Vo, a Vietnamese "boat person" who grew up in Durham, North Carolina. Long Vo's mother tried living in California but returned to North Carolina because she had established strong ties there. A comparison of California and North Carolina Vietnamese showed a stronger community orientation among the North Carolinians and a stronger family identity among the Californians, one presumes primarily because of the smaller number of Vietnamese in the South.[7]

On August 31, 2006, in the University of North Carolina newspaper, the *Daily Tar Heel*, Linda Shen, a senior from Raleigh, North Carolina, whose family immigrated from China, published an op-ed piece entitled "Welcome to the New South(?)." She takes her title, she says, from Kate Campbell's song "New South," which she finds comical. She writes, "The funny thing about a person's identity is its intricate relationship with location, with language, with all things colloquial—strange as it might seem, I've never seen myself as anything other than a Southerner." She mentions immigrating but mainly dwells on things southern, concluding, "Around here all the iced tea is sweet tea, and I'll probably die of starvation before I find a pushcart selling gyros—and that's fine with me."

The immigrant situation varies hugely with education and work: laborers, mostly from Latin America, live in a different world than that of the immigrants from Asia or Latin America who join the circles of the educated professionals or the well-off. Members of particular ethnic groups may encounter special situations. Indonesian Chinese immigrants, for example, may not easily identify with either Indonesian or Chinese immigrants, because they do not necessarily speak Chinese, yet they are not Indonesian ethnics either.

A unifying force is the religious group, the church for many (and here, certain fundamentalist or evangelical churches are more viable than mainline ones) or the mosque or the Hindu temple. Differences in class, education, and ethnicity are leveled to some extent through shared religious identities, which themselves may become leveled to accommodate differences. Some churches, such as Korean Christian ones, even include non-Christians who are Korean: ethnic unity overrides religious difference.

In considering what, if anything, is distinctive about the experience of immigrants in the South as opposed to elsewhere, neither the melting pot nor the multicultural models often applied elsewhere quite fit. Becoming American is not so simple in the South, since a certain anti-American oppositionality (that is, lingering resentment by the South of the nation that conquered the South) is present there, and the tradition of absorbing peoples of multiple ethnicities is not as established in the South as it is in the North, Midwest, and West. Although Americanism and multiculturalism are both threads in the southern fabric, the dominant structure and identity of the South remain dualistic, complemented by a certain regionalism that may emphasize the white node but must include the black one, too, as part of a unifying regional identity.[8] To become dominant, pluralism must accost this dualism. An analogous situation, to a degree, can be found in South Africa, where black-white dualism complements a third stream of immigrant cultures, including "coloreds." The question for immigrants and natives is whether a region will simply add new elements to its traditional dualism as a third stream or, more radically, create a new pattern of pluralism. At present, the first alternative is more evident in the South, but the direction is toward a new pluralism.

In assessing the depth of change, one could distinguish cultures, psyches, and societies along a spectrum from open to closed, from dualistic to pluralistic. A more open society achieves new pluralism with less struggle and resistance, while a more closed and dualistic society resists more. The argument has been leveled against northern liberals that for them integration was easier than for southerners, because the northerners had less black-white diversity to integrate, whereas the South had large black populations, sometimes even a black majority. Some argued that once integration was accomplished—to whatever extent—in the South, it meant more, because more obstacles had to be overcome, and more history worked through to achieve it.

In turning to consider the impact of immigration on the evolving relations between blacks and whites in the South, then, it is apparent that immigration has not entirely superseded the dualism of black against white. A common argument is that the South has a long history of black-white relations, that southern blacks and whites are still working through centuries of oppression and struggle, and that Hispanic and Asian immigrants are newcomers to this history. Thus, pluralism does not replace dualism but, if anything, adds a new layer—a rather superficial one, some would suggest—to the old structure and its painfully evolving process. This pattern is apparent at many levels, from philosophies to practices. Note the Clinton, North Carolina, banquet discussed above, where blacks and whites had arrived at a balance of sorts, including each other in the community while excluding new immigrants, at least for the moment. Charles Long, an African American scholar, asserted at a conference on the "multicultural south" in the late 1980s that southern black-white relations are a "moral problem," whereas multiculturalism is merely a demographic fact. Vincent Harding, another African American scholar, presented a similar argument. Riché Richardson, however, sees southern hip-hop as a minority form encompassing pluralism.[9] At a bureaucratic level, minorities are drawn into diversity and pluralism in yet another sphere—task forces, committees, and projects that may confer status and resources but also consume energy and sometimes, as one minority person put it in a conversation I overheard, are a "lot of crap."[10]

What is lost, what is gained? Pluralism implies change in community, whereas dualism is part of a hierarchical pattern in which black and white were separate and unequal during most of southern history and in most areas of society, though with many areas of intersection and efforts at greater equality. Pluralism implies a variety of cultures espousing an ideal of equality while living with a reality of hierarchy. A pluralistic South would, perhaps, move toward "heterarchy" as various groups find mobility.

In the process, certain kinds of community may erode—in fact, are eroding. When schools were segregated, African Americans built strong communities that revolved around admired teachers, ministers, and others, and these centers of community declined in strength following efforts to integrate schools. Such segregated enclaves might be compared to, for example, "old boy" networks, which were segregated by gender in elite northern settings such as prep schools and the Ivy League. Community can flow from exclusiveness or from being excluded.

Flux and the erasure of boundaries can diminish communities; the challenge is to build new ones and sustain old ones. Hints that this is possible can be seen in the Martin Luther King banquet described above. Awards are given for community service that cuts across lines of race and class. A certain tentative inclusiveness in speakers is apparent for Hispanics and Jews (though not Asians) while anchors of African American identity—song and speech and the composition of head panels—are sustained.

Globalism Emerging

Emerging globalism, then, is constituted locally in diversities of persons and cultures. These include transnational families that span international communities, networks, and cultures in science and the arts. Assad Meymandi, mentioned earlier, was educated at the Sorbonne, and his mother met Puccini, a background he brings to his support of the arts in North Carolina. Yang-je, from Jakarta, Indonesia, and of Chinese descent, learned classical music from Dutch records and comes to Raleigh to conduct. Emmanuel Ax, who plays a concerto conducted by Yang-je, is married to a Japanese woman from Durham. Mohammed Isa, who was an imam in South Africa, now lives in Durham and is a leader in a network that includes Muslims and scholars of Islam globally and locally. Samia Serageldin, a novelist from Cairo, resides in Chapel Hill and belongs to the Islamic Council in Raleigh. These are examples of the local diversity among migrants and visitors that connects to global society and culture, thereby constituting the global locally.

Despite fears of immigrant flooding, terrorism, and global connections, the South is moving not simply from dualism to pluralism but from dualism to a globally infused pluralism. The depth to which this pluralism penetrates in social contexts and in attitudes and values obviously varies by context. Gated neighborhoods differ from poor ones and from those inhabited not by retirees but by active professionals. Attitudes vary from those who embrace to those who resist pluralism. Overall, however, at levels from the demographic to the social and psychological, the change from a decade or so ago is marked. Jim Crow is still with us—there is unfinished business, to be sure, in civil rights and equality—but the configuration and context within which such issues are framed is notably different than in the past, owing to the influence of pluralism.

The move from dualism to pluralism is a broad tendency composed of many subtrends and complexities. The pluralism is new, the dualism old, yet the new pluralism has the power to reconfigure the bedrock dualism that remains. Resulting identities vary in social and cultural locale and in psychic depth, buttressed obviously by economics and demography and emerging politics.

How, then, does a shift from dualism to pluralism as part of daily demographics and social life affect identity? The question was posed by a young woman after I spoke at a Rotary Club meeting in Southern Pines, North Carolina. She was originally from Florida and Alabama and had been a stockbroker in New York. She asked, "When my eighty-seven-year-old grandmother in Andalusia, Alabama, is experiencing pluralism, is this an external situation or also an internal change, a change in her attitude?" I answered, "Both." My answer presumed that internal and external aspects interpenetrate—that change in situation and attitude go together and that "identity" entails both. The question is challenging, however, and deserves more attention.

Consider the varying ways people deal with pluralism. Mary hosts immigrants. Joan marries one. Tom and Veronica adopt a child from Russia. Emanuel adopts Buddhism (or Islam or Baha'i), and Joe eats Chinese food and studies tai chi. Emiliano joins a Hispanic church, and Kim Choong joins a Korean church, each becoming part of a group that shares his ethnicity. Alexander, having migrated from the Northeast to the South, embraces "foreign" cultures in some of the ways noted above—relationships, foods, religions—while rejecting "local" cultures, which he sees as backward, biased, oppressive, and "southern." Tess, on the other hand, loves a full spectrum of music from blues and bluegrass to gamelan, from local to global. Peter keeps his distance from new immigrants and cultures, yet they appear in his dreams—an intriguing occurrence, considering that Joyce Rockwood Hudson, who edits the newsletter *The Rose*, published by Emmanuel Church in Athens, Georgia, suggests that images of foreigners in dreams appear as "shadow" figures, shadows of the self.

These examples illustrate varying kinds of pluralistic identity, some of which are globalist. Yet a dualistic identity could also coexist with globalism. Tess, while embracing a spectrum of world music, might also identify as white in contrast to someone who is black. My second hypothesis suggests, however, that pluralism tends to diminish dualism and press toward globalism. The Andalusian grandmother, one might think, will shift her attitudes about blacks as she embraces a richer spectrum of cultural identities as part of her daily life and worldview. Blacks and whites are no longer polarities in a dualistic and hierarchical universe but instead are nodes within a pluralistic universe.

The granddaughter's question, though, was how internal is my grandmother's change? Does she live in a changed world, does she adopt a changed worldview, or, even more radical, does her own identity change? She would seem to go partway in terms of the first two but probably not all the way in the third. What if she went all the way? Would she leave the church for Buddhism and abandon dresses for saris? Perhaps. But more likely she would retain her culture of origin—however that is constituted—as an anchor and core while entering a trajectory of pluralism.

The trajectory can, of course, go in the opposite direction. From Germany to Rwanda, ethnic cleansing was one way of rejecting pluralism. The Holocaust was extreme but by no means unique. Racial dualism in the South is less extreme, generally speaking, in that on the whole the black-white dualism has been sustained by subordinating blacks without eliminating them. Violence against immigrants, though rare, and fears of terrorists warn of the possibility of backlash.

What grade on the diversity scorecard might these trends receive? Global identities sometimes reinforce liberalization of race and diversity, as in the examples of the Martin Luther King Day banquet and the church retreat. Sometimes, as in the family gatherings, neither global identities nor local diversities are strongly evident. At other times, global identities bypass local diversities, for example when new immigrant elites merge with old native elites, both excluding old minorities from their circles and endeavors; here, global effects take a somewhat conservative turn, at least in the short term. The overall force of globalism, however, would seem to be toward opening up perspectives that sometimes demonstrably, and perhaps often potentially, liberalize relationships—though not necessarily in the specific ways decreed by older liberalism. Affirmative action and school desegregation, for example, gain new meaning as schools and other institutions broaden their concerns to encompass Hispanics.

Globalism and diversity connect, but not always or inevitably or in the same ways. Nonetheless, the larger tendency would seem to be for increasing diversity "on the ground" in life and in work to dispose southerners to a more global-oriented identity, an identity with the wider world.

CHAPTER FIVE

Southern Space

From Sense of Place to Force Field

THE PHRASE "sense of place" suggests the perception of a locale as more than just a physical space, as a territory but also as a psychological space, a place imbued with history and memory, community and experience. In short, "space" becomes "place." The South, it is said, has a sense of place. As Roy Blount Jr. put it, "the South is a place," and, he added disparagingly, "the North is just a direction out of the South."

Blount captures in a phrase a long history of imagining the South as a place. The land of cotton is not forgotten and instead has been "constructed" (imagined, envisioned, conceived) for centuries romantically and critically, in song, literature, and in memory and perception of those who live there and those who have left or never been. Certainly it would be foolish to accept the mythologies as true but it would be equally foolish to deny their truths. One of those is that of "sense" of place, namely that, regardless of what the South as a place "*actually*" is, it is experienced by many as a significant space, which, therefore makes it a real "place"—a place in perception and conception, in memory and in action. One could draw a parallel between race and space; both are constructions of a certain kind of physicality, and those imaginative constructions have crystallized into perceptual realities which, regardless of how they square with biology or geography, are real in experience and consequential in behavior. Accordingly, I do not disparage unduly claims that "the South is a place," meaning that many, native or not, have a "sense" of that place. At the same time, I welcome recent rethinking, especially in literary criticism, of how space is construed in "postsouthern" conceptions to lose old senses of place and to create new senses of place.[1]

Oppositionality is, as Blount's comment indicates, part of a southern sense of place: it is a place different from the North, opposed to it in everything from politics to lifestyle, even endangered by it. To go north is like Lee invading Pennsylvania—moving into enemy territory.

Dualism is also embodied in Southern space and place. Racism is spacism. Plantations had the big house and the slave quarters. Older towns often had, and still have, a version of that arrangement, with houses for whites on the main streets and houses for black servants nearby on backstreets. More recent settlements and towns divide black and white even more, into separate neighborhoods and communities, though division by class and occupation is also noteworthy, for example, separated, stigmatized neighborhoods for workers in textile mills. As Jack Boger, Julius Chambers, and the Center for Civil Rights at the Law School of the University of North Carolina at Chapel Hill document, facilities such as electricity and sewers are frequently lacking in the black areas. They also show how redistricting is being used by political parties to determine how voters can and cannot support minority candidates.[2] Since integration, wealthier blacks do move into previously white neighborhoods, but at the same time developers create gated communities that largely cater to affluent white residents, many of them retirees from outside the South.

"The South is a place," then, in many senses. As a sentimental, nostalgic, and intimate homeland, as a battleground opposed to that space behind enemy lines, as a dualistically divided, racially segregated space.

What happens to the southern sense of place as the South assumes a global identity? Does it disappear, so that one becomes a "man without a country," a refugee, an immigrant in one's own land, a cosmopolitan? Is physical space merely *maya*, illusion, anyway? Or does one retain an inner sense of place identity, as in the old sayings "You can take the boy out of the country but not the country out of the boy?" or "Home is where the heart is"—and the heartless aren't, adding the social dimension? Do the romanticized, mythologized senses of the entire region as a place diminish along with decay of localized spaces—downtowns, farms, and neighborhoods? The evidence suggests that either of the above can happen, but it is clear that global identity need not simply destroy local identity, the local sense of place. Instead, it most often transforms and complicates it—not that it isn't already complicated. This transformation has two main aspects: scope and dynamism. Scope simply entails a larger space: today (or yesterday) we orient to our neighborhood, farm, community, region, or nation, tomorrow to the whole world. Dynamics mean change, perhaps engendering a sense of changeability, flux, and impermanence: our farm is now a shopping mall, my old house a highway. Combine global scope and dynamism, and you get a global force field replacing what may have seemed a smaller, more localized, and less changeable space. An international airport that replaces a farm is an example, for the airport has global scope as well as incessant movement. Uncle Will Schley's land was turned into Fort Benning, Georgia. In protest, he refused to shave. When he died, his beard came to his waist, symbolizing the futility of opposing what has been since World War II a global force field.

Identity and Place

Identity matters. Place matters. Identity and place are two emphases, either of which may entail the other. Place may be seen as subordinate to identity, as one of many identities, including ethnic identity, gender identity, and national identity. Or identity may be seen as subordinate to place, one of many features of place, others of which might include physical or ecological features, geographical location, natural resources, and so on. "Place identity" combines the two concepts, endowing identity with the physicality of space and endowing space with psychology, even holiness. Place identity contrasts logically with global identity, insofar as the global is seen as undermining identity in any particular local space. Yet global identity and place identity in fact play against and with each other dialectically, as is suggested in the notion of grounded globalism.

Among the markers of identity, place is distinctively concrete, based on physical location, just as other identities are expressed in the body, clothes, or food. But place is not merely space any more than food is merely feed; that is, these seemingly material entities have a cultural and mental overlay that makes them matter. Space becomes place when meanings are imputed to it. Wars to defend territories are a dramatic example, for the defended territories assume symbolic meanings through courage and sacrifice. Worship is another example, as it is spatially localized through shrines.

Genealogies and kinship offer more subtle examples of how schemas, remembered and constructed, interweave with spaces. One of my ancestors, Samuel Pearson, built a mill, now known as Yates Mill, in Wake County, North Carolina. I did not know this and had never seen the mill until recently, for I was neither born nor raised in this space, nor do I know any of the local descendants of this ancestor. Yet the mill, now reconstructed and documented, assumes a meaning that links me and my ancestors and descendents conceptually. We are all kin, and if we ever meet, we can assert that kinship even if our "blood" ties are quite distant and we are strangers. This mill, its space, becomes a symbol with meaning, a focus of identity that remains operative by extension to other spaces. While a specific site such as the mill may be identified as ancestral, its spatial identity may be extended more broadly. On my father's side of the family, there is a "Peacock clan of the South" that actually includes persons from outside the South but is oriented around an ancestral site, the grave of an ancestor near a town he named for himself: Pavo, Georgia. (*Pavo* in Spanish means "turkey," and *pavo real* is the term for "peacock.") Clans and kinship are both real and constructed, and they connect time and place, both historically and sociologically, in that people value the link to the ancestral site or sites.

If a clan identity entails a conceptual vision of ancestors dead and gone as well as of relatives still alive and, perhaps, present, all grounded in some site, a regional identity entails a similar vision but on a different plane, on a broader space. The sense of inclusiveness may be broader too, in that blood kinship is not necessary for membership. "Imagined community," a phrase coined by Benedict Anderson, captures the sense of community persons can share even when they cannot gather in one place and meet face to face: they have to imagine themselves as a collectivity, for they cannot see themselves all together at once.[3]

In a vast region such as the South, place or space is the basis for community and identity, but that place identity must be constructed imaginatively on a variety of bases. Origin is one basis: one who is born and bred in the South but has ancestors from outside, or one who is born and bred outside the South but has ancestors within it, may still claim the place identity. Other attributes, ranging from accent to values, enter the mix. Boundaries are porous, yet the sense of relationship to the region, to the place, forms identity, and the salience of that identity does not diminish with its complexity or vagueness.

Boundaries sharpen, moreover, when a regional or other collective identity becomes oppositional: when outsiders and insiders, patriots and traitors, contrast. Space now becomes place in a context of violence, in a territory to be defended, captured, or occupied. At this point, too, the symbolism of family and other primordial contexts charge the place: it is motherland (or fatherland), and those who defend it are brothers (or sisters). Thus the South becomes Dixie, as in "Dixieland where I was born," and organization names emphasize kinship relationships to the place or the political organization that represents it, as in the Daughters of the Confederacy and the Sons of the Confederacy. Even where such explicit symbols and identities are not evoked, however, individuals and groups identify in varying degrees and ways with the South as a place.

Sense of Place and Global Force Fields

Southern sense of place is complicated by change. Forces of change issue, for example, from civil engineering that is unguided (sprawl) or ecological (smart growth, new urbanism, even preservation). The space remains the same, but it becomes a new place. That place is now experienced as part of a force field, as part of the convergence of global and local forces. Even if landmarks are preserved—churches, schools, homes, town squares, meadows, or gardens—they change meaning, for they are now framed by expressways, airports, fast food restaurants, and shopping malls.

Forces of change may also be cultural or mental. *Feng shui* is an ancient Chinese system for creating balance and harmony in your personal space. *Feng shui* experts now live in the South, and some southerners use *feng shui* in designing and organizing their spaces. "Close that door," a woman commands. "*Feng shui* warns that bad forces come through an open door." *Feng shui* is only one of many increasingly influential worldviews—others range in origin from Asian to Native American—that encourage thinking about space holistically, as intersections of physical, mental, and spiritual force fields. Such cultural influences from ancient philosophies merge with new technologies that also transform our sense of space, including cyberspace. Military technologies affect our sense of place, which is now framed by global systems of weaponry and surveillance that extend, even, to outer space with "Star Wars" missile defense systems.

Space sense is influenced, too, from the ground up. Bodies are redefined by practices ranging from acupuncture and yoga to genetic engineering. Tai chi, spreading among the elderly as a way of improving balance, instills a sense of space as harmonized with the body. So do other Asian exercises and alternative medicines ranging from foods to herbs and to art and music that project visions of space. Southern painters, like others, are influenced by Asian landscape. The experimental envisioning of space is apparent in Clayton Colvin's work "Space Cadet," which hung in a show at Material, in Memphis, Tennessee, in his various "stealth art" paintings, and in "Dirty South!" a group show curated by José-Carlos Diaz at Worm-Hole Laboratory in Miami, Florida. These images, exhibited and, at least in part, created in the South, are largely nonrepresentational; when faces appear, they are transmuted by geometric vectors, expressing visually a sense of forces that shape people.

What impact do all of these transformations of space have? Space and place do not cease to matter; the world does not become entirely "cosmopolitan" or a global marketplace where one lives electronically or in airplanes and hotels. Peripatetic businesspeople and intellectuals accumulate frequent flyer miles, but most people move only because they have to and confront huge obstacles in crossing boundaries as refugees and immigrants. The global marketplace exists, but sweatshops are still located in places, not in midair. Asian and other alternative spatial and cultural perspectives may influence southern experience, but they do not erase it. Even cyberspace is a world of messages, while bodies still eat and sleep in locales. Space matters for many reasons. One is functional: governing, including democratic governance, still requires space, as do farming and other activities, including eating and sleeping. Another reason is cultural: humans, like other animals, orient themselves territorially. A third is attitudinal: place matters, but place is mind as well as matter, so the meanings of spaces remain even as spaces change; spaces or places still carry history and meaning, even as they also join global force fields.[4]

Place as a concrete, geographically bounded territory imbued with meaning by history and memory becomes subject to intersections of global forces. Sense of place evolves to encompass connections between places (global environmental issues, for example, are common to many locales) and the inseparability of places from processes that affect them, ranging from unguided development to the preservation of nature. Place is never simple, but the kinds of complexities related to place shift.

What some have termed a southern sense of place entails, first, attachment to particular locales—a homeplace or region; second, fascination with the histories and memories connected to those locales and a commitment to them and their values; third, a fetishization or sacralization, whether elevated (Scarlett returns to Tara) or degraded (Eudora Welty's poor white trash family, the Peacocks, are described as keeping old tires in their front yard and waving at every passing train—still, they do hold on to their yard). In the global shifts envisioned, place still matters, but it is reconceptualized as part of an ecosystem, as resources to sell or develop, and ultimately as part of a world market (defensively, as when people worried that the Japanese were acquiring local land, or happily, as when such acquisitions were welcomed). The Civil War and South of legend, including its ferocious commitment to Dixie, are themselves commoditized as part of global tourism, but even then they are not lost, not yet.

In some ways, this shift echoes histories of thought about space generally, that what may once have been experienced as solid is now "melted into air." Place is no longer taken as given, as just "there," a context into which you are born and whose basis you do not question. Yet its space is felt as special and as an anchor, as one's "spot," to recall an allusion by Carlos Castaneda to the shaman's search for a place from which to launch his vision.[5] But southern images of space are more homely: a house, a yard, a field, or a road that resonates in the poetry and prose and talk of southerners, or more mythological and collective, as in the legends of Lee and the war.

Southern Space

My first two hypotheses treat social relationships: cultural diversity locally, connectedness globally. My third hypothesis brings us back to earth, to the matter of identity associated with place. Yet place is not just space; mind is not just matter. Hence, this coming back to earth entails asking questions of meaning, even of spirituality. We interrogate dialogues between place and meaning throughout southern history and human experience generally. One such dialogue—internal, in this case—involves a story from southern history about Robert E. Lee. At the outbreak of the

Civil War, Lincoln offers Lee command of the federal forces. Lee, at home in Arlington, Virginia, paces through the night, pondering the offer. In the morning, he declines it, stating that he could not lead an invasion of his native territory, Virginia.

Lee put place above principle, at least the principle of national unity upheld by Abraham Lincoln and, by implication, the principles of national ethics (including opposition to slavery, which Lee himself opposed). In effect, he said, "My country, right or wrong," with his country being Virginia, his ancestral home, land, and family—and by extension, the South. Never mind that Lee had himself been mobile, moving from Mexico to West Point, as had his father, who went away to the Caribbean. Location need not imply paralysis. Never mind that he forsook an exemplary career as an army officer, once commander of West Point, to lead the Confederacy. Never mind that he rejected certain leadership at the highest national level for uncertainty and dubious prospects, if any. What he affirmed was a bond to a place, now set in opposition to an outside invading force, the nation. This story of Lee's dilemma defined choice and value for the South and southerners then and continues to do so still. The question is, How do the South and southerners react to the new invading forces, not those of the nation and the North, but of the world?

The southern sense of place was shaped strongly during the relatively inert period following the Civil War. The events of construction, destruction, and reconstruction fostered the growth of mythologized senses of place, of memories, and of histories—including the honoring of the Confederate dead eulogized in Allen Tate's "Ode to the Confederate Dead" and the myth of the Lost Cause.[6] A sense of the South as a place of inner meaning implies also a non-South, an outer realm. Borders such as the Mason-Dixon Line carry a powerful psychology: in crossing it, one has the feel of moving into enemy territory. If, as James McBride Dabbs suggests, southerners identified South as home, then non-South was foreign, not home. Such dichotomizing is common in world cultures, of course, and the South is not as deeply dichotomizing, perhaps, as tribal societies such as the Navajo, for whom homeland is human land and outside is outer darkness, or even as the Germans with their sense of *heimat* (home), the Russians with their *mir* (earth), or many other nations that sacralize homeland as motherland or fatherland. Nonetheless, the South has its own mythos of homelike insularity based in land and buttressed by opposition to the alien and dangerous, which was once (and to an extent still is) demonized as the North.

Occasionally, some extraordinary person would break out of this place mold. By being blind and deaf, Helen Keller was emancipated from the prison of Alabama to become a world person. Any number of others, from Thomas Jefferson and Edgar Allan Poe to Ava Gardner and Bessie Smith or Louis Armstrong and Wynton Marsalis, became world persons, but southern culture on the whole has fed on local more than global orientations. In *To Kill a Mockingbird,* Harper Lee wrote of honor and dignity grounded in a small place. Yet another Alabaman, Walker Percy, expressed irony and disorientation but retained a sense of place: "The engineer" in *The Last Gentleman* finally makes his way back to Birmingham (Percy's birthplace), which is all golf courses and suburbs now, just like the North, except that people are "nicer." Stories set in earlier times—Scarlett returning to Tara, or Inman returning to Cold Mountain—reinforce the boundaries as characters cross obstacles to come back home. (Charles Frazier's novel *Cold Mountain* and the resulting film compare interestingly with *Gone with the Wind* in that although Frazier's hero's home and destination is a mountain, and Margaret Mitchell's heroine returns to a lowland plantation, the more individualistic later novel and the more paternalistic, or maternalistic, earlier one both move toward a home, a place.) Such songs as "My Old Kentucky Home" to "Carolina on My Mind" convey the theme that "There's no place like *heimat*." (The tapestry of associations ranging from folklore to Nazi ideology that accompany the word "heimat" are somewhat analogous to the spectrum of meanings attached to home and homeland in the South.)

We need not exaggerate the uniqueness of the South. The distinctiveness of southern perspective lies in its combination of land, settlement, and war, all of which created a culture of oppositionality expressed in spatial boundaries. In the early nineteenth century, as South Carolinians, Virginians, and Georgians expanded westward, the Charleston writer William Gilmore Sims created a literary sense of a "South" that by then extended westward to Arkansas and Alabama. That sense of a region served to unite—at least conceptually—people who were spread far apart. That sense of regional identity endured for a century and still endures as a construct termed "The South."

This bounded regional space, once invaded by the Union forces, is now invaded by development, urbanization, and urban sprawl. Take Atlanta: Hartsfield-Jackson Atlanta International Airport, one of the busiest in the world, has global reach. It is a connector to the world. Atlanta itself is set in a vast mélange of suburbs, condos, and expressways. In the center of Atlanta are global elements—CNN, the World Congress Convention Center, the Carter Center—encapsulating regional landmarks—among them Margaret Mitchell's house, representing *Gone with the Wind;* the Cyclorama, representing the Battle of Atlanta; and the Martin Luther King memorial representing civil rights—and global/regional elements such as the Coca-Cola museum and Buford Road, a multicultural immigrant area. Atlanta represents a global South, versions of which can also be found in Dallas, Charlotte, Raleigh, and Miami. As in Tokyo, Singapore, and Berlin, elements of history are quarantined and preserved, but increasingly they intersect with global interests. Bob, a builder based near Covington, Georgia, contracts with a firm from India to construct an office building. The design must fit certain models drawn from Hindu cosmology, mirroring in certain ways the flow of fluids within the human body. John Portman, an architect, has taken the Hyatt Regency Atlanta, his first atrium-centered building, and used it as a model for Hyatts around the world.

Global Forces and Southern Spaces

Transition from regional to national to global senses of place are expressed at every level, from public to private. The transition is epitomized by large public events; our four examples are global (the Olympics), national (bowl games), local and ethnic, and an intersection of such levels. The transition is also epitomized in private lives; our examples pertain to the life cycle, travel, and literary representation. All are in southern settings. All manifest a spatial orientation by their structure and symbolism. All are affected by global forces.

THE OLYMPICS

The Atlanta Olympics of 1996 illustrate an adaptation of southern place into global space. The Olympic Games are localized: they must be held in a specific city. Yet they are also obviously global, bringing together many nations. At the Olympics, a special symbolic space is created. For a brief period, this space is a world, in a sense *the* world, because teams and visitors come from all over the world, and billions of people around the world view the games using electronic media.

Suggestive, therefore, is the Olympic map sold in the Atlanta airport depicting the venues at which events would take place. It included the Atlanta sites and the outlying sites around Georgia where softball (Waycross and Columbus) and dressage events (Conyers and Covington) would be held. Far outlying was the site of a soccer competition, which happened to be held in Washington, D.C. The nation's capital became, from the Olympian perspective, merely a province serving the global center, Atlanta.

The games themselves pronounce this geography in their detailed ritual and spatial structure, defining the Olympics and, for the moment, Atlanta as the center of the world. Speakers at the opening ceremony are, first, the president of the Olympic Games, then the mayor, and last the president of the nation where they happen to be held. U.S. national sports, such as baseball and football, are marginalized; they are mere exhibitions (baseball) or not included (American football), while international sports—track and field, soccer, judo, shooting, and dressage—are emphasized. Though such international sports are normally attended by only a few within the United States, they draw large crowds at the Olympics and account for the most expensive tickets. Global trumps national.

The ritual merges and centralizes dimensions of time and space. Space is carefully designed to feature track and field events; they are held in the Olympic stadium. Time is calibrated to move in a sequence toward a finale. The games progress from the opening ceremony to the closing ceremony and from the shortest race (one hundred meters) to the longest race (marathon), advancing in even multiples of one hundred meters to fifteen hundred meters at the midpoint of the games, and culminating in the special event, the marathon, at longer than twenty-six miles. The distances of races parallel the march of time. The races are held within the central space, the stadium; other events are held in outlying areas. The culminating event integrates these spaces: the marathon, which has been taking place on the roads outside, merges into the closing ceremony. In this finale, nature, represented by the outlying areas and the animal energy of the athletes, is merged with culture, embodied in the ordered ceremonial center at the stadium. "The Olympics are a Camelot," wrote Michael Jordan in a paper he did for a course. He described his Olympic experience as taking place in an indeterminate, transitional time and space like that of the mythical kingdom; he was writing as he completed college basketball and was about to enter professional basketball, someday to become a global star.[7]

The South was explicitly present at the Atlanta Olympics, not only in context but also in content, as in the accompanying cultural exhibits and performances, overseen by George Holt of Chapel Hill and including everything from blues to bluegrass, Tabasco sauce to fried chicken. Leroy Walker, an African American who is the track coach and much else at a historically black North Carolina Central University in Durham, was the president of the Olympic Commission.

Eric Robert Rudolph, captured in 2005 after hiding out in the mountains of North Carolina, bombed Centennial Park at the Atlanta Olympics. He reportedly said at his trial that he was protesting a federal invasion of his region. In fact, it was a global invasion. Rudolph foreshadowed 9/11 by bombing a symbol of globalism. He expressed a fundamentalist protest, as did the suicide bombers of the World Trade Center, a symbol of global capitalism. They were Islamic terrorists; he a Christian and southern terrorist: both fought global invasions of space.

What is the import of such Olympic events? One might think they have no impact at all if one visits Conyers and the now-abandoned dressage apparatus. Or if one recalls the bombing or complaints about the heat and logistics, one might think the impact was negative. Memories fade, anyway. Who recalls the Olympics in Montreal or in Los Angeles? Yet Atlanta is now part of the Olympics pantheon reaching from ancient Athens to Tokyo and Seoul, to Athens again, and then on to Beijing. Atlanta has become a world city, anointed by the Olympics, and it has played a part in the creation of a world space.[8]

BOWL GAMES

In scope Olympics are global, and bowl games are national. Top-ranked American-style football teams are pitted against each other, ultimately for a national championship. But the games are regional in location, sited largely in the Southwest and Southeast. The oldest and most important southeastern bowl games are named for plants signifying locales: orange (Miami), cotton (Dallas), sugar (New Orleans), and peach (Atlanta). Typically, a southern team is pitted against a nonsouthern team. The objective of the game is to penetrate the territory of one's opponent, an action that may carry sexual connotations. In any case, the imagery is often of a northern team and a southern team vying by means of violent actions and militaristic strategies to invade each other's territory in a game taking place in a location symbolizing the agrarian South. Perhaps the allusion is to the experience of the Civil War repeated in similar invasions, economic this time rather than military.

However one chooses to interpret the symbolism of the bowl games, they illustrate a national frame in a southern locale: regional territory is a site for national struggle and competition. The Olympics, by comparison, illustrate an international frame in a southern locale: regional territory becomes a site for international struggle and competition. The symbolism of the first suggests place as part of a national force field, while that of the second suggests place as part of a global force field.[9]

LOCAL AND ETHNIC ENACTMENTS

If the Olympics illustrate globalism in a southern city, and bowl games wed national frameworks and regional rivalries and southern settings, a range of other kinds of celebrations use localized settings not featured in global or national media. Outdoor community dramas commemorate ethnicities and histories. For example, *Unto These Hills* deals with Cherokee identity in North Carolina, and Jamestown's *The Common Glory* recalled national history.[10] Highland games, at Grandfather Mountain and throughout the South, are international in celebrating Celtic heritage, in this sense comparable to La Fiesta del Pueblo, in Raleigh, which celebrates Hispanic heritage. Folk festivals, such as the Festival for the Eno, in Durham, mix blues, bluegrass, blacks (usually as performers rather than spectators), whites, and foods—a potpourri. Folkmoot, in the North Carolina mountains, is explicitly international, bringing performers from throughout the world. State fairs, once segregated by race, are now mixed.

These events mark spaces. They are local, and they build locale. They also express globalization by their grounding in physical space. Scots come to a meadow on Grandfather Mountain, as does their Scottish heritage, which is invigorated as they toss the caber and run races in kilts, eat Scottish foods, and sing sentimentally about the Battle of Culloden. Even where international culture is not explicitly emphasized, global connections are often apparent. At a demolition derby held during the 2003 North Carolina State Fair, I acquired, as noted, a Confederate flag that says "Made in China."

In the South, social and cultural configurations have long been expressed through particular spaces. In slavery and later in segregation, divisions were often dualistic, as between slave quarters and the big house or between small and large farms—divisions that required that some people enter through the back door or sit in the backseat of a car or bus and that whites and blacks not sit at the same table, attend the same churches and schools, be buried on the same sites, or play sports on the same fields. Public gatherings sometimes brought groups together while keeping them apart, as when blacks were seated in the balconies of theaters, and whites in the lower sections. While many old separations continue and new ones arise, what is striking are the spaces that do bring together varied groups, for example, a state fair (even an ethnic one such as the Fiesta del Pueblo) or a track meet. At the local high school commencement, the group of valedictorians consisted of six persons, including students from China and India as well as a white American male. The commencement was held inside a gymnasium, but most of these events are held outdoors, implying some kind of relationship to the environment, to space and place. One is reminded of the contrast that Gwen Neville noted between Catholic Communion inside churches and the outdoor gatherings that Protestants favored in Scotland, which led, she suggests, to southern traditions of having dinner on the grounds and other ceremonial gatherings outdoors; here the form is expanded to include multicultural gatherings.[11]

REGIONAL AND GLOBAL INTERSECTION

The symbolism of globalism shares space with the symbolism of regionalism. Silent Sam, a statue of a Confederate soldier, stands guard on the campus of the University of North Carolina at Chapel Hill. Sam has withstood more than a century of post–Civil War history, including calls to tear him down because he is a symbol of slaveholding society. In front of him one afternoon is a celebration by the local Hare Krishnas, who maintain a complex nearby in Hillsborough. The Hare Krishna dancer is singing the epic of the *Bhagavad Gita* from the Indian *Mahabharata*. This tells of Arjuna's dilemma. Arjuna, one of the Pandava brothers, must fight his cousins, the Kauravas. Remembering their shared childhood, he hesitates but is advised by Krishna, the god-charioteer, who reminds Arjuna of his caste, the *Kshatriya*, or warrior-leader caste. To fulfill his *dharma* (his duty and destiny), Arjuna must fight physically, but at least he can maintain his detachment and balance spiritually. Here, then, are two military cultures juxtaposed in one space—the Asian, or global, and the regional. They share values: recall Robert E. Lee's sense of duty (not unlike Arjuna's) and his commitment to fight his "cousins" from the North, not out of anger but because it was his caste duty—or so his decision is portrayed. In any case, this space before the statue becomes two places, a regional place representing history, and a global place representing a certain future.

Time and Space: The Life Cycle

Space and time interact, as illustrated by the life cycle. Global diversities penetrate space for an individual variously depending on that person's age and stage of life. Robert and Louise began life in a dualistic setting, in Deep South white homes with black servants, and they enter old age in a Deep South retirement home that is similarly dualistic, with a white clientele and largely black staff. Their young adult and middle years, however, were less restricted: they moved about the country and were in military service overseas. Their children, grandchildren, and great-grandchildren are at once more peripatetic and more multicultural, marrying across cultures, living abroad, and eating, studying, and working globally. Will they remain so as they enter old age, or will they maintain their largely dualistic demographics in retirement settings? The history of globalization interacts, of course, with the life histories of individuals, which begin in restrictive settings (the womb, then the family) and end likewise (retirement or nursing home, the family, and a grave or urn), while life lived between cradle and grave usually takes place in wider spheres that are also more diverse.

Life cycle pressures may push toward grounding, even if one's inclinations are global. Sophia, a scholar of literature who is of southern origins, chaired a panel at the Modern Language Association called "Feminist Cosmopolitanism" but then gave up a position teaching in New York City because her four-year-old son, Raymond, yearned to return to his home in Maine. While Sophia's outlook at this point in her career and life cycle is flexibly cosmopolitan, Raymond is very much grounded in a particular locale. Raymond calls himself "Logman" because his passion is to pick up sticks outdoors. He is also attached to the sea, and he spoke to the sea when he returned from New York to Maine: "Sea, I know you have missed me." In New York, he felt at home only in the Museum of Natural History, among the dinosaurs.

As funerals and memorial services illustrate, a certain diversity is restored that extends past life into death. Louisa's memorial service in a small-town Methodist church in Georgia includes several exemplifying strands. Pastor Watkins, a black minister, knew Louisa's father and has worked for the family—her father, his children, their grandchildren—for half a century. He enters the church speaking scriptures. The organ then plays Louisa's favorite piece, Bach's "Jesu, Joy of Man's Desiring." Such a celebration of life conjoins black and white relationships in a southern context with European culture—preglobal, perhaps, but nonetheless both inward- and outward-looking in terms of world culture. Beyond geography, the horizons stretch, of course, into spiritual domains that are at once global—reaching back to the Middle East and North Africa and forward to Asia—and metaphysical, transcending any geography. Burial in the grave signifies grounding locally. Secular globalism, however cosmopolitan, cannot equal religion in its expanse, which moves beyond any physical locale at the same time that the grave is dug deep into locale.

Going Away and Coming Home

Soldiers go away, and soldiers come home. Tears and sadness mixed with pride accompany departure; happiness and relief accompany homecoming. Soldiers are the archetypal travelers because they combine movement and return with danger.

Joanna, a college sophomore from Memphis, is on the way to Egypt to study scuba diving. Sallie, from a small town in Georgia, goes to the Australian outback, sky dives and bungee jumps in South Africa, and then, after making her debut in Atlanta, joins the marines. Tashika, an African American premed student at the University of North Carolina, does volunteer work for Hurricane Katrina then interns in Soweto in South Africa.

Sandy was in Tibet studying Buddhism, then she lived for six years in the Caribbean as a massage therapist, and now she lives in San Francisco. She is home in Raleigh because her mother just died.

Rhett is from Atlanta; his wife, Scarlett, also from the South, teaches French and loves to go to Paris. "Scarlett wants to go to Paris," he says ruefully, "and all I want to do is go to Sunset Beach." Rhett's father built much of the campus of a southern university; Rhett oversees thousands of factories globally—showing a radical shift over a generation from a local to a global focus.

In a country and western video, Glenn Campbell goes back to his old daddy and homeplace. So do characters in Louis L'Amour westerns and in country and western music, where being on the road and pining for home joins lost love as classic themes.

All three retirement communities in Chapel Hill are named for nature: The Cedars, Carol Woods, and Carolina Meadows. Bucolic settings are one image that welcomes retirees to the South, whether they are natives returning or newcomers.

The sense of place combines with global impulses in the South as elsewhere: going away and coming home. Place may be imagined as much as real, and home may be where the heart is, but powerful emotions attach to spots called "home" and are accentuated when one is away. *Rindu* in Javanese and *Heimweh* in German signal the global scope of homesickness. "Dig the grave and let me lie!" requested Robert Louis Stevenson in "Requiem," imaging his ultimate homecoming. Margaret, a neighbor, is leaving town. Where are you going? "To the source," she replied, meaning going to visit her mother, at a closer home.

Living in England, in 1981, our family went to Tunisia. Coming back to England was like coming back home. So was coming back to a room in Jakarta after traveling by boat through the islands of Indonesia. "Home" is relative to somewhere else, proving that place is a construct; it is not wedded to a specific space but imposed by us onto a space. This does not diminish the power of that construction.

The South joins a dialectic of going and coming, which entails constructing and relating space and place away and at home in myriad ways. "Home" gains meaning through its relation to "away" and vice versa.

Constructing Foreign Space

My father had a photographic memory of space, where he lived, wherever he went or had been. He would describe a path in Georgia where he found arrowheads as a child, detailing each foot of the path. Mostly he was silent, but if prompted, as he once was by some archeologists, he would unreel such spatial memories. Forty years after he had participated in the D-day invasion, we visited the area of England, near Stonehenge, where he had camped before embarking. Although road signs had been removed then to confuse Germans in the event of invasion there, forty years later he remembered every lane and turn.

Travis was born and raised in North Carolina. He moved to Tokyo right after college and has lived there for thirty years. When he comes home—to North Carolina—he orients to the land and roads of his home area, where his mother and kin live. When he is in Tokyo, he lives in a world of subway systems. In transit, he lives in a world of passports, visas, air tickets, and international flights. That seeming dichotomy of local and home is complicated by further interests. He and Japanese students do research in Oklahoma among Native Americans. He is a brilliant poet and tough administrator who unites those talents within a Japanese space. He is married to a Japanese woman and has two children; the children live in Tokyo and Ireland.

In 1970 I embarked on a journey to visit branches of the Muhammadiya throughout the islands of Indonesia. I first traveled on a boat, sleeping on the deck along with hundreds of Indonesians, and would disembark at each port to visit the local branch while the boat was in the dock. Then I flew to the island of Sumbawa, where I was to take a smaller boat from the western side to the eastern side, Bima, to visit a particularly intensely Muslim branch that had once tried to assassinate President Sukarno on Tjikini Street in Jakarta. On the flight, I noticed a man whom I identified as a Muhammadiyan—just by the way he acted. On Sumbawa, we disembarked together at the town Sumbawa Besar and waited for the boat, which was a week late; we became friends, and he invited me to stay with his brothers and father in Bima, which I did, returning overland on streambeds in an all-night drive behind wild horses in the jungle. In 1996 I returned to Sumbawa Besar. It looked entirely different from the way I remembered it and had photographed it. I am certain the changes were not entirely objective but were constructed by my differing way of experiencing that same space. (I am reminded of a recent dream: I parked my car next to a house and went in the front door; when I left, I could not see the car or road because I had left by the back door, which opened onto a deep chasm that I descended and had to ascend to find the initial space. The disorienting sense of expecting one space and finding another was similar to my return to Sumbawa Besar.)

So here we have three illustrations of how, just as global forces transform space at home, individuals (as it happens, southern ones, here) construct ways of living in space abroad. Nothing is distinctively "southern" about their constructions so far as I can see; the point is that southerners, like anyone else, do stretch their senses of place when they go away, and those stretched conceptions shape their sense of place when they come back home.

Postsouthern Space: Literary Constructions

Literature is prescient—alert to change and dissonance, expressing them in fiction in ways that clarify and articulate what we experience in fact. Walker Percy, the Birmingham-born, Mississippi-raised writer whose philosophical leanings suggested Kierkegaard, disclosed the ironies and instabilities of southern senses of place. In *The Last Gentleman*, the protagonist is a displaced and disoriented—but engaging and sometimes bravely determined—southerner searching vaguely for a place. *Love among the Ruins* is set in a homeplace, of sorts, but that place is undergoing transformation as racial etiquette changes along with the landscape and milieu. *The Moviegoer*, Percy's first novel, projects perhaps his most nuanced and unsettling interrogation of the southern sense of space; it is cogently explicated by British literary commentator Martyn Bone to illustrate Percy's move toward what he, following Scott Romine and others, term "the postsouthern sense of place." Here are some key themes in Bone's explication of *The Moviegoer*. [12]

Binx, the narrator, is a stockbroker who has removed himself from his Aunt Emily's "social geography." Instead of living in her carriage house on Garden Street in New Orleans, he chooses to live in a new suburb, on a street named Elysian Fields.

Despite some disillusion at this capitalistic, development-driven setting, Binx arrives at a proposal to his cousin, Kate Cutrer, suggesting that she resolve her own issues by joining him in marriage and a service station; he has approached a Shell distributor. Binx then visits his mother's family's fishing camp, where he identifies a "malaise" or "everydayness" that has crept into the countryside, even into the swamps and bayous. At this point, suggests Bone, Binx can find no southern place to escape the spreading capitalistic corrosion of place and its correlated malaise—not least because he himself is an agent of it. However, Binx goes to Chicago and its suburb Wilmette, where he visits his Korean War colleague Harold Graebner, whose life Binx finds alien. This trip redeems the South, argues Bone, by contrasting it with the North. Binx perceives the North, specifically Chicago but conflated with New York, as especially naked of soul, personified as "ghosts of the past," including Confederate ones, and particularly driven by urban industrial capitalism. Bone suggests that by this contrast of stereotypes, Binx avoids admitting how much North and South have in common and represses his own earlier fear of that force in the South and his involvement in it. Returning home, he suffers castigation from Aunt Emily—a speech oddly compelling, I felt, even if Bone describes it as "verbal mauling"; in any case, Emily's cultural force compels Binx back into her circle, and he marries Kate, returning to a certain kind of social and geographic identity.

What Percy captures and Bone explicates persuasively is the irony of a southern sense of place not only at a certain time but also anytime. Binx is the liminal actor and perceiver, caught between Emily and Chicago. Binx himself moves gingerly, antennae out to sense the malaise.

The global dimension is only implicit. Sharon Kincaid, Binx's secretary, is from Eufaula, Alabama. She is a healthy, candid immigrant from a small town on the Chattahoochee. (Actually, Eufaula is notable for its main street of antebellum mansions that, one suspects, she did not inhabit, at least not as she is depicted by Percy.) Sharon's localism contrasts with the relative cosmopolitanism of Binx and New Orleans. That cosmopolitanism, suggested only by such hints as his possession of *Arabia Deserta* (an account of hardship and discovery by the nineteenth-century British explorer Charles Doughty as he lived, often sick and desperate, among desert Arabs) doubtless lies behind his rebellion against his heritage. But then that heritage is itself somewhat global, as is the capitalism that sustains his heritage and him. Binx, in the 1950s, is already enmeshed in global force fields (Shell Oil, for one) that are more than capitalistic and foreshadow the more blatant global instabilities to come. (Katrina tragically symbolizes the flooding force that swept away much of the landscape evoking Binx's malaise.)

Percy, then, evoked an emerging southern sense of place, as part of force fields that are partially global. Proustian introspections are perhaps less characteristic of southern sensing of space than are extroverted public events, soldiering, families, and nostalgic evocation of homeplaces, but Percy's sensibilities question claimed stabilities of locale and affirm that place still matters, very much, even to southerners like Binx. After all, Binx did not go to the Arabian desert but merely read about it, and he did not stay in Chicago but merely visited it to discover its deficits compared with home. In the end, at least for the moment, he moves back to where he came from.

Ecology: Nature, Culture, and Global Forces

Place is the human construction of space, which is to say that we build culture onto nature. We do so not only by the most blatant construction (buildings, roads, and cities) and by more nuanced construction (literature or ritual) but also in the ways we try to live with nature: intimately, as a partner, or masterfully, manipulating it but still in deep relationship with it. Living in and off the land by hunting, fishing, farming, and ranching, or learning about it through hiking and bird-watching are obvious examples in agrarian and country settings: you can't do these things in cities except perhaps in restricted ways. Somewhat related are various endeavors that move through space, such as military campaigns or maneuvers. Summing up the multiple ways humans relate to nature is ecology, specifically human ecology. A related concept is the environment, especially our "natural" surroundings, and environmentalism, which is concerned with saving and sustaining the environment. The South has a certain ecology, a natural setting, and southerners practice certain human ecologies, ways of relating to nature in this place. We explore, now, characteristic practices in relation to global forces.

Memory, history, and the southern sense of place are threatened, some argue, by ecology and environmentalism. But are they, or must they be? Certainly, southern ecologists exist. They are perhaps a notable and distinct type, including Al Gore, Thomas Berry, Wendell Berry, Howard W. Odum, Howard T. "Tom" Odum, Eugene Odum, Stuart Marks, and William McDonough. These are all ecologists whose work has both a social and a meaning dimension; they are all more than (less than?) strict environmentalists.

Gore was inspired by Erik Erikson. Thomas Berry is a theologian. Howard W. Odum was a sociologist, and his sons were tuned in to place, though they were scientists. Marks champions subsistence hunters in community context over strict wildlife conservation (animals over humans). The most comprehensively articulated perspective is given by Berry in his "Ecozoic era" theory. Berry traces the history of the world from its origins through prehistory into the present. He portrays the Industrial Age, especially the creation of the great corporate enterprises of the late nineteenth century, as a greater threat to the earth "and all that dwell therein" than the events of all the previous millions of years.

Urgently needed, he argues, is a change to an Ecozoic era based not on exploiting the earth for industrial production and corporate profit but on a balance. Four major institutions—government, religion, education, and business—are implicated in the problem, and all must work toward a transformation. This will entail change in practice and change in culture at the deepest and most comprehensive levels, from values to ritual and human subjectivity.[13]

Berry's vision is ecological and global. While he alludes to the South in one passage (a meadow of his youth), his vision is at a more universal level. Somewhat more place- and practice-oriented is the thesis of Berry's protégé Herman Greene. Although Greene alludes to his own background—his North Carolina farmer grandparents and his Florida agricultural economist father—his profession is law, and his guiding philosophy is Thomas Berry's concept of the ecozoic. Greene has organized the Ecozoic Society, based in Chapel Hill, North Carolina, which publishes the *Ecozoic Reader*. Greene has expressed the ecozoic ideal in various ways—for example, by instituting a celebratory season in a particular Baptist church, developing a sustainable residential community, and applying law to ecological issues. He is the secretary of an international society devoted to envisioning process, including ecological process.

What does global ecology have to do with religion, farming, hunting, fishing, the military, and other traditionally salient streams of southern culture? Preservationism, bird-watching, and nature walks are part of another subculture, but this subculture, too, connects to the environment, to the nature around us, which happens to be in the South. Farmers run the gamut from those accused of destroying the environment—the hog farmers, poultry farmers, and others with massive operations—to those who farm organically and champion seed banks. Hope Shand, who is based in Pittsboro, North Carolina, works and speaks internationally for sustainable agriculture and the preservation of seed resources developed over thousands of years. Hunters are usefully subdivided by Stuart Marks according to what they hunt, from rabbits and squirrels to deer and quail. Of these, the quail hunters most consciously articulate sustainability, because they control the land on which the quail reproduce.[14]

"They are part of our culture, part of our town. To get rid of them would make this town very, very blah," said Jan Gelders of Fitzgerald, Georgia, of the two thousand feral chickens that roam the town.[15] Perhaps Fitzgerald boasts more cultural richness than the chickens alone can provide. At a convenience store there, I overheard a conversation between a male teenager from India, who was helping his father, and a blond teenager with her mother, suggesting a nascent cross-culturalism. In any case, the feral chickens are deemed part of the culture. The same holds for the feral hogs that also roam the area. A giant one, "Hogzilla," was recently shot in nearby Alapaha. First claimed to be twelve feet long and weigh a thousand pounds, Hogzilla is apparently not quite that large, but it is still reputed to be the largest wild boar known.

John Reed tells of a southern farmer who every day took his favorite hog down the road to wallow. A recently arrived neighbor from the North suggested that it would save time to allow the hog to wallow at home. The farmer responded, "Time don't mean nothing to a hog." Chickens and hogs that wander free or whose time takes priority over humans' suggest the theme of southerners as *Naturvölker*, part of nature. An agrarian, quasi-frontier heritage expressed by a fondness for hunting and fishing resonates. Good ol' boys hunt and fish. Nature writers, from Robert Ruark to William Faulkner, celebrate the theme: in *As I Lay Dying*, Faulkner evokes totemism, identifying characters with fishes. In "The Bear," he likewise probes an identity between the human and the animal. The bear is at once a soul brother and a quarry, and hunting him is necessary for becoming a man.

The South also has its great naturalists, from John Lawson and William Bartram to William Coker, but their kind of nonintrusive naturalism—such as bird-watching, trail hiking, and nature walks—has been minor and largely late in coming in comparison with ways of mastering nature, such as farming, fishing, and hunting. Broadening our view to other southern ways of being outdoors, consider golf, football (American style), baseball, stock-car racing, and military campaigns (including reenactments). They are all not only ways of mastering and controlling the environment—moving about it, shaping it, often destroying it—but also ways of subjecting oneself to it—facing storms, sun, wind, insects, and animals.

Globalization is part of the development, as Safari Clubs International, based in Arizona, illustrates. Safari Clubs International oversees safaris that take hunters to game camps in Africa and other "exotic" locales. Stuart Marks, the organization's scientific director, hails from Wilmington, North Carolina, but grew up in the Belgian Congo, where his father was a missionary dentist. Marks earned a doctorate in animal ecology from Michigan State University and studied anthropology at the London School of Economics. He applied both areas of expertise in Zambia, working out a system to divert profits from safaris to sustaining subsistence hunting–based tribal communities. Marks's success in transforming exploitative hunting into sustainable ecology suggests a model for the South to link its own hunting heritage with ecological sustainability as part of the globalizing South.

Southern religionists also exist, famously. They, too, share certain tendencies that, on the face of it, appear to contradict those of the ecologists. Their central theme is a theology that denies the validity of many social and other contextual issues (including environmental issues). They focus instead on individual and spiritual needs, on saving souls as contrasted with saving the earth. Some see the earth, the world itself, as evil, as full of snares and temptations. Yet such a perspective is often connected to a rural background and, for many still, to a culture that honors hunting, fishing, guns, trucks, and the military as a complex that bespeaks manhood. One is used to seeing figures such as the Baptist preacher I heard speak on the steps of the capitol in Austin, Texas, at a gathering to oppose gun control. The preacher praised gun ownership; in fact, he claimed guns as a hobby of his and said, "You fellows have probably seen me at gun shows."

Military bases and military traditions resonate with guns, hunting, and perhaps (though not necessarily) certain kinds of political conservatism. Several such themes came together at a dove shoot in Scotland County, North Carolina. The shoot began with a prayer about a boy who was accidentally shot by his grandfather at an earlier hunt. The boy was imagined in heaven, looking down and blessing the hunt. The organizers, brothers of Scottish descent who were war veterans, expressed contempt for draft-dodging politicians.

The South, then, as space or place, has multiple relations with southerners. The regional identity is historically agrarian, outdoorsy, and "natural," as opposed to urban. Nature is close to self in the Dabbs characterization of the South and is felt intimately. Mastery and Dabbs's "at homeness," intersect in hunting and in other outdoor activities, as illustrated by Faulkner's story "The Bear." Such activities of the outdoorsman contrast with the blatant destruction of nature by the bulldozer and the built environment that result from globalization and urbanization. At the same time, globalization brings more subtle but equally powerful forces, one of which is ecology as a perspective. Ecology and environmentalism oppose destruction of the environment itself, but in privileging the nonhuman environment, these approaches often undermine ways of relating to and thinking about the environment that, whatever their ecological drawbacks, nonetheless build and sustain relations between humans and nature. Examples include hunting, fishing, farming, and ranching, and even building houses, clearing forests, and cutting trees. Such practices exhibit the double-edged combination of mastery and intimacy that characterizes preglobal relations to the environment in the South and elsewhere.

What ties all this together? First of all, these outdoor activities are global in reach. This is true of hunting (Safari Club International), military actions (global), and even celebrations of ethnicity. As Celeste Ray argues, the sort of macho land-oriented hunting-military complex illustrated by the Scotland County dove shoot has merged a certain international theme (Scottish connections) with a Lost Cause heritage, and both the Scottish and the southern heritages are oppositional.[16] They also engage nature through culture, though not in the ways espoused by posttraditional global ecology. Faulkner's "The Bear" brilliantly captures the ambivalence inherent in this pre-ecozoic culture: the deep bond between animals and humans coupled with the human character's determination to conquer and kill the bear as part of his passage into manhood.

Gender issues surround and underlie pre-ecozoic "outdoorism" and ecozoic ecology. The outdoorism is often patriarchal. In the patriarchal stereotype, men hunt, fight, and conquer nature, and women stay home bearing and nurturing children. The ecozoic and ecological vision, by comparison, blames men for their destruction of the earth and honors women for their urge to live in balance with it. Yet for both, the mythos of Mother Earth is prominent. In southern mythology and memory, Dixie symbolizes Mother Earth—raped by the North, defended by the South— and the Lost Cause mourns the inability to defend, remembered poignantly in the Battle of Atlanta and Sherman's March to the Sea. Even bowl games, I suggest, may reflect that theme, and it is certainly pervasive in the huge industry of histories, films, and reenactments. The South's experience resonates with parallel experiences globally, parallel struggles to defend the motherland against invaders. The historical memory of the region, then, converges with the ecozoic vision in a certain reverence for place; that place is often symbolized as a homeplace imagined as female, sometimes specifically as the Mother Earth.

How might these trends connect, if at all? The notion of the force field is a familiar concept: what seems to be mass is actually energy; the table before me is not so solid and inert as it seems. Herman Greene, head of the Ecozoic Society, writes about process philosophy, which captures the same general notion. "Process philosophy" is the name given to the work of Alfred North Whitehead, especially with reference to physics since Newton and extending through quantum and string theory. Briefly summarized, post-Newtonian thinking shifts emphasis from mass to energy, from objects to processes.[17]

Whatever the meanings "process" and "force field" may have in physics, they capture usefully a sense of the global forces as they converge at certain times and spaces to create a place. The implication for "place" is that it is envisioned not as a thing but as a process, a field of force rather than a "field" in the spatial sense. Distinctions between race and place illustrate the change. Race and racism, like spacism, imply fixity of boundaries: one is black or white, lives in one neighborhood or another, attends one school or another, enters through a certain door, or sits in a certain place in houses or buses or cars. North and South are spacist ways of accentuating opposition, the differences in values, ways of life, histories, and institutions of the two regions of the United States. Spatial boundaries such as the Mason-Dixon Line or the Potomac River crystallized the opposition and spatialized the oppositional stance of the South and the North toward each other. Such spacism accented by oppositionalism is part of the sense of place that characterized the South in the nineteenth and twentieth centuries.

Southern spacism is transformed by changes emerging in the twentieth and the twenty-first centuries, but sense of place is not necessarily obliterated. Industrialization, urbanization, and the "development" of new neighborhoods and roads emphasize change, but they also emphasize a certain amount of integration into broader systems. Ecology implies not only process but also integrity and balance. Smart growth is not no growth, and preservation is not duplication, but rather involves sustaining a sufficient core of identity and community while accosting forces of change and acquiring global identities.

The move from sense of place to sense of process (or force field) requires replacing spatial boundaries with non-space-bounded processes, which, however, converge in spaces. The Mason-Dixon Line, racially divided neighborhood lines, and the division of sacred places fix forces in space, or try to and tend to. Such external spots and sites—monuments, battlefields, churches, homes, and other landmarks, that is, marked spots on the land—embody and gain fixity and meaning from internal processes.[18] Together, such externalities and internalities compose history. Other structures—shops, restaurants, malls, highways, and highway rest stops, entrances, and exits—are built over and around them, seemingly dissolving that history as they join global force fields. These spatial transformations crosscut social and psychic transformations, bringing diversity with them, as new immigrants build the roads and malls and staff the high-tech parks, opening worldviews that connect with the globally connected spaces to some degree. Globalizing development and globalizing ecologies clash and connect with each other and with nodes of place, memory, and history in the South as elsewhere. Reordering living arrangements and spatial configurations correlates, though not simply or perfectly, with shifts in identity, as in the trends toward pluralism and globalism. Global identity is manifested both socially and spatially in pluralistic cultural relations among peoples and in force fields linking constructed and natural spaces. Both signify change as part of global identity. The change is partly in mode or aspect and partly in scope. Sense of place becomes both more dynamic and more insecure and broadens in scope toward a global compass.

While accepting that such an integrative trend is under way, however, one should also recognize the flame that still burns—a southern sense of place and heritage that is tied to the defense of territories and the affirmation of manhood, womanhood, and family values. Southern globalism is grounded: it reflects a certain sense of place. Imperfectly captured by environmentalism, Catholicism, or even southern-based ecologism, caricatured by "olde plantation" gated communities and golf courses, expressed by cabins, hunting clubs, boats, and fishing expeditions, by farms and gardens, this "southernness" tones ecology locally as it intrudes globally.[19] Globalism is grounded, even as it transforms that ground.

Globalism is grounded, too, in proximity. Mary is a Floridian, having grown up in a multicultural setting in which immigrants from elsewhere in the United States and from Asia and Latin America mix with those from families who have lived in the South for generations near such globally oriented enterprises as Disney World and Epcot. She takes a job in Nebraska but happily moves back to Florida. Why? That is where she grew up, that is where her family and many friends still live, and that is where she feels at home. Mary is an anchorwoman on television, yet her electronic world does not override her anchoring in her home space, even a relatively cosmopolitan one such as Florida. She returns to a global setting that is spatially grounded: her home.

What is implied, then, for oppositionality? Expressed spatially, oppositionality remains part of the landscape in the South, but it is now situated within structures that subsume it. The Cyclorama in Atlanta depicting the Battle of Atlanta remains prominent, as does the memory of Clark Gable and Vivien Leigh visiting Atlanta for the premiere of *Gone with the Wind*. But these artifacts of oppositional space and others in the South are situated among and interpreted in the context of newer artifacts noted earlier—for example, CNN, Turner Field, the World Congress Center, the Carter Center, the Hyatt Regency Atlanta, and the expressways clogged with cell phone–using drivers. The objective artifacts, the built spaces, constitute the cultural landscape, which is shared.

The globalizing of space challenges boundaries of many kinds—ethnic, racial, and class. Global forces create new ethnic spaces, immigrant neighborhoods, and new class divides, as the well-off head to the airport to travel and the poor use the bus station, the former more expensive and global, the latter cheaper and localized. Environmentalism itself, while opposing the capitalist destruction of the environment, clashes with workers' desires for jobs and hence with industries and businesses, including agribusiness, which is global both in markets and workers. While the global impact on space, then, is not entirely in accord with liberal platforms, the overall effect of flux and change offers new opportunities.

Space and place, together with their visual representations, show how an essentialized oppositional southern identity is altered by global forces that de-essentialize and de-oppositionalize. Spatial redefinition ricochets into modes of making sense, and calls for new frames for making meaning and for framing existence, spatial or otherwise. Such framings engage religion and other spheres of culture and subjectivity, topics of our next chapter.

PART THREE

Meaning and Action

CHAPTER SIX

Meaning

Religion in the Global South

TIME, PLACE, PRESERVATION, tourism, memory, spirituality, horror movies and Halloween, retirement homes, commemorations, reenactments, community legends, Sigmund Freud and William Faulkner, funerals, cemeteries, monuments: the members of this list share a focus on the past. "The past is not past," proclaimed both Faulkner and Freud. (Faulkner's character was thinking of society and its remembering; Freud was thinking of the individual and how repressed memories determine behavior.) Not surprisingly, as globalization presses and change happens, a countermovement seeks past as well as place, a way of connecting to something larger and older than immediate circumstance.

My first three hypotheses all address specific changes—in social relationships locally and globally, in sense of place—and how these changes redefine identities. Identities are immediate, involving who we are as persons or as groups, but identity is not the deepest or largest category of existence. According to theory and commonsense observation, identities are framed by larger questions: What is existence? What are the purposes of life and death? Who I am or who we are is only an element of a wider reality, a wider "Being." Individual identity is a part of that whole. Identities are immediate, but meaning is ultimate. Meaning is found by locating parts in a whole, by placing oneself within a framework that articulates significance for one's life.

A woman parked a van with a New York license plate. She and two teenagers got out and examined a map. "Are you looking for something?" I asked. "Yes, we are. What are we looking for?" she asked her son. A young woman drives a Jaguar with a North Carolina license plate that reads "ATAKLIFE." Quests and attacks (on the "inexpressible") imply meaning. Place and globalization seemingly clash, but both are species of space; the one is localized space, the other, global space. Meaning transcends both. Meaning entails a framework that is metaphysical rather than physical, a conceptual framework in terms of which physical entities, such as spaces, make sense.

What moves us to get up in the morning and go through the day, to live life and do work, to "ataklife"? The answers may vary, from Nike's "Just do it" to a religious treatise on why we are sent to pursue a calling, serve God, or make a difference. Even "Just do it" presumes a certain value system of activism that has its roots in religious and other values and beliefs. In each case, some framework of meaning is operative. Meaning drives action, as we discover when some action seems meaningless and we question why we should do it. Yet meaning is difficult to articulate. Meaning is everywhere and every-when, yet nowhere and no place. For believers, meaning may flow from God and end in Heaven or Hell, which are imagined in place and time as having physical reality. Whether or not such images and categories matter to us, meaning is the total world in which we exist experientially and is a framework for making sense of that world conceptually and for motivating ourselves to act behaviorally.

Meaning entails not only the world—the global world—but the "other-world" as well, the cosmos, the metaphysical world.

Challenges of Globalization: Rationalization, Relativism, and Decontextualization

Meaning clashes with and is challenged by globalization in many aspects. Two key ones are rationalization and relativism; a third is decontextualization. First, globalization entails rationalization and specialization— making tallow into candles and men into money, as Max Weber put it.[1] One becomes obsessed with rationalizing life to make it serve specialized goals, such as profit, the bottom line. Such narrowing threatens those frames of meaning that define the whole, those large metaphysical visions not reducible to the rationalization of means in the interest of specialized ends that drive models of business, government, education, science, and technology, which spread globally, threatening older values. So globalization challenges meaning, and meaning must seek a way to encompass and make sense of globalization.

Globalism also brings with it many varieties of meanings and values, challenging meaning with relativism. Why believe or choose one rather than the other? Where one guiding faith or perspective has reigned, now many vie for acceptance. What seemed absolute is now relative—one option to be evaluated according to need and use or circumstance.

Finally, globalization, like any change, threatens meaning by ripping away context. One cherishes a certain form (say a song or a ritual) wedded to a certain context (a church or temple or a community in which one has grown up). Now, that form is placed in a new context and divorced from the old. The meaning that it had acquired from its old context is shattered, because the context has changed. The neighborhood has disappeared. The church is now surrounded by Asian restaurants and Mexican video stores. The Hallelujah Chorus is sung to advertise toilet paper. Christmas is celebrated along with Ramadan.

Rationalized, relativized, decontextualized: meaning is challenged. Responses range from fetishism and fundamentalism to recontextualizing, reframing. Fundamentalism and commerce are quite similar in that they fetishize. Coke is deemed "the Real Thing" or "It," and the most lavish and loving attention is given to body parts and food. The enormous fascination with gourmet cooking is an example. Fundamentalism is similarly focused on a particular thing, fetishizing scriptures or the details of the rules and practices they dictate. Reframing is a more abstract response, broadening rather than narrowing perspective. Synthesis is one endeavor; another is to make the search for meaning itself a source of meaning and commitment.

Every shift in identity implies shifts in meaning or is grounded in deeper or broader meanings, and the opposite holds true as well. One "becomes" a fundamentalist or an interpretative scholar or an environmentalist, championing a place (such as the Everglades or the Smokies or the entire planet). Identity is a way of branding oneself or a group as part of a particular mode of "meaning making." So each shift of meaning challenges identity, and each shift in identity challenges meaning.

Religion

We seek meaning in all that we do, but of the various modes of seeking and defining meaning, what we broadly term "religion" is a central one. Broadly defined, religion addresses questions about our origins, nature, and destiny—why we should act or live, why we do what we do. Thus religion is central to quests for meaning and to frameworks of meaning. Of course, because it entails action in addition to thought, religion is more than just theology or philosophy, which are cognitive systems. It attempts to enrich and integrate experience—external and internal, *Liebe und Arbeit*, love and work, dreams and life, the reality principle and the pleasure principle—by actions that are at once sacred and practical.

Peter Beyer has attempted a comprehensive account of the relations of religion to globalization. Beyer argues that globalization is an extension of modernization. Modern society developed specialized functions or systems, such as economic systems, educational systems, and health care systems, and then these specialized systems spread globally, replacing socioeconomic class as a key organizing principle and devouring older class-based structures. Religion and meaning-making structures are less specialized, or less simply so, than such functional systems. Religion specializes in nonspecialization, in encompassing the whole, making sense of parts, and bestowing meaning on life. Religion is therefore particularly challenged by globalization because its raison d'être—comprehensive meaning making—is out of step with the thrust toward specialization and expansion of specialized systems that is globalization. Beyer argues, too, that religion addresses the challenge in myriad ways but that these ways are essentially two: fundamentalism and liberalism. The fundamentalist reaction is to dig in the heels and resist modernization (but not necessarily globalization, since fundamentalism globalizes) and, in some varieties, to withdraw from the evil wider society and focus on spiritual and personal ethical concerns. The liberal reaction is to become engaged in issues stemming from globalization, such as the environment, while sometimes losing firm religious anchors. A possible third course is to synthesize globalization and religion, perhaps in a global religion, the shape of which is obscure.[2] Spirituality—turning inward—may offer a transitional medium.

Religion in the South

The South is stereotyped as the Bible Belt, which of course needs qualification. Historically, the South, relatively unchurched during the sixteenth and seventeenth centuries, was settled largely for commercial reasons, while New England was the site of religious missions to escape persecution in Europe and build religious communities in America. Whereas New England was predominantly settled by town communities focused on creating a "city upon a hill," the South tended to be oriented toward commerce, plantations, and the countryside. The Anglican Church was a state church in Virginia until the Revolution, but this religion of the gentry was challenged by Baptists coming from New England, by Methodists from England, and by evangelical camp meetings and other mass movements, all of which combined to make the South palpably religious in certain ways. In the nineteenth and twentieth centuries, mainstream churches—

the Southern Baptists, Methodists (now United Methodists), Presbyterians, and Episcopalians—predominated. These are the denominations whose churches, with some exceptions, are in the centers of southern towns and cities still, whose seminaries and universities are most recognized, and whose members are most affluent and influential. The side streams now rapidly becoming nationally and globally influential include the Pentecostals (Assembly of God, Holiness, and so on). Also important are the African American Methodist churches (for example, African Methodist Episcopal Zion, Christian Methodist Episcopal Zion), further kinds of Baptists (regular, "primitive," and so on), and localized groups such as the Moravians in Winston-Salem, North Carolina, and the German Brethren in southern Virginia. Catholics are prominent in such places as New Orleans, Savannah (with its large population of Catholic African Americans), Mobile, and Memphis and are increasing rapidly throughout the South. Jews have settled throughout the South, though in small numbers. (Some of the oldest Jewish synagogues in the New World are in Charleston and Savannah.) The late twentieth century and the early twenty-first have witnessed increasing religious vitality in the South, with the influx of Buddhists, Hindus, Muslims, Baha'is, and smaller sects such as Zoroastrians.

Stemming from Aldersgate and John Wesley, John Bunyan and the Baptists, the South has featured what Samuel Hill termed "the central theme" of conversion dynamics: that a faith can change a life, that the focus of religion is on saving souls and personal ethics as contrasted to social ethics. The conversion experience, an emotional experience of conviction that one is saved, is central to much of southern religion. The thesis set forth in work by Hill and Donald G. Mathews, in Sinclair Lewis's satiric novel *Elmer Gantry,* and in other caricatures of Bible Belt religion succeeds in capturing southern Protestantism's focus on saving souls by inducing an emotional conversion to Christ, but a broader and more complex perspective is needed to address several crucial points.[3] First, the emotional emphasis on soul saving is hardly present in much southern religion, including especially the liberal Protestant mainline, which continues to attract leaders of society despite the rise of Pentecostal and charismatic churches in recent years. Second, the emotional focus ignores more intellectual dimensions of religious thinking in the South historically as well as recently and currently.[4] Third, the evangelical, soul-saving impulse is by no means exclusively southern and in fact would seem to be as prevalent in other parts of the country, notably California and the Midwest, and the world. Fourth, stereotypes about the Bible Belt ignore secular influences that dominate the larger contexts; the South is indeed a "Christ-haunted landscape"—to use literary commentator Susan Ketchin's phrase from her book by that title— but not always or everywhere. Finally, globalizing influences suggest new variety and even new paradigms and perspectives.

Consider the intellectual objection. The past century of religious thinking in the South among the liberal mainstream, including college students and college-educated southerners, has been dominated by Protestant theologians, often of German background, such as Paul Tillich, Rudolf Bultmann, Richard Niebuhr, and Reinhold Niebuhr, and by inspirational scholar–missionaries such as Albert Schweitzer. This was true and remains true not only in college classrooms but in discussions and practices in many settings: denominational organizations associated with colleges, work camps, soup kitchens, and retreats. For many, such theologically oriented discussions and works were a way into religious thought and practice. The pattern was not and is not confined to the South but is national and international, sometimes led by southerners as part of a global liberal Christian (perhaps ecumenical) culture. While this liberal theological stream found its centers in seminaries inside and outside the South, including Harvard, Yale, Vanderbilt, and Emory, so-called fundamentalist and evangelical Protestantism flourished elsewhere.

In other kinds of communities in the South, quite impressive intellectual debates took place, for example, among Primitive Baptists in mountain districts. Men with eighth-grade educations studied eighteenth-century theologians such as Henry Philpott. "Primitive" evokes images of snake handlers, but in fact the Primitive Baptists eschew such emotionality and emphasize instead "discourse" (their word): careful and systematic exegesis of scripture to discern "types" that symbolize truths about destiny. Equally serious and committed analysis occurred in groups imported from New England, such as the Christian Scientists or the Unitarians.[5]

Of course, individuals of distinctive vision, such as Georgia's Howard Finster, the folk artist, drew notice. The media and scholars in fields such as folklore tend to highlight charismatic figures like Finster and ignore those self-taught individuals who reach high levels of scholarly research and thinking. John Peterson is an example. A dentist in a small town in Georgia, Peterson developed a highly sophisticated series of interpretations of scripture. He learned Greek and Hebrew and read vast amounts of scholarly work, as well as such commentators as Carl Jung and Claude Lévi-Strauss. His technique was deep textual analysis that led him to reinterpret scripture. He traced the historical, cultural, and sociological meanings of symbols in the Bible and other religious texts and found that they formed patterns and implied meanings not customarily inferred. His research, which seems to have been lost, led him to develop a somewhat unorthodox view of Christianity that he taught for many years to the "tree class," a Sunday school class of older men that met under a tree at the local Methodist church, of which they were longstanding members. (My father was one of them.) His view held that the New Testament provided a caricature of the good Jew, namely, Jesus. Christ was a metaphorical figure the Jewish rabbis invented to personify bad practice of Judaism. Later still, he expanded his theory to include the modern world, using symbolic analysis to demonstrate, quite suggestively, how media and advertising were using subliminal symbols to undermine faith and trust in the nation. He never published this work, and his audience was confined to the tree class, captive patients in his dental chair, and those he met at the post office.

Another example from the same place and time is the Reverend Sam Clark. Hailing from another South Georgia town, Warner Robins, Sam did graduate work in English at Princeton University and then moved on to Union Theological Seminary in New York, where he combined brilliant academic work with service among the homeless. Rejecting large city churches, he became the minister for a small chapel in the country. A gifted preacher, he attracted young people from the town, at least one of whom later went into the Peace Corps, though he returned to be a rancher. Sam himself went on to do mission work in Peru and later to take students to work camps in Latin America and Africa.

A third example is Fred Brooks. Raised in eastern North Carolina, Fred is a devout Methodist who is a leader in church and religious activities; for example, he once organized a large gathering to hear Billy Graham. He is also one of the world's most prominent computer scientists. He led the team that invented the first commercially available mainframe computer, the IBM System/360, and he was a leader in virtual reality (one of the earliest renditions was his own church, shown on the television series *Nova*). Such accomplishments earned him the Turing Award from the Association of Computing Machinery, the Nobel Prize of the computer world. Other examples of science leaders with southern religious roots include E. O. Wilson, the Harvard biologist, and Francis Collins, head of the human genome project.

My point is that in the South, as in other places at certain times— New England, Scotland, Germany, perhaps the global South, including Africa and Asia—Christianity has provided a focal identity for thinking, for confronting issues of ethics and meaning, and for broadening horizons globally. When Jimmy Carter held a retreat at Camp David to which he invited commentators such as Robert Bellah to consider issues of society, he did so on the assumption that religion, specifically Christianity, could provide a framework for working out ethical and meaning questions that translate into social action. The Wesley Foundation, Westminster, Hillel, Newman, and other organizations continue to usher students from small-town church (or large-town cathedral or synagogue) backgrounds into university life. Habitat for Humanity, created in Americus, Georgia, by Millard Fuller, exemplifies a southern religious culture translated into global endeavor. Not surprisingly, as David Chappell has shown recently, this same stream also engaged Martin Luther King. It represents a kind of southern Christian thought that united Billy Graham and King within a larger intellectual dimension, of which their work was in part an expression.[6] When considering the impact of global forces on the South, we must grasp the culture and setting framed by religion, but we shall be hopelessly wrong if we stereotype that framework as simply Bible Belt evangelical fundamentalism. Yes, religion is important, and no, it is not just that.

In acknowledging the presence of religion in the South, intellectual or otherwise, one should not exaggerate its pervasiveness. Most of life for most people most of the time is more profane than sacred. In the South, as in many places, sharp lines are not always drawn between church and state, and interpenetration between them is rather casual. An assembly program in high school featured a minister who kneaded bread dough to illustrate his message, after which the football coach stood and said "Man shall not live by bread alone" and then invited people to come out to the games. The casual scriptural allusion suggests common knowledge and a joking familiarity, not a fanatical zealotry. Zealots abound, of course, including Bible thumpers and cross burners, but most pervasive is a friendly hospitality toward the supernatural.

"Religion in its mildest form," as one Presbyterian termed Episcopalianism, accurately describes the religious practice of many southerners. Many, to be sure, are serious believers, and periodically, especially among adolescents, the flame of religion ignites, but most often it is on simmer. When a Javanese friend and I encounter devout Christianity (such as the devotional room of a certain Catholic Filipino) or "fanatical" Islam, I sense that our relatively mild and mixed backgrounds are similar in contrast to the stronger commitments. His mother taught him that simply thinking about prayer and pilgrimage, or doing what others in the neighborhood did, was good enough. Her casual view resembles that of my mother.

In short, the Bible Belt caricature is misleading. Literary figures such as Flannery O'Connor's Haze Motes conjure images of the South as a "Christ-haunted landscape" (to borrow Ketchin's phrase again), a kind of American theocracy after the fashion of the Ayatollah Khomeini's Iran or Calvin's Geneva, all backwoods tent meetings and snake handlers.[7] This picture is distorted, underemphasizing both the intellectuality of much of southern religion and the casual semisecularity of much nonreligious life. Nonetheless, the religious realm, in its own particular way, provides a continuing framework for making meaning of life in the South and, therefore, of change, including global trends.

If the recent South is a religiously shaped but fairly open place, casually religious but not vehemently so for the most part, is this changed by fundamentalism? Is the world polarized by the vehemence of Christian fundamentalism and governmental correlates on the one hand and Islamic fundamentalism on the other? Is Samuel Huntington's "clash of civilizations" occurring in the South as in the world? Muscles are being flexed, to be sure. Pat Robertson and Jerry Falwell in Virginia lead on the Christian right, now joined by novelists Tim LaHaye, who is from California, and Jerry B. Jenkins, who is from Michigan. We also see new divides in major denominations. Southern Baptists were taken over by fundamentalists, driving moderates into reactive postures. Fundamentalism can induce a new oppositionality—against Islam, for example. At the University of North Carolina at Chapel Hill, a summer reading assignment to incoming freshmen, the Qur'an and a set of interpretations, was opposed by the Family Policy Network, a fundamentalist group from Virginia that initiated an unsuccessful lawsuit, and the post-9/11 "forces of evil" rhetoric forced Muslims in the South, as elsewhere, into an oppositional category. The son of Egyptian Muslim immigrants in North Carolina graduated from Wake Forest University, a Baptist university; his French-educated mother writes about southern literature. Yet she is Muslim, a member of the Islamic Council in Raleigh, and she expresses fear of stigmatization and categorization in the newly polarized America. The oppositional force is by no means predominantly southern, but the South is part of it and part of the conservative politics that comes with the new Republican dominance in the South.

As in anthropologist Miranda Hassett's analysis of global Anglicans, described earlier, it is important to distinguish conservative from parochial: one may be global in geographic respects and conservative in theological and cultural aspects.[8] Pentecostals and Primitive Baptists, for example, are often emphatically open to global linkages. Durham, North Carolina, is the central headquarters for one chain of African American Pentecostal churches that stretches up to New Jersey and down into the Caribbean. Primitive Baptists profess that a Muslim in Africa or Egypt is as likely to be chosen by God for salvation as a faithful member of the local congregation. The "Macedonian call" led some Primitive Baptists from the Blue Ridge to the Philippines because a "brother" there felt the need for counsel. I have helped Primitive Baptists initiate services in Hopewell, New Jersey, and in Chapel Hill, to which worshipers came faithfully, driving many miles: "We will go the furtherest to hear the least," they say. Aside from willingness to travel, Primitive Baptists transcend geography if they sustain doctrine. Blue Ridge Primitive Baptists feel entirely at home with the Strict and Particular Baptists of England, with whom they are doctrinally identical. On the other hand, they scorn those who violate doctrine. Several who visited the University of North Carolina's alumni "memorabilia room" exhibiting trophies and awards for athletic achievement judged it to be "idolatry," and they dismiss their lowland Virginian Christian Right as seriously heretical for empowering merely human polities.

Concerning Pentecostalism I think of Doris Barbour, a black Pentecostal minister whom Ruel Tyson and I once interviewed in Durham. We started interviewing on her front porch, but she then invited us across the street to a hot and airless room above a store. A large, tall woman, she put one arm around each of us and expressed a vision she had for us. She then played and sang, concluding that "it takes both the white and the black keys to make music."

Pentecostalism also has broken gender barriers, as illustrated by the presence of female ministers. Black Pentecostal churches are often led by female ministers while male bishops oversee sets of churches. When a female Episcopal chaplain complained about gender barriers in her denomination, I suggested that she become Pentecostal. "Not a helpful suggestion," she replied, doubtless thinking of the prestige she would lose.

These fundamentalist churches, whether Pentecostal or Primitive Baptist, may be rigid theologically and socially, but they show incisive capacity to cut through local divisions such as race, class, and gender at the same time they stretch globally.

While the fundamentalist thrust has gained momentum, so have mystical, naturist, and other movements, including the spiritualist tendencies noted earlier. Joseph's Jewish forebears emigrated from Lithuania to Canada. He was born in Montreal, grew up in Charlotte, and became interested in Buddhism and adept in martial arts. After graduating from college with a major in comparative literature, he spent a year in Israel in a kibbutz, and now he is studying the *Kabbalah*, mentored by the rabbis who lead Hillel. Students and young people join Sufi, Buddhist, Wicca, Baha'i, and fundamentalist Christian groups. One young woman keeps a diary in which she describes her religious reflections; she refers to "my minister" but also to the spiritual influence of birds, sunsets, and her own meditations.

Religion and Globalization in the South

Globalism and religion have a range of southern faces, including fundamentalism. Intersections between the South and the world via religion are many, and we can only hint at them. Missionary relations between southern denominations and churches and the world are vast and longstanding. The best hospital in Indonesia, at Kediri, is Southern Baptist. A former pastor of St. Matthew's Church, an Anglican church in Singapore, was trained in Malaysia by a Baptist from North Carolina. A dental school in Zaire (now the Democratic Republic of the Congo) was established by a Presbyterian from Wilmington, North Carolina. Africa, China, and Latin America are in the backgrounds of many southerners through missionary work, and even the smallest churches maintain missionaries, so traveling and living abroad turns up southern religious presences everywhere. (For example, the Moravian Church in America, Southern Province, whose mother church is in Winston-Salem, North Carolina, lists churches in most Northern European nations, including Estonia, as well as many in Caribbean and African nations.)

Southerners who are not missionaries move out into the world in religious ways as well: a highly placed executive in a global company who is from North Carolina but has long resided in Singapore is taking up permanent residence there and has found a second home in a Singapore church whose congregation is largely Chinese. These southerners abroad are primarily Protestant because the Catholic presence globally is relatively underpopulated by southerners, though they are not entirely lacking. Thomas Berry's sister is an example; she was a nun in India. Places such as Bob Jones University in Greenville, South Carolina, that are staunchly conservative are global in surprising ways. Bob Jones has a museum of world culture containing objects gleaned from missionaries; it also boasts one of the best collections of religious art in the South. Less palatable to many are its relations to Ian Paisley and the conflict in Northern Ireland. And Billy Graham, who lives in Montreat, North Carolina, has spread Christianity globally more than any other person. Graham was asked by an interviewer from *Parade* magazine what he would like to be if he were not a preacher, and he replied that he would like to be an anthropologist so that he could better understand the variety of cultures he has encountered.[9] The global mission of Graham and others is, of course, illustrated by thousands of churches.

Although the global relations of the mainstream churches have been enduring, it is the Pentecostal movement that has been most active globally in recent years. The number of countries into which Pentecostalism has spread is remarkable, as in the number of conversions its adherents have effected. The unexpected influences of Pentecostalism that one encounters around the globe are equally striking. On an overnight train from Yogya to Jakarta, I once shared a compartment with a Chinese Pentecostal en route to Singapore, to a major revival led by Billy Graham. In Jakarta, I attended a meeting of the Full Gospel Businessmen's Association led by Sumatran Batak Pentecostals and heard a testimony that, had it not been in the Indonesian language, would have been like many I have heard in Durham, North Carolina. In Singapore recently, I attended a Pentecostal church with a woman from India who was of the Brahmin caste but converted to Pentecostalism after having a vision in which she saw Christ. What all this suggests is not simply that Pentecostalism is a partially southern-born, globally spreading religion but also that it is crossing cultures and ethnicities, which, after all, Pentecostalism has done in this country since its beginnings at Azusa Church in Los Angeles.

Note, again, that the apocalyptic trend, marked by a huge readership of Jenkins and LaHaye, intersects with southern preachers, notably Jerry Falwell. Jenkins is a Michigan native, however, and sales of the Left Behind series are high in the Midwest as well as in the South. Falwell's lieutenant at Liberty University is Turkish, a convert from Islam. A byproduct of the global spiritual tidal wave is that local distinctions in the South, such as black or white, and national distinctions, such as northern or southern, as well as global distinctions, such as American and Turkish, blur as people join in a larger movement seeking spiritual meaning.

Beyond the Christian sphere, the South sees greatly increased diversity, most visible in the physical presence of places of worship: mosques, Hindu temples, and Buddhist meditation retreat centers. The penetration of global organizations is evident also. Decades ago, in Singapore, I encountered Ahmadiyya, the Pakistani-based international and (in the view of orthodox Muslims) "heretical" Islamic movement. Now I meet a member of Ahmadiyya in Raleigh, North Carolina, represented on a panel discussing the opera *Samson and Delilah*. A certain multiculturalism for southern "natives" accompanies the arrival of diverse immigrants. Taoist devotees meet in Covington, Georgia, and Hindus, Muslims, and others from Asia or the Middle East form networks of kinship, friendship, and ethnicity or religious commonality that reach across the South, not only in cities but in small towns as well. Even though such ethnic and religious newcomers tend to form enclaves, considerable interchange with "natives" is apparent.

"Wan," a Chinese Singaporean, received in Singapore a photograph of Sai Baba, a South Indian guru, and put it in her suitcase as she traveled to

Edinburgh. At a time of lonely despair in this foreign place, she looked at the photograph and experienced solace. Some months later, she moved to Chapel Hill and had a similar experience. She then discovered other devotees of this guru. In Chapel Hill, Wan met "Jane." Wan returned to Singapore, followed by Jane. Jane met Wan in Singapore and went with her to a temple. Wan gave Jane a photograph of Sai Baba, which Jane took back to Chapel Hill, where she included Sai Baba in her own meditations; Jane is actively Christian. Jane has since met Indians who live in the South who are followers of Sai Baba and who communicate with each other by e-mail. This example illustrates how a global meaning penetrates the experience of both an immigrant and a "native" in the South and how both join a global network that includes the South in its system of worship. A final point is that these interconnections are not merely intellectual, theological, or cultural, but also "embodied."

On a country road in a remodeled tenant house is a massage therapist's practice. Stewart Walker grew up in Raleigh, the son of a Harvard-educated lawyer from there. Stewart majored in religious studies at the University of North Carolina, learned massage therapy, and stayed for some time in an ashram in India. He founded a holistic health center. A sturdy, straightforward, and independent person, Stewart left the center and has his own practice. Without advertising or a listing in the phonebook, Stewart has built a reputation locally, nationally, and internationally for healing injuries and relieving pain when others have failed. He does so entirely by the manipulation of muscles, guided by his precise knowledge of anatomy. No mantras, rituals, herbs, or other Asian practices are invoked, though Stewart privately meditates on the guru with whom he studied in the ashram. His patients testify to having chronic or acute pain healed or alleviated by Stewart. Do Stewart and those he treats reflect features of the Indian teachings and perspective that he follows, even though he does not teach them verbally or deploy them explicitly? The answer is yes, through embodiment.

Jane, the Sai Baba devotee noted above, is also a patient of Stewart's. Fifty years ago, at the age of sixteen, Jane was in an automobile accident.

Ever since, she has suffered constant neck pain, which Stewart is the first to have alleviated. It was after becoming Stewart's patient that Jane met Wan and was introduced to the teachings and image of Sai Baba. Stewart has stated that, in essence, his practice is worship. He mentions H. B. Jeffery's model for healing: the healer must address the level of the patient's suffering and then must also see through that suffering and "evoke that which is already perfect."[10] While such philosophies may implicitly inform Stewart's practice, the practice itself is anatomically scientific massage. Culture is transmitted through embodiment, not only through word or creed.

Identities, whether expressed in ethnic relations or in sense of place, gain meaning through framing within wider perspectives, notably religion. The South, stereotyped as a Bible Belt of fundamentalists, has a complex religious heritage within a largely Protestant framework that is not nearly as simplistic as the stereotype suggests. Although earlier diversities (such as Muslims brought over as slaves) were erased, southern religion has sustained global connections all along, and this abiding globalism has been amplified recently by new diversities. Southern religion has often strengthened the oppositional regional identity, sanctifying the Confederacy or its extensions, but the balance is shifting toward a global identity encompassing not only evolving Christian movements of world scope but also arriving world religions. Religions, whatever their provenance, energize and bestow meaning on the South's global identity.

Shifting for a moment from the South to global and historic perspectives, one might consider trends in world religions and also trends in the study of world religions. Simplifying greatly, three stages of study are discernible in the past century or so. In the late nineteenth century, European scholars classified religions according to varying stages of evolution, such as primitive and civilized, and saw a divide between their own European cultures, which they perceived as civilized, and much of the world, seen as primitive. During the early and mid-twentieth century, many scholars attempted to dissolve the divide by intensive study of particular communities and their religious practices in largely non-European settings. By the late twentieth century, as globalization engendered new connections within the varied settings and traditions around the world, the connectivity itself, as well as particular practices, became a focus of study. Study therefore paralleled practice: the history of the study of religions paralleled the evolution and spread of religions globally, in that increased connectivity among world religions spurred study of that connectivity. The U.S. South, like other places, now manifests many of the world religions; at the same time, approaches to study and understanding of religion in the South as elsewhere have evolved—but differentially. Academic or liberal approaches veer toward global or objective views, seeing the various religions as equal or as threads in a world tapestry, while sectarian approaches may actually engage more deeply with newcomers while perceiving them as rivals or intruders or, worse, as heretical (or, better, as fellow believers). In this landscape of the practice and study of religions, the South is somewhat distinctive in its Christian commitments, but that context should not be exaggerated or stereotyped, as it sometimes is in dialogue with religious communities globally.

What about liberal or conservative impacts? Within Christianity, classical liberalism, as found in northern-based social gospel movements, found expression in the South in civil rights efforts by southerners as well as northerners, yet head-on reform was often eschewed by southerners in favor of spiritual or soul-saving endeavors. The latter emphasis has become globalized in Pentecostal and other movements that have huge followings globally. Conservative in social ideology, soul-focused endeavors can be socially explosive in drawing diversity into spiritual community. Unexpected combinations are apparent: as Carie Little Hersh's fieldwork in the Naval communities of Norfolk and Virginia Beach, Virginia, shows, the same people who follow Pat Robertson occasionally also follow New Age beliefs. In both instances, their beliefs emphasize inner improvement and global connections more than social improvement. Beyond Christianity, the impact of Islam, Hinduism, Buddhism, and other Asian or Middle Eastern religions is largely inner-oriented as well. The effect, then, has been to deepen and broaden southern spiritual perspectives and experiences in a direction that is socially conservative in immediate impact yet potentially liberating in its overall gestalt.

Potentially liberating how? A suggestive text comes from remarks by Secretary of State Condoleezza Rice at a recent Southern Baptist convention in Greensboro, North Carolina. Rice begins by identifying herself as southern, from Birmingham, Alabama: "In the South we have an expression—yeah, there's some folks out there from Birmingham. I can hear them. We have an expression for people who were raised with religion. We say they grew up in the church." Rice continues by applauding Southern Baptist service globally—digging wells in Banda Aceh, for example. She then shifts to foreign policy and the need to liberate oppressed peoples. This brings her to racial oppression at home, and she states that, evolving from that oppression, the United States has made progress, symbolized by the fact that if she serves out her term as secretary of state "it will have been 12 years since a white man was Secretary of State of the United States of America." She concludes by telling about a note she received from a man at Centreville Baptist Church in Centreville, Virginia, who informs her that his Sunday school class is praying for her.[11]

The themes are these. As an African American she affirms a southern identity. As a Protestant (Presbyterian) she affirms a shared identity and even spiritual unity across racial lines with Southern Baptists. As a secretary of state, she traces implication for global strategy. The last point reminds us of the place of religion in global conflict as well as in unity—the fight against terrorism as a religious and cultural struggle as well as political and military one. That struggle takes us beyond the southern region into the "clash of civilizations" that threatens the world and the role of the United States as leader and liberator. However conflictful the foreign policy core of Rice's talk, the framing of the text, how it begins and how it ends, confirms the potential of religious identity to at least envision transcending dualisms through a larger meaning that has a global link.

CHAPTER SEVEN

Subjectivities

Meaning Making in the Changing South

SUBJECTIVE EXPERIENCE is the subject of this chapter, expressed in such areas as dreams, spiritualism, and the arts. How do such expressions reflect global influences? Does globalism penetrate only economics, politics, and public spheres, such as commemorations of race relations, institutional worship, and architecture and city planning? Or do global influences reach into private spheres, into the inner life, as in dreams and spiritual quests, and efforts at popular expression of experience, such as the arts? If so, how, in what forms and contexts? And how may subjective expressions enrich and shape global identities?

These questions are at once revealing and difficult: revealing because only if the "far away" penetrates the "deep within" does it profoundly shape identity, and difficult because the "deep within" is hidden, expressed in symbols that must be interpreted. Here, I offer only the beginnings of such interpretation, enough, I hope, to capture emerging currents of experience and sketch some themes and trends suggested by a sampling of expressions. I begin with spirituality, then consider dreams, and finally turn to the arts and how they give popular—local or global—expression to inner concerns. Concluding, I explore the place of subjectivity itself in the emerging global identity of the South.

Spirituality

Robert Sardello and Cheryl Sanders, founders and codirectors of the School of Spiritual Psychology in Greensboro, North Carolina, lead a workshop of some fifty persons for the Triangle C. G. Jung Society, an organization devoted to the study of subjects related to the Swiss psychiatrist Carl Jung. A majority of those attending are white women; one man is black, and several are white. Most of the people are middle-aged or older. They meet at Binkley Baptist Church in Chapel Hill, but the context is Jungian.

Robert and Cheryl open the session with several questions and a statement: "How can you find your way through the collective consciousness of a materialistic fear-based culture without being oppositional or feeling like a victim? Where can you go for an anchor point? You go to the place of soul and spirit." The group is asked how to get to that place. A woman remarks, "I go quiet, I am, but feel as in a battle zone." Another woman adds, "Also the natural world is a catalyst, grounding me through my feet even more than my breath, even after seventeen years of meditation." A man continues, "like water in a vessel, seeking balance by seeing both sides of it." Joe, from Smithfield, a regular attendee of the Jungian meetings, remarks: "Sardello speaks of fear around us, as an autonomous entity, not confined to events. As Roosevelt said, we fear fear itself."

Robert asks what silence is like. A woman, a Quaker, says it is like taking a bath; it "differs when you are alone or in a group." A man added that it was "as if the group puts fear on a shelf." Joe said that he would hear an energy sound. The woman then added that silence was "a place from which I can attend, pay attention."

Cheryl instructs us to go mentally into our "homes," be present to things that hold memory. Next Cheryl and Robert shift to finding silence by relation to the dead. Cheryl asserts, "The dead wait for us to remember them holistically." A man (Tom, the younger one, seated next to the black man) asks, speaking in a country accent, "How can I separate demons from gods?" Cheryl replies that he should ask her angel to contact his angel. Robert tells of a patient whose uncle was successful. The man tried to emulate his uncle but failed at everything. He was fixated on a stuck piece of that uncle when he needed to remember the dead holistically. Robert stresses that we should try to see the dead from their viewpoint, not ours. He advises: "Cry for older people, that's painful for them; cry for children, that's soothing for them. God cried first." (Dreams of the crippled, sick, or dead depict them as whole, as well, because the soul is whole.)

Now Robert prompts an exercise: "Close your eyes and enter darkness." Then he reflects, saying that this darkness is luminous, infinite yet intimate, as a Muslim mystic said, a place that is no place. You go somewhere in it by creating, not by making it up but by perceiving that darkness so it becomes. Cheryl illustrates: "I go into a chapel that is small, but inside, the walls disappear, and it opens to the infinite universe." She continues: "To relate to the dead, perceive who they are now. They teach us who they are; they draw us into greater life, how to perceive by the heart not the head, by their spirituality." Robert explains: "In darkness you meet you and non-you at once. You get there because you meet you there. If you forget that, you are in trouble, for you meet something from somewhere else (something alien). You build the image as in *Bild,* the German word for "image." Now do an exercise building an image of a dead person." Joe asks how he can relate to his ninety-five-year-old mother who has Alzheimer's. Cheryl responds that the senile bring a gift, teaching us how to be present with the dead; they have a life force, yet no memory. Finally, Cheryl asks people to put attention on the heart, later on the "warts" in the heart. This produces emotional choking-up by the younger man, Tom, who alludes to a father who beats his son daily.

What is one to make of this? The context is a Jungian workshop held in a Baptist church; such workshops are held by the Jung Society monthly, and many who attend this one regularly attend the others as well. They usually involve exercises in introspection, inquiries guided by Jungian teachings and Jungian analysts. This workshop is distinctive in that it has a spiritualist focus. God is not mentioned frequently. Instead, inner states that partake of larger consciousness and spiritual terrains are invoked and shared. Key are relations with dead or nearly dead parents or with others, imagined, activated by memory, and, sometimes, disturbing, as in the last example. Dealing with these is the psychology aspect of spirituality.

Notice the themes broached in this session: identity, self, parents, past, memories, and the dead. What does each mean? Why or how do these experiences acquire meaning? Into what kind of perspective do they fit? During such a session, one seeks to "get in touch with oneself," to explore that self, as an aspect of a wider subjectivity—a kind of collective unconscious in Jungian terms, and to share thoughts, feelings, and memories in a group. The goal is to get beneath or above confusing diversities and complexities of life by turning inward; the psychology is nuanced—to sense, cognitively and experientially, the interweaving of perceptions, fears, and questions.

Is this kind of discussion peculiar to Chapel Hill? No. Jungian groups have developed throughout the South—Charlotte, Birmingham, Athens, Norfolk, Richmond, Atlanta. They affiliate sometimes with psychiatrists or other mental health workers, sometimes with churches—usually Episcopalian.[1]

Jung is not the only figure nor is Christianity the only affiliate for spirituality and inward searches. Rumi, the Sufi poet, has been translated by Coleman Barks (raised in Chattanooga, Tennessee, and a long-time resident of Athens, Georgia); his translations are reportedly the best-selling poems in the United States, and he was granted an honorary doctorate by Tehran University. Chapel Hill hosts a flourishing Sufi order, and large festivals there have attracted Sufis from all around. The core Sufis are Turkish, but participants include locals. They do engage in the *dikhr* (chanting Quranic scripture toward a trance) and other rituals. Buddhist meditation centers, Taoist study centers, and New Age movements such as Wicca dot the South. Meister Eckhart, the medieval Catholic mystic, is followed by Eckhart Tolle, a contemporary spiritual guide; Alice Walker tries shamanism. Spirituality, meditation, and inner search are elements of all of these, building on mystical histories in the many traditions. Yoga exercise, herbal medicine, vegetarian diets, ecology, and feminism interwoven into a Jungian focus on "wholeness" are salient themes as well. "New Age" is a label some give to all these "journeys," and they are more associated with the West Coast and New Mexico than with the South, but they are here.

The logic of spirituality is simple: one turns inward, seeks an indwelling spiritual source of meaning to cut under and over confusing diversities and changes in external life. How is this global? It is global not only in content but in context: where denominational creeds tend to separate, "the spirit goeth where it listeth," crossing and dissolving boundaries. Sufis, Buddhists, New Age spiritualists, Jungians, and Rumi converge in a subjectivity that blurs objective distinctions and unites myriad cultural streams. These Jungian spiritualists join a global stream of discussion that began when Gautama, to become Buddha, sat under the Bodhi tree, or when Sufis fled Baghdad in the thirteenth century to travel across China to Southeast Asia. Buddhist and Sufi streams have come together among Javanese Sumarah meditators in Yogyakarta, Java, a movement claiming a resident of Chapel Hill, David Howe, who then took it to Brazil, while German transcendental meditators came to Yogyakarta. The common theme is inner search.

How is this southern? A central theme in southern Protestantism is a certain subjectivism, an experience of inner spirit. "How is God dead if he is alive in my heart?" sang Pastor Don at Bethel Pentecostal in Durham, North Carolina. Pentecostalism itself has one strong source in the South but is global, and one should instantly warn that this subjectivism, stereotyped as salvation and sanctification experience, is by no means present in the most prestigious and established southern churches, although it has become a counterpoint even in these, in the South, as throughout the world. Certain southerners have contributed remarkably to subjective spirituality. They range from Coleman Barks, who translates Rumi into poetic English, to Shirley MacLaine, the actor from Virginia who espouses New Age spiritualism, to Billy Graham; all have touched world chords of inner life. Shamanism, Pentecostalism, and spiritualism are certainly not distinctly southern; they are global, but they can resonate with southern religious experience of a seemingly more provincial type.

Why now? Spirituality and mysticism are ways of addressing change and diversity, ways of discovering an inner self anchored in an infinite self that transcends the uncertainties of life. Consider the great poem "Serat Kala Tidha" (Poem of a Time of Darkness) of Raden Ningrat Ronggawarsita of Surakarta, Java. The poem begins:

> The lustre of the realm
> Is now vanished to the eye
> In ruins the teaching of good ways
> For there is no example left
> The heart of the learned poet
> So coiled about with care
> Seeing all the wretchedness
> That everything is darkened
> The world immersed in misery . . . [2]

As Benedict Anderson notes, this expression of despair regarding change and decline was followed by an organization, Budi Utomo, that reflected and nurtured mystical traditions yet led to nationalistic movements.[3] Paradoxically, the inward turn is part of an outward leaning as well—to embrace a global spectrum, stretching particular traditions, weaving together traditions, reaching beyond to discover a ground of meaning that can subsume the change and complexity that comes with globalization and other aspects of contemporary life in the South as elsewhere.

Locales

Commentators such as Saskia Sassen emphasize the central role of cities in globalization, yet an equally central role is surely played in the religious and subjective sphere by rural domains: think of monasteries and convents, forests and jungles, or mountain retreats.[4] In the South, the globalizing currents of subjectivity flow strongly not only in cities but also in rural areas—in mountain or seaside retreats—and, even more strikingly, woven into the life of small towns. Who would expect, for example, that Tifton, Georgia, would be a site of a Journey into Wholeness workshop? These workshops are opportunities to explore self and spirit within a somewhat Jungian perspective; the one in Tifton was sponsored by the Episcopal church. As a wider example, here is a sketch of another small Georgia town (call it "Blackwell") illustrating something of the variety and penetration of global currents in religious and related subjectivities.

A brother and sister who live in Blackwell have each married and have grown children. The sister married a staunch Presbyterian who was then a farmer and is now a builder and developer. The brother married an Episcopalian. The sister and brother grew up Methodist, but each has moved toward the spouse's denomination in different ways. The sister, late in life, went to seminary and became a Presbyterian minister. The brother and his wife began attending Daoist meetings and participated in self-development workshops in Taos, New Mexico; she has written several novels and works with an editor in Taos. They constructed a labyrinth on their property and have held celebrations that involve walking the labyrinth. The master of ceremonies is a Native American, originally from Asheville, North Carolina, who now lives in the Southwest. There is also a poet and a band with one instrumentalist originally from Florida, now in New York, and a Canadian. The brother, a banker, is ecologically oriented toward smart growth and new urbanism. He has built green spaces and a compact community. His brother-in-law, a builder and developer, builds warehouses, apartment buildings, and other structures. He is a fervent Democrat and populist who argues against the elitism implicit in ecology: a farmer loses land value because ecologists block development.

His son headed the bank until it was bought by a larger, global one. The ecologist banker's daughter, after making her debut in Atlanta, joined the marines and was stationed in Asia.

This family, quite central in the life of this community, both dynamic and forward-looking while deeply rooted, living where they were born, illustrates the complexity of social fabrics, southern or otherwise. The nearby camp meeting, which happens to be attended by the mayor, may still play a role in community life and at one time may have connected, in a glancing moment or two, with this family; they can tell about folksy things to an outsider if requested to do so, and the Daoist/ecologist invests heavily in preservation. This is grounded globalism but globalism nonetheless, rooted in a place and shaped by it but connected to currents of the world.

In sum, whether in globally oriented Research Triangle, North Carolina, or in a small-town setting, one can find an assortment of spiritual and subjective quests, signaling the significance of this theme in southern life. No single "global religion" is apparent in either place, but layers and strands of meaning are. Meaning making and meaning receiving are occurring, grounding globalism by weaving strands into localized lives and subjectivities.

Fundamentalisms

Is the South, then, dissolving into spirituality—subjectivist and multicultural individualistic explorations of inner experience? Has it finally followed the lead of Thomas Jefferson, who famously declared, "I am a sect myself"? These trends, striking to be sure, must still be seen in the context of Bible Belt fundamentalisms that surround and perhaps dwarf them in thunderous proclamation and stern admonition. Even if salvation and sanctification through transformative emotional conversion and Holy Ghost possession share with spirituality a subjectivist emphasis, the large denominations—especially Southern Baptist but also Pentecostal and even to a degree Methodist and Presbyterian—also bring moralism. Personal morals still loom powerful, as in opposition to drinking and gambling; yes, Florida, Virginia, Georgia, South Carolina, and North

Carolina have instituted state lotteries but only after vigorous opposition from Baptists and others. Moral relativism implied by spiritualist quests for one's personal truth and guidance contradict moral absolutes espoused by the more fundamentalist churches on the basis of the Bible and the word of God.

Djuhertati "Tati" Imam Muhni and I are driving down I-85. She is Javanese, living in the Kraton neighborhood of Yogyakarta, all of whose residents are supposedly related to the royal family, part of the milieu that produced the poem quoted earlier: an aristocratic meditative spiritualism indebted to Buddhism, Sufism, and Javanism, which includes reverence for the kingdom and the associated order. Tati is also fond of Faulkner and of southern literature, which she has read from childhood.

Yogyakarta is home not only to the Kraton but also to the fundamentalist movement, Muhammadiyah, founded in 1912 by K. H. A. Dahlan, in the shadow of, but antithetical to, the Kraton. Tati and I talk animatedly about parallels between the South and Java. Eventually we shift into Indonesian language, entering the world of Java. We come to an exit leading to Bob Jones University. We turn off and drive into the campus, where Tati glimpses a clean-cut young man. "Muhammadiya," she jokes, nailing a parallel in Java to fundamentalism in the South, both in counterpoint to spirituality.

At the time, the fundamentalist strength was greater in the South relative to spiritualist; in Java the larger Javanese culture and its spiritualist roots were greater than fundamentalist Islam. Today, it is the opposite: the fundamentalist influence has grown in Java, and the spiritualist has weakened; however, in the South, spirituality has perhaps grown. Whatever the ratio, in each place and elsewhere, the two streams form counterpoints that constitute a context for subjectivity.

Dreams

Dreams, according to depth psychology, offer at once the deepest and the most cryptic clues about what experience means. Despite disputed efforts to dismiss dreams as such sources of insight, both experimental and clinical evidence continue to demonstrate this use, and, in any case, dreams speak for themselves, at least suggestively. What kinds of dreams do U.S. southerners, native or immigrant, report as they experience global transitions? No single occasion is available as with the work of Lee Zahner-Roloff, who reported the dreams of white and black South Africans on the eve of the transition from apartheid, but a sample can be described that are at least suggestive of themes. The following dreams would seem to express meanings concerning the experience of globalization. The first set are my own dreams, reported in sequence, beginning in the early eighties and concluding with a dream in summer 2006. The next dream was told to me in 2004 by a Chinese woman in her thirties who moved to the South from China in her twenties. The last dream was told by a white southern male in his sixties.[5]

In the first, I walk down a street in Chapel Hill, North Carolina, and encounter a panhandler who is a third-world person, perhaps an Indonesian or a Mexican. I wish to give him something but have no change, so I decide to give him a bill and take change from what he has collected so far. But my bill gets mixed up with the money the man has in his tin cup. Then the panhandler says, "I'm afraid my money will be stolen. I wish I had American Express traveler's checks." I tell him to just go inside the bank he's sitting in front of and exchange his money. He replies that they would not admit a beggar and suggests I do it for him. I go in the bank and exchange his money for traveler's checks, but when I walk out I realize that the checks are in my name. When I point that out, the panhandler says, "Well, I've always wanted to travel." The dream ends with the two of us setting off to travel together.

In a second dream, I am in a phone booth somewhere in another country. I emerge to see Arabs fighting each other, and then I see an Arab fighting a European and beating him—in fact, spanking him. As I proceed, I am asked to fight as well. I refuse and walk further. I encounter an old black man, like Uncle Remus, who is sheltering my wife. I feel secure.

In the third dream, my dog runs away, and I chase her. She goes into the house of some Latinos, and I enter too.

In the fourth dream, I meet, and then merge with, become, a short, olive-skinned man (the dreamer is tall and ruddy).

Here's a brief attempt at interpretation: in the first dream, the dreamer gets involved with a third-world figure. Here, on a familiar street, the world comes home to him, invading his life in the figure of a panhandler who wants international financial credit and security. The panhandler is not a businessman, an academic, or someone else we would imagine as a world traveler, but is instead an impoverished beggar. In the second dream, the southerner finds himself in a foreign place and sees conflict between inhabitants of different areas of the world, one an Arab and the other a European, similar to the dreamer and reminding him of a British man he once saw in Singapore who was being defeated in a badminton match by a more agile Chinese opponent. The dreamer finds solace by returning to a familiar, stereotyped traditional figure, an Uncle Remus—a figure he remembers from childhood in the South. The figure is sheltering the dreamer's wife. This scene returns us from foreign and cultural conflict, with threatening Arab figures, to old-fashioned black-white paternalism, with the paternal figure being the elderly black man. In the third dream, the dreamer again encounters an immigrant culture here at home, as in the first dream, but this time he enters the home of the immigrant, and the fact that this immigrant has a home and that this home is inhabited by a family suggests they are here to stay, not just on the street, as in the first dream. Still later, this dreamer, tall and ruddy, dreams that he is a Greek immigrant, short, stout, and olive-skinned. As such, he encounters some who look at him askance. Here, it seems, his identity has shifted still further along a spectrum of engagement with the "other" to the point where he becomes, at least in a dream, the other.

The Asian woman, J, dreams that R and A, her American (southern) friends, invite someone to visit them and to stay in J's room, which is in their house. J is concerned that her room is too messy or dirty. R has a beautiful Chinese pallet, but J thinks it's too nice for the visitor to sleep on. R walks on it, saying it doesn't matter. Then J sees a dog, which has beautiful eyes. She gets down low to see it eye to eye. It says, "Your mouth is too big, to the point it hampers your breathing," and it kisses her on one corner of her mouth. This last insight seemed huge in the dream, says J, even though it is not logical anatomically except that a mouth could be so large as to block the nose.

What meanings might one attribute to this dream? Perhaps the mouth expresses J's breadth of multiculturalism—too big, too much, too varied—while the dog expresses a focus, a grounding and grounded focused affection. That part of J is requesting attention. The bamboo pallet signifies China. R is her American side, failing to honor her Chinese side.

T, from North Carolina, dreams of the Christian dilemma of one and many, monotheism and polytheism, resolved by the Trinity: God in three persons. A beautiful woman, like Grace Kelly, appears, encumbered by a skirt with too many pleats. For two hours, he lies awake, struggling to resolve this dilemma of pluralism. The content is not global necessarily, but the issue is. The near-resolution, named Grace, is like Christian grace and also like what Jung would term the "anima," in either case a source of creative energy that potentially cuts through the paralyzing masculine logics. But she herself is paralyzed by the pleated skirts, perhaps a hair-splitting kind of pluralism that fails to capture creative energy that could ignite a deeper unity.

When Freud published *Die Traumdeutung* (*The Interpretation of Dreams*) in 1900, he began with one of his own dreams. The dream depicted a former patient, whom he calls Irma, as well as a friend, Otto. Freud interpreted the dream as "wish fulfillment," as symbolically expressing his wish to excuse his failed treatment of Irma by attributing an organic disorder to her and as getting back at Otto by blaming him for a dirty syringe. In short, interpersonal relations were the focus of this dream as well as many others that Freud presents. Later Freud's onetime protégé Carl Jung presented a series of dreams beginning with a dream about a hat. Jung does not interpret this dream in terms of interpersonal relationships but rather as expressing cosmic themes; the hat is seen as a symbol in mythology. Jung himself moved, then, toward themes he regarded as pan-human, universal, rather than the localized interpersonal contexts illustrated by Freud. Jungians, however, link universal themes to local ones, as the South Africans reported by Zahner-Roloff did when they interpreted certain symbols as connoting both inner concerns and outer concerns such as racial relations on the eve of ending apartheid.

Freudian, Jungian, and other approaches to dream interpretation can be deployed to interpret the dreams cited here, but I focus on the manifest content rather than on the latent psychology in these dreams. What is the geography expressed in these dreams? What realm of life is of concern? In contrast to Freud's Irma dream, which focused on intimate personal relationships within a local social circle, these dreams are global. They treat relationships with immigrants or foreigners, the experience of living in a new country as compared with one's native country, issues of pluralism, and the experience of a certain kind of global identity. Natives and immigrants demonstrate by their dreams that global experience enters deep layers of subjectivity.

Community Dreams: The Orange County Project

In spring 2005, Orange County, North Carolina, invited its citizens to depict their dreams visually and to describe and interpret them verbally. Hundreds did so, and their paintings and commentaries were exhibited in several venues: town halls, a museum, an arts center, and a cafe. The community dreams differ in context and form from the personal dreams. The community dreams are displayed to the community. While one might expect this context to skew contents, in that an individual might be reluctant to reveal all to a public, the dreams are nonetheless quite revealing. They are numerous, hundreds of them, and they represent a diverse sampling of the population, ranging in age from a year and a half to eighty or so and including, to judge from names, some persons of Asian and Latino origin, though most names are of European origin. A few deal specifically with a conflict between characters, and those that do, depict the characters as mythological or archetypal, for example, a dragon and a human, rather than as ethnic. Many, however, portray scenes, and these include foreign and fantasy landscapes. Characters in these scenes are also sometimes foreign and fantastic, for example, monsters, machines, and spiritualized figures, such as a woman in a nightgown or evening dress in a ghostly setting. These depictions expand the imaginative universe, generally, including globally, mirroring spiritual and world themes as dimensions of dreamed vision.[6]

Art, Architecture, Literature, Dance, and Music

While religion, including spiritual expressions, may be the most obvious and organized mode of meaning making, secular culture, too, is creatively probing and expressing experienced meaning. The content of the arts reflects subjectivities similar to those of dreams, but the context is necessarily public: one must address an audience. Accordingly, in looking to the arts for global content, one also queries the kinds of subjectivities that are shaping the public, whether that public is local, regional, national, or global. For example, the South traditionally has conveyed, in music and literature, an agrarian world—one of cozy peace in Stephen Foster, oppressive tragedy in blues, feisty independence in bluegrass, tortured patrimony in writers from William Faulkner to Tennessee Williams, and romantic defeat in that most international epic of southern writing and film, *Gone with the Wind*. All this is so well known as to bear no more commentary, but the question here is whether—and how—the arts of the South, and about the South, express and shape a global identity. Addressing this question, I offer only "a lick and a promise," not a full survey of southern arts and literature but a few suggestions of ways this domain is and is not moving globally.

At an external level, the influx of international elements is obvious and is illustrated by music. A Carrboro, North Carolina, world arts festival, kicked off by the Korean American Ong sisters, featured a Javanese gamelan that drew an overflow crowd.[7] Elsewhere in the state, Bald Head Island hosted international artists from Macedonia. Balancing the arrival of international influences, indigenous artists go global. The Indigo Girls of Atlanta press global ecology, and the Dixie Chicks of Dallas condemn the invasion of Iraq. Hip-hop is multiethnic and global.

In literature, global identity is emerging variously. Shannon Ravenal has edited anthologies of so-called southern short stories. My perusal of the anthologies and questioning of Shannon confirm that much of what has been written is oriented locally more than globally. She says immigrant writing in the South is only gradually entering the canon. On the other hand, more informal literary expressions of global themes are evolving. An example is a symposium I organized at the first North Carolina Literary Festival, held in Chapel Hill in the late nineties. I titled it "Far Away and Deep Within," and participants were local authors with immigrant experiences that they wrote about. Lilian Furst, who came from Vienna, Jun Wang from China, and Daphne Athas, whose paternal ancestry is Greek, read from their works. Then psychoanalyst David Freeman commented on why their "far away" origins and journeys to a new place prompted the "deep within" feelings and reflections expressed in their writings.

As a model for globalizing identity penetrating deep structure of literature, consider Salman Rushdie's *Satanic Verses*. While a tale pertaining to Muhammad is a counterpoint, the main plot is about the struggles of two immigrants—from India to Great Britain—to connect identities that are both Indian and British. One has married a British woman and become a virtuoso speaker of several British accents that represent acquired identities that eventually plague him as he rediscovers his Indian identity. The other immigrant, the hero, rediscovers his Indian identity when he goes home to be with his dying father and reunites with a voluptuous and brilliant Indian woman. Deep structural transmutation and stresses of identity are symbolized by monstrous embodiments, such as satanic horns. Whether such deep-structure global identity is evidenced in southern writing, notable elements are, and one can discern trends.

In the movie version of Tennessee Williams's *Suddenly Last Summer*, the aristocratic southern heroine, played by Katharine Hepburn, tells her young male visitor, played by Montgomery Clift, that two places she has always wanted to go are Chicago and Hong Kong, implying by her arch intonation that both are so foreign as to be beyond her approved world.

In Williams's time, this was funny and sounded foreign in the context of New Orleans. Would it be funny today, when small-town southern women go to Hong Kong for weekend shopping trips? In any case, the artistic effect comes by dropping an exotic allusion into an insular setting. (A parallel from real life is the local businessman who wanted to import coffins from Indonesia to sell at Wal-Mart.)

Global penetration can come by such an insertion of the foreign into a domestic time-place unity. In the Williams example, only a name is given. In other examples, a foreign character may be prominent. In *The Heart Is a Lonely Hunter,* the novel by Carson McCullers, an important character is a Greek man in the small-town setting of Columbus, Georgia. A Greek figure is also a focus of Daphne Athas's *Entering Ephesus.* Compare these examples with Alice McDermott's *Charming Billy,* set in an Irish American New York neighborhood that is itself transnational and transcultural. The focus is on the local hero, Billy; the foreigner, Eva, the Irish girl, the lost love of Billy's youth, is shadowy, rarely present. While the New York setting merges cultures and nationalities, highlighting the local hero and deemphasizing the foreign one, the less diverse southern setting accentuates the foreigner as standing out.

What is the role of the outsider in southern literature, the violator of inward-looking community norms? Sometimes the outsider is heroic, as in the case of Atticus Finch, insider to the community but outsider when he opposes it as the upholder of the law and universalistic norms in Harper Lee's *To Kill a Mockingbird.* Sometimes he is inhuman, for example, Son in Peter Taylor's story "A Long Fourth." Taylor, who came from Tennessee, sets the story—about a white doctor, his matronly wife, and their black cook—in Nashville in the early twentieth century. The couple's son, who is called simply Son, has come home to visit from New York, bringing with him a young woman, Miss Prewitt. Son is the intellectual, the theorist, who excelled in school but is cold, even cruel, in his treatment of his mother and Miss Prewitt, who is in love with him. He stands on the porch, conversing abstractly with Miss Prewitt about equality and race relations while his mother suffers her immediate crisis with the cook and the father. Sometimes, the hero is in between: in Walker Percy's *The Moviegoer*, he is detached, ironic—with a touch of the global (he has, as noted, one book, Doughty's *Arabia Deserta*, an account of travels in Arabia)—and embedded in the familial and hierarchical. Sometimes he is wild, like William Faulkner's Thomas Sutpen, in *Absalom, Absalom!* who moved to Mississippi from Haiti, bringing with him a gang of wild blacks to build a new plantation. The southern heroes stand a bit above the common herd. (Remember, too, the southern patrician in Mark Twain who stood down the crowd in Missouri.) They are not quite global, and they are certainly not multicultural, but they are universalistic. Maybe Inman in Charles Frazier's *Cold Mountain* is of their ilk, the lone hero against the mob, the mountain man who fought for the Confederacy but abandoned it to walk alone.[8] This structure is adapted somewhat to the global outsider, the Jewish wise man in Carson McCullers's novel, the more marginal Greek father in Athas's. "Parker's Back," by Flannery O'Connor, depicts a native southerner who travels extensively, then imports global culture back to the South in the form of tattoos: "Imagine Queequeg from South Georgia," suggests David Davis, the literary scholar at Wake Forest University, who is thinking of the area where he grew up. But the global person remains too much an outsider to fulfill the hero role.[9]

Some southern novels brilliantly depict minority cultural perspectives—Josephine Humphreys' *Nowhere Else on Earth* is an example. Focused on the Lumbee Indians of Robeson County, North Carolina, this novel may not be global, but it is multicultural, entering the world of the Lumbee in a way they themselves affirm. The poetry of Dave Smith and Charles Wright brilliantly evokes global themes, and localized southern writings earn global resonance. Outside published literature, papers by my own students—Hmong, Vietnamese, Cypriot, and Turkish—perceptively comment on their adopted region. Immigrant writings seem largely excluded from the canon of "southern writing" so far, but Lan Cao's *Monkey Bridge* is notable.[10]

David Payne's *Back to Wando Passo* stretches identities across boundaries of time, space, and race. Three contemporary characters, Claire, Ransome, and Marcel, parallel three nineteenth-century characters, Addie, Harlan, and Jarry. The third character in each trio is part black, the first two white. However, the white and black men are brothers, by a father whose mistress is Afro-Cuban, and Claire turns out to bear some of that mixed (white and Afro-Cuban) heritage. Ransome, Claire's "husband," who identifies as white "trash," is possessed by spirits from the Cuban ancestors and becomes Jarry, the nineteenth-century black, or part black. Payne's engrossing narrative resembles that of Rushdie in that it describes the experience of crossing racial, temporal, and ethnic-cultural-national boundaries. Doing so, Payne pioneers in uniting the historic and global South—fiction that grounds globalization.

Elizabeth Spencer, originally from Mississippi, wrote *The Light in the Piazza*, a novella that became a Tony Award–winning musical. A mother and daughter from Winston-Salem, North Carolina, go to Italy, where the daughter and an Italian youth fall in love and plan to marry. The daughter is somewhat retarded, which causes the mother to struggle with the question of whether their marriage should occur. She concludes that it should, only to encounter resistance from the boy's father, but she converts him to her point of view. Her husband, back in Winston-Salem, resists even more strenuously, but she refuses to bend, telling him the wedding is going to happen. In this story, then, a global romance transforms everyone except the husband who had stayed home. The daughter falls in love, and the mother, who is rather attracted to the courtly Italian father, transcends her previous subordinate obedience to her husband to come into her own as a wise and strong person. A foreign context joins romance in transforming identity.

African-American writing perhaps deserves special attention when asking whether movement from localized to more global themes can be detected in the literary imagination. One might begin with classic *Beloved*, by Nobel laureate Toni Morrison, and move to a more recent example, Paul Beatty's *White Boy Shuffle*. *Beloved* is set in a household in Ohio but in relation to the slave South, from which the heroine has escaped. The world depicted is that of black family and community, with whites merely on the edge. Threat as well as poignant love comes from Beloved, a ghost of the child the heroine killed while escaping a slave owner. The *White Boy Shuffle* is set, first, in Los Angeles. The hero, an African American, has southern slave forebears but is primarily identified by his white and cosmopolitan connections. He is born and raised in a white neighborhood and has to learn to behave "black" after his mother moves him and his sisters to a black neighborhood. His friends there include a Hispanic tough guy and eventually, after he moves to Boston, a Japanese woman. While *Beloved* is deeply serious and *White Boy Shuffle* is farcical, the comparison does suggest opening of the African American world in a global multicultural direction that is shaping identities.

Resonances between southern literature and the world enable localized worlds to be global while retaining locale. As scholars Michael O'Brien, C. Vann Woodward, Jon Smith, Deborah Cohn, and others have noted, the South's history of defeat and colonization bonds it with other Souths— with virtually everywhere, including Europe, that has also suffered: hence the global appeal of southern epics from Faulkner to *Gone with the Wind*. As Drew Faust and others have described, Scarlett O'Hara has world popularity (recall the Takarazuka Revue, the Japanese all-women shows that staged *Gone with the Wind*). While Faust thinks this is because Scarlett is a feminist, one might find even more resonance between her struggle as a self-reliant woman in a traditionalist order and similar situations of women everywhere than between Scarlett, women everywhere, and cutting-edge feminism.[11]

Music is more obviously global. Take the musicologist Alan Lomax's Global Jukebox. Lomax, the son of John Lomax, a collector of prison songs in Texas, grew up in Texas and initially collected and played folk music and blues. He moved from local to global in the fifties and later developed cantometrics, choreometrics, systems of analysis incorporated into his Global Jukebox, which correlates dance and song style with cultural regions globally.[12]

Music heard in the South, as in other parts of the United States, combines global and regional or ethnic influences in varied ways. "Classical" music, whether sacred or secular, largely derives from Europe. Blues, jazz, gospel, and hip-hop are strongly influenced by Africa. Shape notes, bluegrass, and folk music adapt (but do not copy) British traditions to local styles, as in the mountains. Musical forms and ethnic communities sometimes coincide: in New Orleans Creoles played European classical music, and jazz was created by blacks who left sharecropper backgrounds for New Orleans. Such events as the Festival for the Eno, next to the Eno River in Durham, North Carolina, and other folk music festivals are multicultural sites, hosting folk music from communities ranging from Valdese, North Carolina, settled by Waldensians from the Italian Alps, to blues and bluegrass. Such festivals now edge into newer immigrant variations, such as Latino mariachi music or popular music from India, and combine cultures performatively, in contrast to literature, which must do so reflectively, as part of single-authored plot and experience—writing a story or poem is, perhaps, a slower process than the management of musical performance groups or individuals, hence the greater speed in the performances mirroring globalism.

Visual arts are at once intuitively closer to me, as one who grew up drawing, but I find visual arts intellectually enigmatic as expressions of southern identity. I note only the impressions of immigrant artists, such as Nerys Levy and Faith Germishuizen. Setting aside their depiction of recognizable foreign scenes, they show nuanced and delicate flux and dynamic processes. They contrast with a more traditional artist such as Annette Swan, who depicts, albeit in an impressionistic mode, figures in family photographs. But her family portraits resemble those of Emiliano, a Mexican immigrant, who in turn admires Frida Kahlo. Clay Colvin's "Space Cadets" press experimentally toward crossing the boundaries of visual form.

A further question is how art forms are incorporated into built environments. While this topic is partially covered in the discussion of space, focus here is on representations incorporated into spaces. Coffee shops and delicatessens—The River Nile in Dothan, Alabama, and Southern

Seasons in Chapel Hill, for example—exemplify global or, at least multi-cultural, milieus through foods, drinks, or condiments framed by murals, in the instance of The River Nile. Ty Ty, Georgia, boasts one of the most striking unions of art and nature. Now known as the Ty Ty Bulb Company, this locally created nursery out in the country joins global flora with large representations of paintings from Van Gogh and other late nineteenth-century Europeans mounted along the highway leading into the nursery. A recent visit turned up an assistant from Italy together with locals who explained that much business comes through their web site.

Globalist architecture of southern origin is famously illustrated by John Portman's Hyatt Regency Atlanta. David Davis reminds us of the contrast between the dull exteriors and glittering interiors in Portman's hotels—signifying, perhaps, an inward-looking regionalism beneath the blatant globalism?[13] Agreeing with the interior focus—think of the signature glass elevators from which one can view the lobby and all the floors—one might interpret this as globalist in comparison with the signature feature of the agrarian South: the porch. The porch looks out onto local spaces—fields, lawns, and neighborhoods. Portman-style hotels, high-rise air-conditioned office buildings, and shopping malls all create interior spaces cut off from local downtowns and neighborhoods that consequently deteriorate into crime-ridden wastelands, whereas those interiors are wired into global electronic and commercial connectivities.

Dance, sports, and other physical activities also show global influence. The choreographers and performers at the American Dance Festival, in Durham, North Carolina, for example, combine salsa, yoga, ballet, and other dance forms from many cultures. Azis Bhattarai, from Nepal, was on the Chapel Hill, North Carolina, high school football team. Jun Wang, who was a collegiate champion in tai chi for China, has moved to Chapel Hill; she professes to feel no preference for living in China or here. Years ago Alan Lomax plotted types of dance by choreometrics, and types of music with cantometrics, seeing each as linked to a particular region, including the South. While this distinctiveness remains evident, blurring and mixing proceed.

This brief glimpse at subjectivities expressed in the arts does not document deep structural expression, that is, transformation of regional identify into global identity as a dominant pattern; however, the currents apparent in this content move at levels far beneath the surface. The arts are changing shape, and the "far away" does influence the deep within.

Psychology in the South

The U.S. South could be characterized broadly as polarized in its relations between objective and subjective, possessing a dualistic subjectivity (obliquely parallel to its traditionally dualistic sociality). On the one hand, it is formalistic, concealing and suppressing subjectivities beneath manners and status. On the other, it is exuberantly subjective and emotional in certain spheres, such as in music and emotionalist religion. The two tendencies connect to class, with the formalism more elitist, and the expressiveness more populist.

Following from this characterization, a third tendency or approach to subjectivities has been underdeveloped. This could be considered middle class, or bourgeois: an instrumental approach akin to capitalism where the subjective is manipulated rationally to achieve given ends, whether success or "adjustment." Resistance to this approach is illustrated by the profession of psychology, in its varied guises and schools, in the South.

The South has in many ways resisted the impulses of Western-based psychology as an academic discipline and as a treatment. John Watson, the South Carolina pioneer in behaviorism, stands as an exception to the tendency of academic psychologists in the experimental mode to originate and affiliate with centers outside the South: think of B. F. Skinner at Harvard, Kenneth Spence at Iowa, and Ernest Hilgard at Stanford. In psychiatry, Corbett Thigpen, the Georgia-born author of *The Three Faces of Eve*, is another exception. While Freudians and Jungians, often migrants from Germany or Austria, clustered in New York, Chicago, and San Francisco, until recently psychologists and psychological clinics or counseling services were rare in southern towns, and even in cities by comparison with elsewhere in the United States. Why? Perhaps a reluctance to be introspective (similar to the British sentiment "dread introspection"), or a reluctance to manipulate (as children, my sister and I found it comical to read in *Parents* magazine instructions about holding family council meetings as a way to manage relationships), or a belief about intrinsic sinfulness that holds unlikely any true change through therapy and education. Tales of Skinner's putting his own children through a Skinner box rankle, suggesting the mechanization of humanity. Whether or not Skinner did this, the story was told as scandalous.

Since World War II, however, psychologism has gradually penetrated the South: VA hospitals that pioneered in clinical psychology, schools that adopted educational psychology, and community mental health clinics, psychiatric hospitals, and private counseling practices that brought psychiatrists, psychologists, social workers, and psychoanalysts. Theories and practitioners were often from outside traditional southern cultural streams. They represented the European-derived psychoanalytical traditions and American behaviorist approaches developed largely outside the South.

Certain foci of these imported psychologies and therapies misfit the values of southerners, just as they would conflict with values of many other cultures. One is the extreme emphasis on the individual. A second is mechanistic procedures. A third is self-help, or self-manipulation. Portia is from Atlanta, a brilliant and creative woman from a well-off family. She married a man from a small Georgia town, where he had a large prominent extended family. Portia's therapist, based in a large city, encouraged her to "do her own thing," to attend to her own needs in contrast to the expectations of her in-law family. So she began avoiding their family events and pursuing her own creative interests. While this strategy of individualism at the expense of family and community was, perhaps, therapeutic, it probably contributed to her eventual divorce.

A counterexample, however, is Lucy Daniels, the granddaughter of Josephus Daniels, the founding editor of the *Raleigh News and Observer* and a secretary of the navy. Growing up in a prominent family in Raleigh, Lucy was a precocious teenager who wrote *Caleb, My Son*, a best-selling novel about the divisive effects of the *Brown* decision on an African American working-class family in North Carolina, and was awarded a Guggenheim fellowship for further writing.[14] Finding her writing blocked, she underwent psychoanalysis and eventually became a clinical psychologist. As an expression of her gratitude to psychoanalysis, she created the Lucy Daniels Foundation, located near Raleigh and with archives at Emory University in Atlanta. The foundation is a major center for psychoanalytical education and practice.

Many further examples of the impact of psychoanalysis and psychology in the South could be cited, ranging from writers and intellectuals such as the Georgian novelist Lillian Smith to practitioners such as Granville Tolley, a Virginian psychoanalyst who directed the Dorothea Dix Hospital in Raleigh; Roger Spencer, a Chapel Hill analyst and writer originally from Vienna; and Vann Joines, director of the Southeast Institute, which follows transactional analysis. Such influences, however, have been confined to restricted areas or recent periods. As a teenager in south Georgia, I found one psychology book in the local library, by William James, and there were no psychologists practicing in town. To learn what a psychologist does, I got on a bus and went to the state psychiatric hospital in Milledgeville, where I talked with the staff psychologist, who oversaw thousands of patients. Such state mental health hospitals have been and still are—despite deinstitutionalization—the main site of treatment for mental illness. "Going to Milledgeville" was a synonym for going crazy and being institutionalized. Such institutions are, of course, not peculiarly southern but reflect national and global histories of mental hospitals. Many years later, I heard about and met psychologists, psychiatrists, and psychoanalysts in the South, including a few from the South, mainly in locales such as large cities or university towns. Only recently have psychological clinics appeared in small towns. Of special note is the concurrent development of psychotherapy and cultural diversity. Visions Inc. was founded in Rocky Mount, North Carolina, by three black women, including a lawyer and a psychologist. Working with transactional analysis, including with the Southeast Institute, their workshops and therapies work through ethnic or racial relationships by psychological exploration.

Psychology thus spread in the South late and only to a limited extent, though it profoundly influenced certain persons and circles, such as the Jungian, Freudian, and transactional practitioners noted above. Inner searches in the South usually occur under the aegis of religion and, secondarily, in the arts, as in music and writing. But even here the South was often discouraging, and great writers and musicians often had to leave the South, though they continued to write or sing about it. Nonetheless, these twentieth-century developments, representing both European cultural influences and northern American urban ones, paved the way for more broadly global subjectivities of the late twentieth and early twenty-first centuries.

The role of psychology as a discipline or practice in relation to such forms of subjectivity as spirituality, dreams, and the arts is oblique but perhaps suggested by the image of the horse and rider. The workhorses and racehorses—those who do the work and run the races—are guided, coached, cajoled, and rescued (and sometimes, tragically, killed) by their riders, trainers, owners, and other supporting figures. Here the artists, dreamers, and spiritual seekers are analogous to the horses; they do the hard work and run the fast races in the subjective realm, and the psychologists provide guidance and support as well as certain degrees and kinds of understanding. Some, like Lucy Daniels, combine both roles: they create and analyze creativity. Psychology, then, is a distinctive, somewhat abstracted part of the stream of subjectivity that flows in the global South.

Subjectivity in the Global South: Content and Context

How deeply and broadly do global themes penetrate southern subjectivities? The question can be answered at two basic levels, context and content. *Content*: In what sense do global themes infuse subjectivities in the South? *Context*: How are these globally infused subjectivities distributed in the southern landscape as part of the culture and society? Combining content and context, we can assess impact on identity, that is, how deeply the subjectivities are global, and how broadly these global subjectivities are distributed as aspects of a cultural identity.

CONTENT

All three of the expressive spheres—spiritualism, arts, and dreams—show global content. Spiritualism often is global in identity—for example, if it is Buddhist or Sufi; even Christian spirituality has European and Middle Eastern linkages. Thus the vehicle itself brings global identifications. The content ranges through local and global concerns—Joe's mother, life and death, God and godhead, or guiding spiritual forces. The arts, more overtly in music than in literature, it seems, bring multicultural expressions. Such expressions are identified with assorted world cultures yet are now on the stage locally. The content in musical forms brings varied subjectivities, expressed as different scales and vocal styles as well as different instruments. An example is Chapel Hill's Javanese gamelan, noted above. The gamelan consists of distinctive percussion instruments tuned to certain scales quite different from those of Western music. To listen to or play the gamelan transports one into a distinctive subjectivity. Literary expressions are less mathematical than music and more concrete, in the sense that settings, characters, and actions are the vehicles expressing global subjectivities. Dreams as reported here are similar in form regardless of the culture of the dreamer; they depict narratives expressed through characters in scenes. In what ways are these narratives, characters, and scenes global or globally oriented? The tensions and possibilities of interacting with a different culture is one theme. The white southern male and the Chinese woman in the South expressed this theme in their dreams. The scene may be local or foreign. What of the wider global framework implied by such cross-cultural interaction? This is expressed mainly by implication in the personal dreams, by who the characters are and where the scenes are set. Community dreams sometimes explicitly express globalism as a slogan. The personal dreams focus concretely on a story and scene; the spiritual vision and community dreams may refer, more abstractly and explicitly, to some metaphysical or global concept, such as God or peace. Whatever the form, whether spirituality, arts, or dreams, a wide range of global content does emerge. One can affirm, then, that global forces penetrate "deep within," shaping subjectivities in the South.

CONTEXT

How broadly distributed are such subjectivities? The southern landscape, physically and culturally, is suffused with subjectivities expressed in various forms, expressing various contents. We have noted temples and other buildings, and meetings such as readings or meditations. Global orientations pervade these to a degree. These global subjectivities, expressed in religion, arts, and dreams, are woven into a culture that also includes myriad subjectivities that are less obviously global—themes about family, community, and work in more localized aspects. If, the southern landscape is, in Susan Ketchin's apt phrase, "Christ-haunted" and, in Walker Percy's, "ghost-haunted" (referring to ghosts from history), one might conclude that it is also "global-haunted"; ghosts of the past, which themselves derive from older foreign sources such as Caribbean voodoo, are invaded by spirits of the future and the wider world. Noteworthy is the spread of such subjectivities into towns, rural settings, and urban organizations.

IDENTITY

Subjectivities, in content and context, then, energize and shape southern global identities as they coalesce, to an extent, into a synthetic, regional or global identity. That identity gains form and substance as it is manifested not only in concept, in space, and in social relationships but also in vessels of subjectivity such as spirituality, arts, and dreams. How broad and how deep this subjectivity is can be judged by observation and introspection; what can be concluded is that it does exist. Imagine southern identity as a kind of *Geist*, a spirit or cultural complex expressed in the myriad ways noted—temples and readings, therapies and meditations, performances and manifestos. Globalism infuses that identity, which is also infused with localisms (which themselves reflect older foreign histories); the whole gradually takes root in the regional setting. The commentator Peter Beyer wonders whether a global religion will emerge around the world.[15] Our observations in the South suggest that global culture is emerging to be sure, as in the sphere of religion, but patches of subjectivities illustrated by dreams, spiritualism, and the arts, as well as in more abstracted domains such as psychology, hint also at less formal, more localized, and less integrated varieties of subjectivity—weeds in the garden, so to speak.

Thank God for drunkards, children, and the United States of America.
CHARLES DE GAULLE

Yes, I oppose gay marriage. I also oppose marriage of man and woman.
DAVE "MUDCAT" SAUNDERS, Virginia progressive Democrat

CHAPTER EIGHT

Politics

Is Globalism Liberal?
Is a Local Focus Conservative?

ASSERTING THAT the South is orienting itself around the global brings to mind two assumptions we often take as givens: that the South as a region is a bastion of conservatism and that to orient around the global means to become more liberal. We need to examine these assumptions in light of the actual contours of the globalizing South. Obviously, given the South's influence on the nation and, partly through the nation, the rest of the world, the policies the South favors will matter. I want to suggest that the assumptions I have just brought up are problematic for examining the South's present and future for numerous reasons. There is a much more productive way to think about the South—and for southerners to think—and that is to think in terms of grounded globalism.

"Liberal" and "conservative" carry many meanings, and some argue that they are therefore meaningless terms. This conclusion does not follow, for if nothing else they are politically salient labels, even if used primarily as epithets and insults. Listen to parliamentary debates in Great Britain, where "conservative" explicitly labels one of the two major parties, or follow the blue/red state arguments in the United States. My solution to the problem of the complexity and ambiguity of the labels is to simplify for the sake of analysis. I shall therefore define and illustrate enough of the two orientations to capture their gist as needed to pursue a specific question: how do and how might these orientations interact with globalism in the southern context? Contrary to some stereotypes, neither is necessarily anti- or proglobal, but within the southern context, a certain kind of liberalism or conservatism can fruitfully accord with grounded globalism—which serves not only as a method but also a philosophy.

Liberal and Conservative in the South: An Illustrative Text

What do "liberal" and "conservative" mean in a southern context? A manifesto, *Where We Stand*, published in 2004, is an excellent text with which to address this question, for it states the position of liberal southerners, compares it with the conservative position, and explains both the origins and implications of liberalism and conservatism for the South and the nation. *Where We Stand* addresses the following key questions: (1) What are liberal as opposed to conservative ideals, as perceived by self-declared southern liberals? (2) What has been the history and process by which the South has influenced the nation in a liberal direction? (3) What has been the history and process by which the South has influenced the nation in a conservative direction? And (4) what is the impact of this influence on the nation? We shall add a fifth question: How has global identity affected all the above?[1]

The title, *Where We Stand,* reflects the liberal stance of the book in contrast to the rather conservative stance of a 1930 work, *I'll Take My Stand: The South and the Agrarian Tradition,* by "Twelve Southerners." Anthony Dunbar, who edited *Where We Stand,* and other scholars see the

earlier work as protesting the destruction wrought by industrialization—
in this sense foreshadowing current environmentalism—and as unrealis-
tically trying to turn the clock back to an agrarian way of life that entailed its own abuses, including racism. The new statement instead looks
forward.

Among the many contributors to the more recent collection, three authors—Jimmy Carter, Sheldon Hackney, and John Egerton—and Dunbar represent the book's perspective in a certain classically progressive,
or "liberal," stream. Carter and Hackney assumed prominent national
roles in the Democratic Party, Carter as president of the United States
and Hackney as director of the National Endowment for the Humanities under Clinton; the third, Egerton, a Tennessee journalist, has advanced the influential thesis that the South has shaped America in a conservative direction. All three are white males who are from southern
states: Georgia, Alabama, and Tennessee, respectively. Together they locate liberalism regionally, nationally, and, with reference to foreign policy, globally.

Jimmy Carter provides a foreword that states key tenets of liberalism generally, with special focus on the role of American foreign policy.
Carter asserts, first, that the United States is the "strongest [nation] on
earth" militarily, economically, politically, and culturally (9). "Should we
be proud and complacent because the military expenditures of the United
States equal the military budgets of all other nations on earth?" he asks
(9). No, he answers. Instead we should be "the champion of peace . . .
the leading champion of freedom, democracy, and human rights" (9).
We should protect the environment and alleviate suffering. Here Carter
introduces the concept of globalization. We benefit from it, he says, and
"the benefits of globalization require us to be accountable to other peoples who sometimes are affected negatively by our success because they
lack the resources to compete with us or even the knowledge and ability
to cooperate with us" (10). "The greatest challenge facing the world," he
argues, is the "growing chasm between rich and poor peoples on earth,"
a chasm that can hurt rich as well as poor, causing the rich to fear and

suppress the poor (10). "Democracy, peace, and human rights suffer under such conditions," Carter writes (10). Carter, then, states key tenets of liberalism, calling for the nation to uphold these in the world, in contrast to the conservative foreign policy currently practiced.

Anthony Dunbar explicitly identifies "the Southern liberal tradition out of which this book springs" (16). He elaborates: "Always a minority force—whether speaking against slavery, segregation, or the oppressiveness of a society in which power and privilege reign supreme—progressive voices in the South have learned that opposition to injustice is a hard duty, not an enjoyable right. . . . They have learned from the leadership of Southern blacks that the misuse of power must be attacked frontally" (16). Acknowledging that the authors of all the essays are white southerners (13), he, like several of the authors, also acknowledges their allegiance to the civil rights movement and to black leadership of it, stating that the "South has given good and bad," the civil rights movement being good (13).

Dunbar, then, affirms values similar to those of Carter—the obligation to overcome injustice and inequality—but orients them locally, regionally, rather than nationally and globally. Civil rights is Dunbar's focus, in contrast with Carter's human rights. Liberal tenets are expressed by both, but with reference to different domains: regional for Dunbar, global for Carter.

In his essay, "Identity Politics, Southern Style," Sheldon Hackney elaborates how the conservative view became part of southern white identity, which also shaped national ideology. Hackney states: "The race-baiting used against white liberals in the South was a way of suppressing dissent, and it had the added benefit of reinforcing the Southern white identity. . . . [W]hite [southern] liberals . . . were marginalized at home, and they were also vulnerable to pressures from the cosmopolitan North where they desperately wanted acceptance and support. They were cosmopolitans living in a parochial culture" (187). Hackney asks why this southern white identity became so strong, so tenacious, so "unmeltable" (188). His answer is that "Southern white identity was created out of conflict with the North," specifically the abolitionist movement (188). "It was that movement that created a consciousness of commonality," he explains, "because it was perceived by whites as a threat" (189). Here, as elsewhere, Hackney espouses the thesis that an outside threat, the abolitionist movement, was the stimulus for southern solidarity and identity. (In an interview, he rejected the argument that states' rights rather than slavery was the South's motive for secession, suggesting that states' rights was merely a means to sustain slavery.)[2]

Hackney then turns to the recent South and its conservative identity. He traces the history of "the rise to covert national power of the political leaders of the white Southern identity group between 1938 and 1968 in coalition with non-Southern Republicans, the undermining of that 'system' by the Civil Rights Movement and the Voting Rights Act of 1965, and then the flight of Southern whites to the suburbs and to the GOP" (189). He notes that six of thirteen House managers of the impeachment trial of Bill Clinton were white southern men; in contrast, the witness list of people from the enemy camp "looked like America," with "2 Jews, 2 blacks, 2 women, and one Greek/Italian hybrid" (193). He concludes that "Southern white ethnic animosities happened to coincide with the animosities of the stalwart core of the New Republicans: the cultural conservatives and the religious right" (193). Here the threat-generated southern identity behind secession from the nation evolves into a politico-religious conservatism that shapes the nation. This is what commentators mean when they say, as Hackney did when he was interviewed, that the South lost the Civil War militarily but won politically—also culturally or ideologically, one might add, in the sense of merging the South with pillars of contemporary U.S. conservatism, traditionalists, the Religious Right, neoconservatism, and libertarians.

As an antidote to this neosouthern, neoconservative identity, Hackney calls for a national and southern identity that is capacious enough to encompass both blacks and whites as well as those of other ethnicities. Southern identities, he urges, need to "become more complex, more entangled with the kudzu of the heterogeneous world, more implicated in the American identity's embrace of the universal values in what Gunnar Myrdal called 'the American Creed' " (196).

Hackney adds a historical perspective to our understanding of southern conservatism. While affirming tenets of liberalism, he traces the alternative ideology as it took hold of southern identity and then converged with the ideology of national conservatives, "the stalwart core of the New Republicans: the cultural conservatives and the religious right." The result, if we follow Hackney's analysis, is the current dominant U.S. ideology. From a liberal perspective, Hackney's analysis may appear a depressingly cogent explanation of how we arrived at the current national political situation. Yet the explanatory power of Hackney's account, because it relies on a particular confluence of historical circumstances, may offer a glimmer of hope for change, given the increasing salience of globalism in shaping present and future circumstances, especially in regard to southern identity.

The concluding essay of the book, by John Egerton, is titled "The Southernization of American Politics." Egerton's argument resonates with Hackney's and adds detail about the political events that led to what he terms the "southernization of America," which includes the rise to dominance of conservatism. Egerton begins by noting that U.S. founders were largely southern: four of the first five presidents were from Virginia, and nine of the first twelve, from below the Mason-Dixon Line. For a hundred years after the Civil War, however, southern presidents were taboo; southerners were not selected for the U.S. presidency. Between Andrew Johnson of Tennessee in 1865 and Lyndon Johnson in 1963, each of whom gained office through the assassination of a president, the only president of southern origin was Woodrow Wilson, who built his career as an educator and governor in New Jersey. Despite the lack of southern presidents during that century, however, southern senators and representatives exercised considerable control. In 1950 the Democratic Party was under the control of southern segregationists; blacks were excluded from the vote by the poll tax and other means. Then came the *Brown* decision, the Montgomery bus boycott, and Martin Luther King. Lyndon

Johnson engineered the Civil Rights Act of 1964 and the Voting Rights Act of 1965. By 1974 the GOP had gained control in the South. Following Nixon's Watergate, Jimmy Carter became the first Deep South Democrat to win a Democratic nomination for president, and he won with a margin of two million votes in seventeen southern and border states. Reagan then beat Carter badly in 1980, however, carrying all the southern states except Carter's native Georgia.

Egerton concludes by summarizing the results of Republican domination in the South and, with the support of the South, in the nation. He states their conservative ideology as follows: "The role of government is to fight wars, aid in natural disasters, uphold their version of Judeo-Christian values, [and] secure the ruling class and their assets against terrorist threats" (213). Their " 'hot-button issues' include gun control, abortion, capital punishment, school prayer, homosexuality, immigration, even race" (213). The conservatives pander to the Religious Right and big spenders. All of this represents "the southernization of American politics," in that any party needs the allegiance of the region to win, and with that allegiance comes influence, or at least a convergence of interests and values uniting southern and nonsouthern conservatives (197). Despite emphasizing the overall tendency of southern influence toward conservatism, Egerton asserts that southern presidents—Truman, Johnson, Carter, and Clinton—have done more to expand the rights of blacks than all others since Lincoln (221).

The essays gathered in this book make clear the strength of conservative southern orientation and its effect on the nation and, often by extension through the nation, the world. They also lay out the alternative perspective, liberalism, and some of its implications for the region in arenas such as civil rights. Where does globalism enter this picture? Clues are given by the text, with reference to conservative foreign policy, for example, but *Where We Stand* focuses primarily on region and nation, not world. The South's historical trajectory within the nation takes precedence over its current and future engagement globally. However, *Where We Stand* usefully elucidates liberal and conservative perspectives, which leads to our question: what is the relation between these perspectives and globalism?

Terms and Permutations

"Liberal" and "conservative" are points along an ideological spectrum, "global" and "local" along a spatial one. "Liberal" and "conservative" are labels constructed for multiple purposes—to identify policies or philosophies and to win votes or destroy opponents. "Global" and "local" at some level may simply identify a spatial orientation, but these too take on values, as when one is denigrated as parochial or provincial, denoting backward or ignorant, or when globalization is seen as destructive, and foreign ties are viewed as disloyal. So these are not perfect analytical markers, and any analysis of their relationships will be imperfect. Nonetheless it can be suggestive to explore combinations and permutations. Be warned that to do this analysis succinctly we must simplify drastically, distilling rich variations into categories, near-caricatures, providing just enough detail to perform the argument.

"Conservative" and "liberal" each sum up a complex, sometimes contradictory set of values. How might we simplify and quickly summarize each term? A simple exercise is to change nouns to verbs, to ask what conservatives do, or profess to do. If we choose one word, we might say that conservatives conserve, while liberals liberate. Then, we might ask, where do they do it? Again, choose one word: globally or locally. Clearly both kinds of actions can be done in both places. This exercise demonstrates a simple point: both kinds of action or ideology apply in both kinds of domains, globally or locally. This is obvious, but it warns against the easy assumption that conservative is localized, that is, provincial, and liberal is global, cosmopolitan.

One can then identify four combinations—liberal local, liberal global, conservative local and conservative global—and characterize how each ideological orientation plays out through each spatial orientation, broadening or deepening the impact of the ideology in question.

LIBERAL LOCAL (GROUNDED)

Civil rights is a local analogy to human rights globally. "Local" runs a gamut from neighborhood to nation but is focused, as we say, "at home" as opposed to "abroad." "Liberal" applied locally, in the South and elsewhere in the United States, entails reforms in restrictive voting practices, segregated real estate, and unequal educational and vocational opportunities. An example is the fight against redistricting when it is designed to deprive certain constituencies of their ability to elect candidates whom they see as representing them. Another example is affirmative action, which attempts to level the playing field by advantaging previously disadvantaged minorities. While grassroots movements are crucial, so is legislation enforced by the courts.[3]

Locally focused, liberal values in the South are expressed by a long line of black activists, from Martin Luther King on, and by liberal whites as well. Recent examples include Governor Winter of Mississippi and such journalists as Ralph McGill and Hodding Carter. Civil rights and equal opportunity in race relations exemplify a major thrust of liberalism in the South; other concerns include poverty and education, areas in which progressive governors such as Terry Sanford led.

LIBERAL GLOBAL

The United Nations exemplifies global liberal (sometimes flawed) efforts at fostering human rights, peace, and economic development. In the South, the Carter Center and many other southern agencies, ranging from RTI (Research Triangle Institute, North Carolina) to Stop Hunger Now, pursue a similar agenda. Prominent southerners promoting a spectrum of interests from civil rights to human rights have included Johnnetta Cole, Andrew Young, John Lewis, Jesse Jackson, Martin Luther King, and Jimmy Carter. Atlanta-based CNN is liberal compared with Fox News and much more global: CNN founder Ted Turner gave a billion dollars to the UN, and CNN competes with the BBC in international spheres, where its coverage and format are quite different than they are domestically.

In the religious sphere, the liberal Protestant streams are less obvious than the conservative ones but are nonetheless prominent. Many Presbyterians and Episcopalians, and some Methodists, illustrate liberalism both theologically and socially. Baptists vary widely, and the Southern Baptist Convention has shifted to a conservative focus, ousting moderates and liberals, yet historically Baptists such as Billy Graham can be seen as liberating in a very basic way—as undercutting social distinctions by giving priority to spiritual ones. "Are you saved?" is the ultimate criterion, not one's social status. Globally, therefore, Graham's campaigns have been a liberating force for millions.[4] Note also that Carter is a Baptist, though he differed from his church on racial issues in early years. The Archbishop of Canterbury once described the Church of England as an "old lady" muttering irrelevantly in the corner of society;[5] the Southern Baptists and similar denominations are more like robust but green young men.

An essentially liberal or liberating motive joins and perhaps is fueled by a global sphere and global concerns. A basic problem with idealism is that the rationalizing thrust diverts from a humanizing one, and global involvement that presses home the world's suffering doubtless humanizes liberalism.

CONSERVATIVE LOCAL (GROUNDED)

Conserving the existing order is a leitmotif from which flows a variety of policies and actions. Promoting business by encouraging free enterprise minimally regulated by central government (hence minimally taxed) is a key policy of local conservatives. A general value is placed on honoring the local order, which may incline toward the status quo, customs, respect for the existing way of life, and so on. In the South, this sometimes admirable ethic has also promoted slavery, segregation, and the oppression of minorities and the poor. Perhaps more positively, it has also promoted states' rights, which may be seen as a kind of populism that involves realistic skepticism about bureaucracy and central government. Today southern conservatives may declare themselves libertarians; formerly they were just individuals, for example, E. L. Fowler, the gravestone maker in Tifton, Georgia, who burned his car on the town square to call attention to his refusal to pay federal taxes.

Locally focused conservative values may be expressed, too, in valuing traditions, whether they be bluegrass, quilts, and pottery in the mountains or hospitality and courtesy in the lowlands. Courteous relations among the races and classes may of course shade from kindness to maintaining the status quo to oppression—but they may also move in reverse order.

Conservative individualism finds expression also in free enterprise as value and practice: in banking on business, entrepreneurial drive, and ingenuity rather than on centralized government. In the New South, Atlanta synthesized free enterprise, harmonious race relations, and progressive local government in their slogan "the city too busy to hate." Here, conservative and liberal merge into pragmatism.

Leadership in general inclines toward conservatism because to succeed, those in authority must realize that their decisions and actions have consequences. They are "accountable" in a way others are not and, hence, are disposed by that factor to be careful and deliberate. Prudence, learned from experience (one's own or that of others), weighs against drastic, sudden, or large-scale change unless circumstances force it. (The analogous principle in biological evolution is Romer's rule, which states that organisms change only when circumstances force them to, elaborating Darwin's law of natural selection.) Such considerations may or may not be entirely logical, but they are plausible and widespread enough that they sometimes provide a basis for philosophies of leadership and are oftentimes experienced as part of the psychology of leadership.[6] That revolutionaries become conservative when they gain office is a truism, as is the observation that retired presidents and generals regain the freedom to speak their minds when they give up their authority. The plausible pairing of conservatism with power is experienced alike by heads of state, chairs of committees or boards, owners of businesses, and parents: as leaders we take on a burden of responsibility and accountability that we leave behind when we step down.

The South displays a spectrum of leadership styles. One aspect is the assured traditionalist, what Henry Adams termed "the Virginian's habit of command," referring to Roony Lee, his classmate at Harvard and the son of Robert E. Lee. Yet another is the pragmatic, as in the capitalistic entrepreneur who favors individualism: give me freedom to do it my way, and the proof is in the pudding. A third is the silver-tongued orator who rallies opposition against tradition and, like Patrick Henry, Sarah and Angelina Grimke, Huey Long, and Martin Luther King Jr., claims the sanction of religion or morality for rebellion. Traditionalists, pragmatists, and evangelists of change alike are subject to the psychology of Romer's rule, to a disposition to conserve, amplified by the status of leadership and diluted by the freedom to rebel that comes from not assuming leadership or from giving it up. Roony Lee's alter ego is Johnny Reb, the rebel, who when intellectually unleashed becomes the radical and when moderated the liberal.

The slogan "Think globally, act locally," often identified with liberalism or enlightened globalism, is misleading. It seems to remove responsibility and leadership from locals (they merely "act") and place it with globals (they "think"). Splitting global thinking from local action, one also splits responsibility from locale—the place where one lives; you have to live with what you do—and gives it to planners who do not live there. This is an irresponsible liberalism that should be tempered by a responsible conservatism: care about how you lead and how you act, because the consequences are where you live. (Irresponsible conservatism is another subject; the point here is to begin to explain a rationale for responsible conservatism as a component balancing responsible liberalism, both of which could contribute to grounded globalism.)

There is another problem with splitting global thinking from local action: locals think too, and local knowledge is essential for local action. Local knowledge and local thinking challenge global knowledge and thinking that is too general, not tuned into local context, not grounded. Liberalism tends that way when it is utopian, espousing one path for every place—ideals that reform locales. Conservatism dwells in locale. A conservative tunes into particularities locally—local needs, local individuals, local groups: "all politics is local," as Tip O'Neill famously said, though the Massachusetts congressman combined localist politics and a certain liberalism. Such a conservative relishes locale, happy as a clam in that place, whatever its faults. Liberalism, bent on change in the image of a broader ideal, is unhappy with that place and its faults. A result is that the conservative learns more about locale, knows more about it, and works in terms of it. By this argument, then, the conservative can teach the liberal about "grounding," tuning into locale.

This is simplified, of course, an outline of the logic and consequences that tend to develop with each disposition, conservative or liberal. In practice, behavior is more complicated, often mixing the two.

CONSERVATIVE GLOBAL

Conserving the existing order becomes a global project when one combines global concerns and conservative values. Such a view may be fueled by perceived global threats. National defense motivates global strategies to protect and conserve, first and foremost the nation and, secondly, a proper world order, which may be defined as democratic, free, and capitalistic.

Such a perspective is sometimes termed "neoconservative" and paralleled with previous "empires," suggesting that the United States currently strives to rule the world as did the colonial empires of Europe. In his foreword to *Where We Stand*, Jimmy Carter, quoted earlier, contrasts this view with a more liberal one when he notes the military strength of the United States. He proposes that we should be "the champion of peace . . . the leading champion of freedom, democracy, and human rights," perhaps implying that such championing should be the emphasis rather than control.

The South is involved in global conservative policy by supporting conservatism generally (if one agrees with the arguments presented earlier), thus shaping a conservative emphasis nationally that is then expressed globally. One could trace more specific influences, as well, such as that of the conservative U.S. senator Jesse Helms, a southerner who chaired the Committee on Foreign Relations; Helms's memoir *Here's Where I Stand* can also be fruitfully compared with *Where We Stand*.

Here, then, are four combinations linking each ideology to each spatial domain. The lesson here is that globalism or localism can both be are-nas for both kinds of action, liberal or conservative. The next step is to trace how these aspects—liberal, conservative, global, and local—interact dynamically as a process: how do political ideologies take shape as they ricochet off each other and move between local and global contexts?

Dynamics

The combinations show ways that ideologies and spaces, global or lo-cal, connect. Each spatial orientation and ideological orientation can and do coincide. Their juxtapositions reveal seeming contradictions as well as creative combinations. Immigrants may be global in background but localized and conservative in orientation, relieved by and appreciative of their current situation compared with their previous one and apprehen-sive about their status. Blue-collar minorities are not necessarily liberal in all respects. Their religious beliefs may coincide with conservatives', for example, in being global yet based on apocalyptic eschatology. Be-ing conservative religiously does not necessarily imply being conservative socially and politically, or parochial and localized spatially, and it may inspire global liberalism. Given the contradictions and creative combina-tions of spatial and ideological orientations, it may be helpful to step back and explore them more grossly, in terms of how they unfold as processes. Consider four scenarios.

One can argue, first, that globalism leads to liberalism—that the con-servative tenor of the South, and thus the nation, will be tempered or shattered by global forces and global attitudes. But one can also argue that the impact will be in the opposite direction, buttressing conservative attitudes, perhaps in reaction to threats from outside. A third argument is that globalism is neutral, that it can enhance either conservatism or liberalism. After exploring these arguments, I will go beyond them to argue that a more complex configuration—grounded globalism—rather than a single ideology shapes the South and, by extension, the nation and the world.

Social dynamics entail two basic kinds of relationships: direct and dialectical. Liberal or conservative ideology may directly dictate action; examples were given above. Often, however, the ideology enters the process dialectically, as part of an action-reaction scenario, where conditions and predispositions act and react, resulting in a particular ideological tilt. I explore both kinds of dynamic, emphasizing the dialectical.

My argument also distinguishes content and context. Liberalism, like conservatism, has a set of tenets, some quite specific, that are part of the content shaping and being shaped by the South. Global processes affect and are affected by this content in human rights, the conduct of war, or the treatment of the environment, to name just a few examples. In content the South arguably tilts toward conservative in religion, in politics, and in support of the military, although an important liberal dimension is salient.

Context, however, is more complex and diffuse. The context of the global forces includes the South's broader identity with the world as well as its grounding in the region and nation—the South's grounded globalism. In the Anglican case, for example, if the American South identifies with the global South, it may reject the ordination of a gay bishop but engage the world on broad and deep levels that transcend or cross barriers of race and place. This process, though rejecting a specific liberal content, creates a liberating context. This liberation could potentially lead to various liberal contents—to, for example, human rights or world peace, approval of gay bishops or abortion—but in any case, the process is a form of grounded globalism in that it retains a link to grounding in a place while connecting to a grounding elsewhere. An example seemingly far from the Anglican is Pat Robertson's style of evangelizing and missionary work through a world media organization. Based in his native Virginia, he transcends regional, racial, and national boundaries yet exports his own somewhat regionally linked brand of conservative Christian Americanism. Robertson's fellow Virginian and sometime ally Jerry Falwell further illustrates a theologically, socially, and politically conservative movement that extends globally, as when Falwell debated at the Oxford Union (Falwell's Liberty University, by the way, boasts one of the top debate teams in the country), or when I stopped at the Liberty University bookstore and bought a textbook on world religions that decently treated Islam, Hinduism, and other non-Christian faiths, suggesting a globalism more open than the stereotypes of the Christian right suggest. The larger thrust, then, of even these conservative movements is toward transcending or moving toward an inclusive yet grounded frame and away from differences or oppositions, including racial or regional ones. Liberals should attend to context instead of simplistically assuming that conservatives are racist parochial idiots.

Does this notion of context and broader process obfuscate the distinction between liberal and conservative and the real consequences of each ideology? This is a danger, but the larger perspective is necessary to trace real consequences as they are worked out in actual situations. For the South, the picture shifts from red state or blue state designations to broader and deeper assessments of regional direction that encompass but are not reducible to the liberal-conservative dichotomy.

Globalism Liberates

Globalism liberates, we have argued, by expanding the framework of southerners from nation to world. This can free the region from its oppositionality within the nation, for nation is no longer the dominant frame within which to locate identity, oppositional or otherwise. Transcending the oppositionality of a regional identity focused against the North or nation breaks a link in the chain that binds southerners together against the outside, whether outside is North, nation, or world, and it potentially dissolves differences inside the South, such as those between blacks and whites.

Is such liberation liberalism? Certainly there are parallels. *Where We Stand* contrasts itself with *I'll Take My Stand* by affirming principle over place—not grammatically, since "where" implies place, but philosophically, asserting principles of liberalism first, then applying them to the South. Yet the liberal ethic as stated in *Where We Stand* and in similar elaborations differs from the global South identity perspective in key ways. First, the global process is not taken into account in its impact on the South. Globalism is not treated as a strong factor in domestic, specifically regional, culture. Liberalism is envisioned primarily within a regional and national context, a preglobal perspective. Such a perspective is not confined to *Where We Stand* but can be found in other contexts as well. In a major conference that aimed to examine the liberal agenda for the South, the panel on religion was confined to liberal Protestant Christians, black and white. Excluded from the conversation were conservative Protestant Christians, Catholics, Muslims, Buddhists, and the others who now worship in the South. The discussion was liberal in values yet somewhat parochial in scope.[7] Where the global is considered in a domestic context, moreover, it is considered in limited respects, either in its multicultural expression (that multiple cultures are now present owing to new immigrants) or in its economic impact (loss of jobs). The totality of the global process entailing how world forces penetrate local identity is not grasped.

Where the broadest scope of globalism is considered, it is dislocated from the domestic, as when Carter links it to questions of foreign policy. Linkages between domestic and foreign are seen primarily as applying ethical or ideological principles to ever-broadening arenas. Liberalism is applied to the South, then to the nation, then to the world, and the emphasis is on the movement from inside to outside—local to global—rather than on the reverse, the global influence on the region.

What if the global dimension were recognized? How might a global southern identity shape southern liberalism? One possibility is that the liberal agenda would be amplified and more inclusive, hence strengthened. Another is that it would be diluted, weakened. An example of both possibilities can be found in the domain of civil rights and human rights. The shift of focus from civil rights to human rights could work to enhance both concerns by grounding civil rights in the wider human issue, or it could divert attention from pressing local injustices in favor of global concerns.

Blacks and others committed to civil rights sometimes express worry about the dilution of the local by the global. They say, "Yes, globalization is happening, as exemplified by immigration; new minorities are present, and new forces must be recognized. So, yes, we must broaden the frame. However, there is unfinished business. Schools are resegregating, and prisons are filled with young black men. Historically the greatest moral obligation is to the blacks. So civil rights, domestically, must remain paramount in policy and action." Others argue for including global concerns. They say, "The South is globalizing, and new immigrant minorities suffer from violations of their civil rights, as do older minorities. Further, such violations are global, occurring everywhere. We must ground our global concerns in local ones while framing the local ones in global principles. Amnesty International should work with the NAACP, for example." In her Martin Luther King lecture, Johnnetta Cole exemplified the extension of concerns from civil rights and equality for blacks to concern for recent immigrant minorities; she reflects global perspectives.

Which position one espouses varies with one's status and the circumstances. Younger, more internationally oriented minority advocates tend to take the global position, and older, more domestically oriented minority advocates who have a long history of struggle locally tend to gravitate toward the local. Events prompt a divide between the two camps, as the Hurricane Katrina disaster in New Orleans has: local blacks term it "our own tsunami" and complain that the relief effort was greater for that Asian crisis than for this local one and, specifically, that poor blacks are the victims here and are ignored.

Julius Chambers provided another example in a commencement speech delivered at the University of North Carolina at Chapel Hill. Chambers, formerly a lawyer for the NAACP, named several white North Carolinians who defended the rights of blacks: William Friday, Terry Sanford, and Frank Porter Graham.[8] William Friday is the founding president of the University of North Carolina as a sixteen-campus system. Terry Sanford was the governor of North Carolina, the president of Duke University, and a state and U.S. senator. Frank Graham was president of the University of North Carolina from 1932 to 1949 and was then named ambassador to the United Nations. Of the three, we might ask, who was globally oriented and who was locally oriented? Graham became a globalist (ambassador to the UN), and Friday and Sanford were primarily oriented to the state and nation, not to the world. Chambers himself carried out his struggle for civil rights within a state and national framework. He was the first African American to graduate from law school at the University of North Carolina, where he edited the law review and was first in his class; he finished his career as chancellor of North Carolina Central University. By comparison, Condoleezza Rice, also an African American from the South, a native of Birmingham, Alabama, moved in a global direction. She studied the Russian language and, following an academic career, became George W. Bush's advisor for international and military affairs and then secretary of state. Thus she moved into a global space, but hardly in a liberal direction, inasmuch as she, together with others, champions conservatism. These comparisons are in part generational: Friday, Sanford, Graham, and Chambers were civil rights–era champions, and Rice is of a later generation. But the comparisons also illustrate how globalism may or may not coincide with liberalism.

The civil rights–human rights struggle, then, demonstrates a dialectical process. The liberal ideology of civil rights can be enhanced by globalizing it into human rights, thus enlisting and engaging all humans of the world. Yet those engaged in the struggle locally may resist, recognizing the danger of diverting and diluting. And globalism may, as Rice illustrates, take a somewhat conservative turn.

Globalism Enhances Conservatism

Globalism can enhance conservatism directly. Regimes simply expand their control globally while sustaining the given order, and the global expansion itself empowers the regime and its control as well as its ideology. The process is also dialectical: threat and resistance accompany globalism, thereby enhancing conservatism.

Globalism exhilarates but also terrifies. Uncertainties join threats: with globalism come terrorism and outsourcing. In *The Clash of Civilizations,* the Harvard political scientist Samuel Huntington describes two major threats to the West, Islam and Asia. And the two threats first noted issue from these civilizations: terrorism from Islam, and outsourcing and economic takeover from China and elsewhere in Asia. These threats may send one back to the bulwarks, including religion. Religious conservatism, whether Christian, Muslim, or other, demonstrably represents a reaction to globalization, according to Bruce Lawrence, the Duke University scholar of Islam who analyzes fundamentalism across world religions. Peter Beyer, the University of Toronto sociologist of religion, identifies two reactions to globalization, liberal and conservative. Religious liberals join world trends, becoming environmentalists and feminists; religious conservatives resist them, hunkering down in the foxholes. Religious liberals, argues Beyer, are so caught up in social movements that they are in danger of diluting their faith, while religious conservatives may withdraw from engagement with the wider society to focus on ritual and spiritual concerns.[9]

The military exemplifies the conservative reaction, building the bulwark domestically, shoring up homeland security, and then shifting from defense to offense, invading foreign soils to destroy a threat. Religious conservatism reacts analogously, building a bulwark spiritually among the converted, invading the lands of the unconverted, evangelizing, and fighting the ultimate threat from the devil. Both military and religious reactions of these kinds draw support from the South. The military and its sense of duty are rooted in southern tradition, politics, and geography; the South boasts numerous military bases. Southern Baptists and Pentecostals are two of the major Protestant denominations that are expanding in this way, Southern Baptist being the largest U.S. denomination, and Pentecostalism, also in part forged in the South, now the fastest-growing world Protestant movement.

This "reaction thesis"—the notion that militarism and fundamentalism are reactions to globalism and its terrors or confusions and that a key source of their energy is the South—is useful, but only to a point. It does not fully explain the conservative ideology, either in politics or in religion, for these ideologies are systematized ways of thinking and believing shaped by many forces, whether philosophical, theological, or strategic; they are proactive, not merely reactive. Yet the main point is that globalism can enhance conservative ideology and practices in a range of ways. Globalism spreads them. Globalism creates circumstances that evoke them. And globalism justifies them, proving their validity: yes, terrorists do attack; yes, jobs are going abroad; yes, the world is chaotic and needs control.

Liberals are mystified sometimes that those who would seem best served by liberal policy support conservatives, including conservative religion. One explanation is that they gain by doing so. Why did poor miners in West Virginia, normally Democrats, vote against Gore in 2000? Perhaps because Republicans spread the word that "Gore will take away your guns." More complex is the allegiance of poor blacks to conservative religion (which is sometimes linked to conservative politics). Alice is an example. Poor and devout, her devotion to Christianity leads her to be sympathetic to the eschatologies set forth by evangelicals and fundamentalists—that is, to favor a conservative theology and, hence, perhaps a conservative ideology, even though her socioeconomic interests might go in a liberal direction. (Theological doctrines include the idea that the apocalypse is imminent; hence, issues such as conservation and recycling, even economic development and AIDS lose importance; on the other hand, as Pat Robertson and others argue, the Jews should control the Gaza strip, for Revelations can enact itself only if Israel is in the hands of the Jews. Alice emphasized that above all we must leave it to God, for God must be in control.)

Fundamentalist and conservative religion can carry global implications that are also liberal. Jeff is from the Blue Ridge Mountains, and he is a Primitive Baptist preacher. He is also a Democrat (probably) and global. Jeff took the Foreign Service exam and scored very high. A husky, strongly built young man, he was assigned the job of tracking down AWOL soldiers and bringing them back to service. This job took him around the world. Once, he was in London, riding on top of a double-decker bus, when he spotted a set of books in a bookshop window. He got off the bus, bought the set, and brought it back home to Ashe County, North Carolina, for his friend Eddie, another Primitive Baptist preacher. The books are the collected works of an eighteenth-century British theologian, Henry Philpott, who is a favorite source for the Primitive Baptists. The theology is Calvinist. Because Jeff and others believe that only God, not a human organization, can dictate truth, they oppose the Christian Right. They are fundamentalists, however, in that they are led by the Scripture.

The example of Jeff rebuts too simplistic a notion of fundamentalism that equates it with religious conservatism or parochialism. Primitive Baptists are remarkably global in their Calvinist view that God has decreed who will be among the elect, and God's scope is ecumenical and global: the saved are as likely to be Muslims in Cairo as Christians in Ashe County. Some may be children of God, but no one can know if they are—the "dread presumption" of Calvinism.

Sherman reportedly said of Grant, "He supported me when I was crazy; I supported him when he was drunk. Together, we supported each other." Globalism and conservatism are not such strange bedfellows, nor are those who are theologically conservative and socially and politically liberal.

Globalism Is Neutral

Connectivity per se can give whatever ideology is considered a global scope. Anglicans in the American South join the global South; fundamentalists globalize conservatism through world missions. Liberals expand human rights via Amnesty International or protect the environment by means of the Kyoto treaty. Is globalism, then, a neutral agent, simply a way of expanding in space whatever ideology is professed? It does appear that it can be a medium for either conservative or liberal ideologies. But is the medium also a message? Would not the sheer process of global expansion liberate and thus move in a liberal direction? That is, at the level of content, specific tenets of liberalism can be spread globally, just as can specific tenets of conservatism. But at the level of context, the act of globalizing itself is expansive, and in this sense liberating: liberating in space and hence in ideology as well. The psychology is of liberation; does this imply liberalism?

Consider an example particularly prominent in the South: the military. The military globalizes. That is certain. But that action and reactions to it can go in an either liberal or conservative direction. The military is central in the South economically, politically, and in identity, and it brings home national loyalties and global orientations. The military is arguably the most regional, national, and global of southern institutions in a context where "the rubber meets the road," a domain of action leading to death in defense of national life.

"From the halls of Montezuma to the Shores of Tripoli": the Marine Corps hymn announces global reach. American military traditions have inculcated a southern perspective across the world that penetrates deeply and widely. Everyone, it seems, has served (or has fathers, uncles, sons, and sometimes mothers, aunts, sisters, and daughters who did), often "overseas." Many military bases are in the South. Retirement and military bases often go together for soldiers in the South. West Point—not the Ivy League schools—was and often still is the highest educational aspiration among southern high school students.

Almost all my male relatives of my father's generation were in World War II. When they came home, they brought back a certain globalism. My father directed the firing of both American and British ships during the D-day invasion, including the *Tuscaloosa* and the *Black Prince*. He brought home a few French and German phrases, a nostalgia for "Lili Marlene," and comments about French and German habits (admiring of the Germans). My uncle was in Merrill's Marauders in Burma, a commando unit, and later pioneered in organizing a special forces group in Thailand; he described Asians and Asia to us who had never known one or been there. The only real foreigner I met growing up was a French war bride from Algeria, another example of the military's global reach connecting us provincials to the wider world.

Academic impacts of the military on the South are as considerable as the informal familial or community relations to the world already noted. Pashto is taught at Fort Bragg, along with numerous other languages unavailable at most colleges or universities, and global thinking in terms of strategy, tactics, and policy are part of military culture. The global reach of the American armed forces connects the South and the world in a myriad of ways.

Culturally, institutionally, and individually, moreover—one might even say spiritually—the military is salient in the South. That is not to say only in the South, though the writer Tom Wolfe argued as much in *"The Last American Hero,"* which points out that Wilkes County, North Carolina, has produced more Medals of Honor than New York City. Sergeant York of Tennessee and Audie Murphy of Texas sustain that heroic tradition; York was the Tennessee mountaineer who reportedly captured a number (the exact number and circumstances are debated) of Germans in World War I, and Murphy was a hero in World War II who later acted in Hollywood westerns. Military academies such as the Virginia Military Institute and the Citadel also nourish the tradition, despite—or because of—their issues surrounding their admitting women, which they have now overcome and moved past. Large military bases such as Fort Benning and Fort Bragg exert huge economic effects on local communities. Traditionally for young men and increasingly for young women, military service is a rite of passage. Along with athletics, especially football, the military is the surest way to prove manhood, and for the majority of southerners, military experience speaks in a political candidate's favor.

The impact of military presence on the nation is well known. The military is credited with racial and regional integration at a national level. Integration of blacks and whites in the military was a catalyst for their integration in civilian life, though discrepancies between the two remain an issue; blacks serving heroically in combat were still treated as second-class citizens in the segregated South and elsewhere, but where military and community coincide, integration is often notable, as in the Virginia Beach area, reportedly the most integrated community in America, owing to the military. Similarly, though some southerners were ambivalent about fighting for the federal government, their doing so, often heroically, in the Spanish-American War, World War I, and World War II was important in reuniting the South with the nation.

In short, for southerners and the South, the military forges global and national connections to the region. That forging coincides with rites of passage, especially for men. An equally intense union of the global and the personal rites of passage is rare, occurring perhaps among missionaries and anthropologists but for few, if any, others. Terms spent abroad in the Foreign Service or for multinational business employment may be longer but are likely not as intense. In addition, this process is two-way. Just as the military propels people into foreign places, so does it bring foreigners to the South, from places such as the Philippines, Puerto Rico, Samoa, Europe, Japan, Korea, and Vietnam. Marriage is a link, but so is friendship, as when Southeast Asian highlanders settled in Greensboro, North Carolina, because of ties to American soldiers with whom they had fought in Vietnam. American protectorates are strong sources of such immigration; hence, for example, many Filipinos live in Virginia.

Military endeavors connecting global, national, regional, and personal identities also address the deepest issues of meaning, especially in the realms of life and death, evoking polarized emotions and perspectives regarding the morality of war that are related to identification as conservative or liberal. Such polarization, too, is part of the fabric of southern culture and identity. Consider two recent Memorial Day commemorations in North Carolina, one in the state capital, the other in a small town nearby.

At the commemoration in Raleigh, taps began and ended the ceremony. A concert band played Sousa marches, national anthems, "The Star-Spangled Banner," "My Country 'Tis of Thee," "America the Beautiful," and the songs of each branch of the military. The main speaker noted that more than a million soldiers had died in the many American wars from the Revolution to the war in Iraq. Describing headquarters at an American camp in Iraq, he said the Iraqis, who normally talked loudly, were quiet in one place: a shrine set aside to commemorate the fallen American soldiers. These they honored. While the official symbols at the event were national, most of those present appeared to be veterans and other locals. One group, for example, was named Southern Bikers.

In the town of Carrboro, taps also began and ended the ceremony, but there was no band, and there were no uniforms. Women representing the Ethical Culture Society presided. Music was by guitar and voice, a duet written by Bobby Sands of Belfast and sung mainly by a soprano, and a baritone solo about the composer's father, a miner who joined the Marines at fifteen, and the consequences for him of serving. The speaker noted that Memorial Day is set aside to remember the fallen in battle, and slogans always tell us to remember: Remember the Alamo, Remember the *Maine*, Remember the *Lusitania*, each a sacrifice in a war the United States went on to win. Yet each of those memories, she noted, is used to inspire further war. She wished to institute the memory of wars to evoke peace. In her speech and later in other presentations, those remembered were not soldiers but civilian victims of war from Iraq, Afghanistan, and elsewhere.

The two ceremonies would seem to have little in common except that both began and ended with taps, and both were memorials. They shared a common purpose, remembering the fallen, yet those they remembered differed. The views of war expressed at each differed as well, as did the rituals, their participants, and their ideologies. Common to both were the interweaving of local, national, and global perspectives and their connections to ultimate concerns, such as war and peace, life and death. These concerns, oriented globally as well as nationally and locally, can take on liberal or conservative shades. (For example, at a memorial service I witnessed recently in Tifton, Georgia, the head of the Veterans of Foreign Wars singled out a young black man as someone aspiring to uphold the values of service for the country—a liberal aspect in that it publicly signaled racial integration.)

While military commitments incline conservatively in the sense of protecting, defending, conserving the nation, those commitments lead to global engagement, and that engagement can lead, dialectically, to liberal or even radical leanings, whether by the soldiers or former soldiers themselves or by civilians. After the war, Robert E. Lee refused to march in step.

Grounded Globalism Reconfigures

Globalism is not an autonomous force but part of a configuration. "Grounded globalism" names such a configuration. Global, local, liberal, conservative, and other forces form a force field. The result depends on how the various forces interact, shift, balance, and tilt. Both "global" and "ground" define a framework, a context, within which values such as conservative and liberal are shaped and shape. This field is not shapeless, however; it does have vectors, and these push in certain directions, as is illustrated by the dialectical processes described. A key dialectic is global grounding.

Globalism grounds; that is, it enhances identities with locales. This thesis would appear self-contradictory: does not globalism demolish local identity? The seeming contradiction masks a dialectic. As even globalists conclude, globalization "constructs place." Globalization casts people into new spaces in which they create places, such as expatriate communities. In fact, globalization entails deconstructing and reconstructing place. This insight, reflecting the experience of immigrants and cosmopolitan intellectuals, should be compared with that of locally rooted individuals who go abroad and come home again, or hope to, as in the case of the military, a vastly global machine that is grounded in actual home communities and images of home created by those who are away but plan to return.

Consider a familiar proverb, "Absence makes the heart grow fonder." The proverb may apply to travel as well as romance: the fondness is not only for the loved one but also for the place, home. Here is another dialectic, rather the reverse of what psychologists term "approach-avoidance." In that process, the closer one comes to something, the more one wishes to avoid it. But here, the more one avoids it, the more one wishes to approach it.

Beyond physical travel, psychology and ideology engender dialectics between going away and returning home. Global identity arguably can intensify local identity, not only because broadening horizons may teach about local ones, but also because of the psychology suggested by the proverb—that moving away sets in motion a counterforce of moving back, or a desire to do so. The grass may seem greener on the other side until one goes there; then the greenness of the first side becomes evident. A similar pattern is seen in the immigrant who, having moved, puts down roots and adopts conservative ideologies. Wearing the insignia and pledging allegiance, the immigrant claims the new locale, and a conservative ideology can reinforce a sense that the newcomer's affiliation is not new but timeless, part of a utopian history.

At a collective level, the grounding of globalism is illustrated by movements such as preservation and regionalism, both of which have arguably increased with globalization and certainly have gained new meanings. Closely related are heightened concerns with preserving the environment and with memory and documentation of the past—ironically, through electronic technology. Preservation and conservation would seem to converge with the liberal drive to sustain the environment and to contradict policies enacted by conservatives that tend to destroy it. In the South, as elsewhere, this kind of concern goes beyond the simplicities of liberal versus conservative. A distinction, often implicit, is between sustainability as a liberal goal and preservation as a conservative one, where sustainability refers to the physical environment and preservation to the built, human one.

Regionalism is a related trend. Regionalism and globalism are in dialectical relationship.[10] As globalization proceeds, nation diminishes somewhat in importance owing to the breaching of national boundaries opening the way for regrounding regionally. The European Union thus creates a committee on regions and builds socially, politically, and economically around regions—Bavaria, Scotland, Brittany, and so on. Far from disappearing because of globalization, regionalism can transform itself into new and sometimes stronger forms.

Dialectical possibilities are inherent in each orientation. Localism can lead to sympathetic engagement, which expands to globalism; so could conservatism in localistic and human groundings lead to liberal ideals, and vice versa.

People

Alice is a black woman, fifty-five years old, from Ozark, Alabama. She has nine children. A son is a sergeant in the military who has been overseas. A daughter is a helicopter mechanic at nearby Fort Rucker. Alice is a devout member of the AME Zion Church. She corresponds with Billy Graham. She says that she agrees with Jimmy Deyoung, an evangelical minister located in Jerusalem, that Bush may be an agent to eliminate the anti-Christ Saddam. Her theology is that God is ultimate, though the devil is currently asserting power; one must leave it to God.

Archie is a white man, probably about seventy, who lives in Shalotte, North Carolina. He has been a truck driver all over the country, but he hurt his back and now drives a taxi. A large, powerfully built man, he used to do two hundred pushups a day. His mother was Cherokee. His son, in the military, is a sergeant who was stationed in Guam who hopes to retire in Australia. Archie appreciates family and food, and, in counterpoint to his life as an itinerant truck driver, enjoys being at home, yet he is proud that his son, through the military, is globally oriented.

Clarence Jordan was a white Baptist minister in Americus, Georgia. A pioneer for civil rights, he created an integrated community. His nephew is Hamilton Jordan, who was Jimmy Carter's campaign manager. Another nephew is a fervent Republican who lives in Florida and joins his Republican orientation with a rather cosmopolitan fascination with alternative medicine—global influences in herbs, diet, and health.

Jennie Smith is a young white woman from the Tennessee mountains. After attending college at Furman University, a Baptist school in South Carolina, she spent several years under the auspices of a Baptist mission doing community work in Haiti, becoming so adept in the dialect that she served as an interpreter for Haitian refugees detained at the U.S. naval base at Guantánamo Bay, Cuba. She then earned a doctorate in anthropology. Her dissertation, which was based on participant observation of grassroots organizations in Haiti, was published by Cornell University Press.[11] She heads an anthropology and sociology department at Berry College in Rome, Georgia, where she works with Latinos, work she describes in her article "The Latinization of Rome." She combines a Baptist background with an intense commitment to service and an astutely critical liberalism.

The lesson to learn from such sketches of individuals is the obvious one: that the themes of interest to us—ideologies and orientations, global or local—interweave variously in the lives of people and families in the South. Global, liberal, conservative, and localized do interconnect, but not always in ways stereotypes would predict.

Transformations

At the individual level and at the group level, the spatial (global-local) and ideological (liberal-conservative) interact, generating not only combinations, but also transformations: movements within a life trajectory.

Simply to move, to leave one place and go to another, can stimulate change. Military service, study abroad, and religiously sponsored work camps provide, according to many witnesses, "life-changing experiences." The U.S. senator William Fulbright, according to his widow, had one such experience when he moved from Arkansas to Oxford as a Rhodes Scholar. The result, eventually, was the Fulbright program, which is global and liberal.[12] (Worth mention, too, is Cecil Rhodes. The son of an English vicar, he went to South Africa to work at mining and underwent a transformation from green youth to domineering empire builder, resulting, among other things, in Rhodes Scholarships, which, whatever the values of Rhodes himself, have been transformative in a variety of directions.)

Religious conversion can spur localism and globalism. Jimmy Carter was a nuclear submarine commander when his father died. He returned to Plains, Georgia, for the funeral and realized what his father had meant to the community in comparison with his own career, which was global but not anchored locally. Carter returned home and plunged into community work and farming. He ran for political office but was defeated, which prompted a religiously motivated self-examination, then further political efforts culminating in his campaign and election as president. During and after his presidency, he attempted to advance an agenda that is liberal and global while remaining strongly grounded locally.

Conservative surroundings can spur liberalism: the southern liberal and northern liberal are sometimes contrasted, in that the former often works against the grain of the context, and the latter often works with like-minded liberals. Both may end up with the same ideology but through different histories. The same may be true in oscillation between local and global orientation: the provincial who becomes global may share an outlook with the one raised in a more cosmopolitan style. Combinations and transformations are the life forces that energize ideologies and contextualize them.

Syntheses or Synergies: Grounded Globalism

Can these dizzying complexities be distilled into a single perfect model? On a road in eastern North Carolina, according to Marion Oettinger Jr., a Kinston, North Carolina, native who now heads the Rockefeller museum in San Antonio, was a sign that read, when he saw it back in the seventies, "The Perfect Person." The sign led to a farmhouse. In the front yard was an old chair, high on a platform. Seated in the chair was an old man, and underneath was another sign reading, "The Perfect Person." [13]

The image is quintessentially southern in the discrepancy between the ideal and the reality. A spiritual ideal envisions a kingdom of God, but earthly reality enacts the kingdom of man, and these men are, in Christian doctrine, fallen—thrown out of the Garden of Eden and subject to the suffering and evil of life on earth. For Flannery O'Connor that discrepancy was especially evident in the South and is illustrated in her grotesque characters. The perfect person caricatures perfection.

The word "fallen" implies a certain grounding, as in fallen to the ground rather than ascended into heaven, into abstraction. "Sense of place" implies such grounding, thus connecting to the local. But does not "global" in its fullest sense include grounding, connection to locale? To be global only, without grounding in locale, is to be global superficially, like one who has visited every airport or website but gone no further in engaging with varied places. True globalism implies immersion locally, here and there. Thus we speak of grounded globalism. This notion can lead to a relationship with conservatism. A conservative orientation in the sense of attachment to place could plausibly lead to a grounding of globalism that is potentially more powerful than abstracted, or ungrounded, liberal globalism. Abstracted liberal ethics—as human rights, for example—may lose power or impact if they are not grounded in locale, in the particularities of context, or they may gain power by such grounding but in so doing edge into attachment to place, which leads toward conservatism. The point is that grounded globalism provides a context, or force field, within which liberal and conservative tendencies interact. A plausible result is a more viable liberalism, which, however, absorbs some conservative aspects, such as attachment to local orders. The perfect person is a caricature of the one who is ungrounded but in fact fallen to the ground, buried by the counterforce to his own perfectionism.

Charles De Gaulle and Mudcat Saunders, in the epigraphs to this chapter, are cryptic and wry satirists of a certain perfectionism. De Gaulle equates the mighty U.S.A. to children and drunkards, and Mudcat equates gay marriage to heterosexual marriage by rejecting both. Both writers lump together something revered, the nation or marriage and family, with something lesser or questionable. In so doing they, in Rodney Needham's phrase, "disturb the tranquility of axioms," in this case axiomatic patriotism and family values. By disturbing perfectionist absolutionism, that is, absolute adherence to an entity or value, they open the door for contextualism, a kind of situational ethic that draws us into considering context when evaluating and acting.

Grounded Globalism as a Context for Ideologies

What is the potential of grounded globalism? Global identity itself can potentially liberate. Inasmuch as global identity entails deepening engagement with the world while sustaining grounding in locale or locales, this engagement can broaden and deepen awareness of issues and needs, of people and places. The result is not necessarily precisely liberal policies but perhaps evolution away from narrowly conservative ones—in fact, away from orthodoxies of ideology generally through forging vision in context.

How might such vision in context configure for the South? Positions stated telegraphically look like this:

What the South Might Become

1. Global, in that the South is emancipated from regional constraints, including oppositionality in its paralyzing aspect
2. Local, in terms of affirming place, relationships, family, and humanity
3. Liberal, in its concern for environment but not in a mode of inhuman environmentalism, and in its advocacy of human rights but not in the mode of "one size fits all"
4. Conservative, insofar as it affirms and preserves local history, tradition, and family values, excepting elements of oppression, cruelty, inequity

What the South Might Eschew

1. Globalism, in the sense of unanchored globalism
2. Localism, in terms of an insular, parochial localism
3. Liberalism, in the vein of doctrinaire platforms violating context, community basis, and human basis
4. Conservatism, in the style of paternalistic top-down control

Grounded globalism is an orientation rather than an ideology, one might suggest, and its main orientation is toward context. Therefore a list of tenets should point toward context rather than abstracted platforms or policies, and context will affect and change ideology. Take as an example the Anglican global South's conflict with the Episcopal North. This conflict is depicted as between conservatives and liberals, but consider further. The global South orients toward grounded globalism. That is, it shapes doctrine and practice by context. That context is grounded in local practices that are widely rooted. These include family values, among them

African social structures based in kinship and marriage, where who one is depends strongly on who one is descended from and on which group one marries into. Not just African but Asian social fabrics, even in very urban areas such as Singapore, Shanghai, or Tokyo, are rooted in kinship and marriage. Global South Anglicanism also includes spirit-filled worship, which has broad and deep groundings in, for example, shamanism entailing spirit-possession and healing, and in Christian movements of Pentecostalism and the like that affirm spirit-filled worship. Such Global South heritage finds a certain affinity with U.S. South roots as well, echoing African influences as well as white emphases on clan and family reflecting agrarian background. And what about John Wesley at Aldersgate in London? Did not his spirit-filled worship influence the South as well as most of the Protestant Christian world, fueling camp meetings, Methodism, and, today, world Pentecostalism? So here is a broad and deep grounding of globalism shared by the global South and the American South. Threatening it is northern liberalism in certain tenets or tendencies, including the support of gay rights and the right of women to have abortions—perceived by conservatives as undermining family values in a deep sense—and a certain conservatism in worship style.

Who is liberal and who is conservative? One might argue that liberalism in a broader sense would affirm the nigh pan-human values of the global South, recognizing the issues raised by specific liberal tenets that violate these. Grounded globalism here would encourage liberation in the broader sense rather than liberalism in the narrower sense; that is, globalism offers liberation from a specific cultural orientation and ideology to welcome cultural orientations that are broadly based, while "to ground" is to seek an accommodation of globalism to local contexts. Admittedly, such a synthesis is difficult to defend: does one really wish to deny gay rights or the right to abortion for the sake of pan-human family values? A synthesis is difficult to propose in a debate, when one is forced to choose between limited options and does choose, but in practice accommodation is necessary.

Outsourcing illustrates another issue in globalization: an ungrounding of factories by moving to places overseas where cheaper labor is available. Nike and Russell contrast among makers of athletic goods. Nike, based in Eugene, Oregon, subcontracts with factories abroad. Russell, based in Russell County, Alabama, chooses to keep local factories and employ local workers. Once comparable in sales, Nike pulled ahead through out-sourcing and advertising. After weathering a period of criticism for its lack of ethical concern ("Just do it" being a statement of Nike ethics), Nike became a leader in industrial human rights. Russell quietly contin-ued to support the economy of Russell County by employing workers locally and producing for global markets as well, but not so visibly as Nike. Who would win the grounded globalism award? Nike is conser-vative in its business practice in the sense of outsourcing as a mode of uninhibited free enterprise; Russell, seemingly more liberal, is almost so-cialistic in sacrificing profit for the communal good. Yet Nike is a leader in industrial ethics at outsourced factories. Nike is more global, Russell more local, with Russell practicing a variety of grounded globalism.[14]

Heather is an Olympic-level equestrian who lives in a southern state. She owns half a horse, that is, a half interest in a horse; the other half is the property of a local horse farm owner. Heather competes internationally on the horse. Heather's half of the horse is global—she rides it interna-tionally; while the owner's half is local—her property at the farm. The two owners divide somewhat like King Solomon's women, in that one claims the horse's global half, the other the local half, but the horse itself practices grounded globalism. Olympian aspirations and ideals, some-what liberal, motivate the rider, whereas business concerns, somewhat conservative, motivate the owner, and the horse, one hopes, is happy with both.

Grounded Globalism in Region, Nation, and World

Hackney, Egerton, and others argue—and political strategists believe—that the South's vision shapes the nation and, conversely, that a national candidate must appeal to the South.[15] Currently the direction of southern influence is seen as conservative. The thesis, then, is this: The South is conservative. The South has gained influence in America. Conservative America has gained influence in the world. Thus the conservative South has, through the nation, gained influence in the world. In this view, southern conservatism strengthens national conservatism, which affects the world conservatively. A second option, like the first, presumes strong southern influence on nation and world, but in a liberal direction. Southern liberalism could strengthen national liberalism, which would yield a liberal impact on the world. Into these two scenarios, insert the global factor. If globalism liberates, could it build liberalism in the South, in turn shaping nation and world, as did the American Revolution?

A third option is grounded globalism. In this perspective, southern ideology is a configuration, a force field that interweaves conservative and liberal strands spurred by global forces that are grounded in the regional context and other localized contexts around the world. Such a perspective affirms global forces and needs but grounds its globalism in awareness of local realities, which include poverty, racism, custom, tradition, place, and family, while affirming innovation, justice, and peace.

Can such a configuration shape wider domains, such as the nation or beyond? Any answer to that question would hinge on more than the configuration itself, including, for example, political strategies that bring one party to power rather than another. On the one hand, a configuration more accurately mirrors a situation because it reflects context and complexity; on the other, simplicity may carry the day. The South has ridden the conservative horse into national influence; a team of horses—conservative, liberal, global, local—could pull the wagon into the ditch. In-between parties sometimes fail.[16] To dilute conservatism in the South may cut Samson's hair, sapping its vitality and strength. To complicate liberalism could divert from its idealism and focus. To push and pull in global, local, conservative, and liberal directions, sequentially or simultaneously, depending on what flies now, then, and tomorrow, is the work of political strategy and beyond the work of this chapter, which is to set forth patterns that can result, not to detail how to achieve those results. Still, politics as the art of the possible demands a vision of possibilities.

Float like a butterfly, sting like a bee.

MUHAMMAD ALI

The man of action is always ruthless. No one has a conscience
but an observer.

GOETHE

Conclusions

WHAT MIGHT WE CONCLUDE? We might conclude that the
South has changed importantly in recent years, that it is changing still,
and that globalization—that is, interconnection with the world—is an
important part of that change. Specifically, a pillar of southern identity—
a sense of opposition to the nation—is being transformed to the extent
that the South acquires a global identity. Because race and place are key
domains of southern experience, we have explored how globalization is
increasing the South's social and cultural diversity and is complicating the
sense of place experienced by both native and adoptive southerners. As
identity changes, so do frames of meaning: religious, artistic and political.
The South is arguably at a turning point: by adopting an outward-looking
integrative identity with the world, it is reversing the inward-looking and
oppositional identity it acquired when it became the South. Dabbs's depiction of the southerner at home in the South expands and is enriched

by the wider degrees and new ways southerners, in various guises from native to immigrant, feel at home in the world as well as in the South.

I trust that the argument expressed here—that southern lives, identities, and meanings are becoming more global—will provide a helpful perspective, a fresh view of a region typically seen from a local or national rather than global angle, a way of interpreting events and experiences unfolding now and later. Seeing the South globally, we glean information and interpret experiences and events that local and national viewpoints obscure. As we see the South from a new viewpoint, we also see studies of the South in a fresh way, and as we see many other new points of view about the South—native, immigrant, local, and foreign, sometimes remarkably similar despite physical and cultural distance—we may be moved to act in our own lives to recognize and extend connections to the world outside the South and to the outside world within the South.

In short, this study offers a model. This model is presented, brashly but respectfully, as an alternative to the dominant model followed by most scholars, journalists, and lay people. Their model correctly and cogently focuses on the place of the South within the nation. I focus, alternatively, on the relation of the South to the world. I argue that within the history and worldview of the South, globalization matters, especially recently, and that it matters so much that other models, including the national one, must be seen as part of the global overview rather than as the dominant, guiding focus. I explore this global perspective not only illustratively but also systematically. This is not a historical argument about how the present differs from the past but rather an argument about what works best to conceptualize the South now and to envision, even shape, the foreseeable future.

The Seven-Step Model and the Global Identity Hypothesis: Far Away and Deep Within

The seven-step model has three main stages: past, present, and future. The first five steps trace in our past the familiar process of regional identity leading to opposition to national identity and then to secession, defeat, and resentment. The sixth step is observable in the present and in the South's recent history. It proposes that a shift to a global perspective can overcome—at least partially and perhaps radically—the paralyzing identities resulting from steps one through five. The seventh step, a hope for the future also based on the actions of southerners in the recent past and in the present, seeks a return to a version of the first step—regional identity—by grounding global identity in a local context.

I argue, then, that the reorientation of southern identity away from local, specifically regional, opposition within a national perspective deeply transforms attitudes and culture. The process is somewhat paradoxical: the focus on the far away, the foreign, changes an oppositional identity that is deep within person and culture. In concluding my elaboration of this argument, I invite you to consider not only its particulars but also its premises.

The polarity between one and many animates much human thinking, from debates about monotheism and polytheism to approaches in science and philosophy. Take empiricism versus rationalism, for example: does one move from facts to theory or from theory to facts, from many to one or from one to many, from parts to whole or from whole to parts? Such a polarity often reflects an interdependent, cyclical process: the many are changed by changing the one; the parts by changing the whole. In psychology, behaviorism and gestalt are major schools of thought. Behaviorists contend that learning is best explained as building item by item, through behavioral stimulus and response, while Gestalt psychology teaches that one learns by reconfiguring the whole framework of understanding, the gestalt. In anthropology, the gestalt approach has been the dominant one for over a century. Structures must be transformed as wholes, gestalts, if impact is to be "deep within." In religion a similar notion of inner transformation obtains. When one's ultimate framework of meaning is transformed, one's reality is seen differently, *is* different.

What the gestalt psychology, anthropological, and religious approaches share is a conclusion that change, deep within self or culture, occurs by means of a shift of the overarching framework, or guiding paradigm.

Echoing this orientation, the argument here is that connection to the global, the far away, can be and sometimes is the stimulus to change the gestalt that orients the South—a change that is potentially profound, deep within in a psychological sense (evidenced in subjectivities) and in a cultural sense (evidenced in values).

The Copernican revolution, which changed our way of looking at the universe and, with that, ourselves, provides an analogy. In the new geo-psychology of the South, the North is no longer the center around which one revolves and against which one revolts. Instead the world becomes the center, relegating the previous center to one of many. Thomas Kuhn, in *The Structure of Scientific Revolutions*, taught us that when experience contradicts an accepted explanation of how the world works, and the contradictions pile up and cannot be explained, other explanations gain credence, and eventually a new explanation that accounts for the anomalies becomes accepted. He termed such a transformation a "paradigm shift." The replacement of an old paradigm by a new one involves more than merely cognitive change, more than simply amassing evidence explained by the new paradigm and unexplained by the old; it also involves emotional change akin to a conversion in religion. In *The Protestant Ethic and the Spirit of Capitalism*, Max Weber argued that market-dominated society emerged in the same way, that such a shift was necessary to break tradition, shatter custom, and create a movement that remolded human beings into rationalizing Calvinist-capitalists.

In this work, I also identify a paradigm shift. The regional paradigm of the American South, forged in war, resides deep within as an oppositional identity. It can be transformed only by a powerful force. That force comes from far away, in the form of connections with the rest of the world, with global forces. These do not operate alone, to be sure; they join national and other influences in changing the region. Globalism is the catalyst, however, crucially energizing a configuration of processes to affect deep within.

That depth is evidenced here by breadth, by effects observed across a broad spectrum, from race to place, economics to religion, and by changes felt deep in the psyche and seen in the private spheres of life. To be sure, impacts vary, and for many they remain shallow. No earthquake or tsunami, they are more like other natural processes known in the South—erosion, for example, or its misguided antidote, kudzu—that spread gradually but become pervasive, transforming eventually but profoundly.

Findings

In this work, I have identified three trends. The primary one is a shift from opposition nationally to integration globally (hypothesis one), which, I argue, is a shift from a sense of place to an awareness of force fields (hypothesis three) and is manifest, variously, in diversities and pluralism (hypothesis two). The three trends correlate, overlap, and intertwine, yet they are distinct from each other. Further, all three can be evidence of globalization but are not exclusively or necessarily so, for they connect to other phenomena as well.

DIVERSITY AND GLOBALISM (HYPOTHESIS TWO)

Take global thinking and diversity. The two can go together, but they are also distinct trends, as is shown by how they can be witnessed in different domains. Retirees, leaders, or the affluent may be movers and shakers in globalization but not reside in diverse communities; bankers and business people who promote globalization in their work may move in circles that include few of the new immigrants in face-to-face relationships. This is partly because of class differences: new immigrants, who are often working-class, live and work in different spheres from executives, whose plans are made in office meetings and on golf courses. Diversification in schools and on construction sites or farms reflects globalization, just as do the planning activities of the executives, but the domains differ.

Similarly, those who are shifting toward a force field sense of place do not necessarily lead in the diversification of neighborhoods or workplaces. The "Think globally, act locally" slogan can be an unfortunate fact as well as an ideal. Global thinkers may often be isolated from local actors, such as the diversifying workers. That there is such a gap between planners and actors is, of course, one of the criticisms of the World Bank, the UN, and other multinational organizations, and it is as apparent in the South as elsewhere. Yet much thought and work about diversification is distinct from global thought and work. This is illustrated by the Methodist retreat discussed in chapter 4: diversity, for this group of Methodists, is an issue that stems from globalization, inasmuch as it concerns diversifying their membership to include new immigrants, but it also includes many other issues, such as diversity of gender and sexual orientation, and the absence of African Americans in the congregation.

The trends and questions do overlap, however, and logically imply each other. If one starts with diversity, one moves toward globalization, and vice versa, as each entails the other. Diverse populations, for example, link their host regions to diverse homelands, and globalization trends spur migration, which results in diversity.

PLACE AND GLOBALISM (HYPOTHESIS THREE)

A corollary to diversity on southern ground is a new experiencing of this ground. Sense of place mirrors and shapes attitudes about the global and the local: place is locale, and becoming open to the global implies stretching one's sense of locale, ultimately to include the world and perhaps beyond (space stations and galaxies, for example). As one stretches, one ceases to stand in place exactly as one did when one was confining one's posture and movements to a single spot, so the spot itself shifts in its meaning, even if it remains the same physical space that it was before one stretched (or before the force field stretched, to shift to the wider global system). The locale is no longer local only, not that it ever was; it becomes blatantly global.

An example: visit an old building anywhere, say an Anglican or Armenian church in downtown Singapore, where the building itself is preserved intact, but the surrounding context has changed and is constantly changing in a global city. Raleigh and Atlanta resemble Singapore in that designated buildings, often churches, are preserved as their context changes. At the Longview offices near the Exploris museum in Raleigh both contents and context, inside and outside, are being transformed into an explicitly global symbol. Longview was a church, and the church building is preserved. The space is the same, the church structure is the same, but the references and uses are transformed. At the pulpit, in place of Christ, are references to Carl Jung and Margaret Mead. Stained glass windows now refer to Sun Yat-sen rather than scripture or apostles. Next door, at the Exploris museum, global forces are made explicit through exhibits and events that inform visitors about globalization.

Nearby stands the state capitol, where the statues commemorate the past two hundred years, especially the late nineteenth century, when whites reasserted dominance after Reconstruction by building statues of their leaders; and near that is the legislative building, where the state motto, *"Esse Quam Videre"* ("To be rather than to seem"), adopted in 1893, claims a certain classical Western tradition as part of the state's history. Now that this older complex is counterpoised to the global one down the street, however, its meaning has transformed. Where it may have once signaled an apex of power in a local context, it is now a local node in a global, urban context. In such juxtapositions, worldviews collide, represented in spatial arrangements and in architecture.

My third hypothesis maintains that force fields replace an inert sense of place. Essentialized stereotyping of the South's sense of place form part of a certain period of history, class of people, and habit of work distilled into particular images by song and literature—by "My Old Kentucky Home," "Carolina in My Mind," and so on. This take on the South as a place remains viable in some respects. These songs are as much about image as they are about behavior, projecting nostalgia for an imagined agrarian society. William James caught himself in another kind of nostalgia, for the unspoiled nature of the frontier South. Traveling in Appalachia he was appalled when his mountaineer wagon driver proudly showed how he had cut down trees to make a clearing. Only when the man demonstrated the necessity of doing so to survive by farming did James admit his naïveté in idealizing unspoiled nature while ignoring necessity.[1]

The South is no longer that old place; it is neither plantation nor frontier, but something new. Current perspectives include the varied and clashing approaches of developers, conservationists, and ecologists. The developers create sprawl as they house and move the South's multiplying, urbanizing population. The conservationists or preservationists try to conserve or preserve built or natural environments. The ecologists who shade into environmentalists take a "scientific" view, often defining "science" narrowly as measurable techniques for analyzing what is considered the natural world.

The notion of force field helps to connect these perspectives, because it redefines place from an inert "home" to a location that is still located but is part of multiple forces. Globalization and globalism foreground the force fields, which were there all along, before and after. The genius of Thomas Berry's ecozoic philosophy, for example, is it that weds a universalistic worldview to a certain sense of place. The Universarium developed by Stan Gibson of Toronto dramatizes Berry's worldview via electronic media and a planned traveling theme park designed "to draw citizens into the for-real, hands-on project of creating a sustainable future." Gibson and his colleagues call for ecological education and action by regions—a strategy consonant with grounding globalism in the southern region or elsewhere.[2] An ecozoic approach moves beyond mere critical deconstruction of sense of place, beyond the literary postulate of a postsouthern place—the argument that a sense of the South as a place was always or has become an illusion, and therefore we should cease to speak of the South as a place. Space is not postsouthern, I contend. That notion essentializes the South, as though the region disappears when one loses some older construction of it. A more productive strategy is to acknowledge the forces constructing place, as in the instance of the South, in order to understand and shape them.

OPPOSITIONALITY TO GLOBALISM (HYPOTHESIS ONE)

The shift in emphasis from oppositionality in a national frame to global orientation represents the most fundamental change, for it entails a shift in worldview—indeed, in basic ways of experiencing as well as of viewing the world. In the vein of the Copernican revolution, there is decentering and recentering: the wider world rather than our particular locale becomes the focus of orientation, after which nothing is the same. Such a change is simple to state but difficult to grasp, yet it is profound for several reasons. First, for some of us, this shift in worldview may happen suddenly, as a shock: culture shock is an example, usually experienced not at home but away from home as one gets disoriented and, one hopes, reoriented. Second, for many of us, especially when our global context is not far away but is at home, the shift is not sudden or total but gradual, unnoticed, rather insidious, and it may wax and wane with context. Still, whether sudden or gradual, whole or partial, far away or at home, the overall effect is profound and multileveled. Originating far away, the impact is potentially deep within, because the most fundamental moorings of our perspective shift.

Or they don't. At one meeting of the board of World View, an outreach program for primary and secondary schoolchildren, a teacher from Robeson County, North Carolina, Nila Chamberlain, stood and said, "I bring greetings from the Flatlanders. We in Robeson County believe that the earth is flat; hence, we will fall off the edge if we leave Robeson County. So we would rather be unemployed in Robeson County than have a job in Raleigh." Nila exaggerates, of course; Lumbee Indians, whose largest concentration is in Robeson County, range up and down the coast as hangers of sheetrock, for example. But the Lumbee, who are so intermarried that two Lumbee names (Locklear and Oxendine) dominate the county, are strongly localized, it seems. Flatland philosophy neatly underlines the opposite of the new global worldview—the assertion that the earth is round, so if you go far enough, you will end up back home. As children we used to think that if you dug a deep enough hole, you would get to China. This is globalism in a naïve sense, since it asserts that two ends of the earth are linked, that the world is one. As adults today, we do not need to dig the hole, since we can easily travel to China, but going there is not being there in the sense of becoming part of that world.

Sydney Rittenberg has done this remarkably. Raised in Charleston,

South Carolina, Sydney went to China with the army and then remained. He mastered several Chinese dialects and accompanied Mao Tse-tung on his long march. He was the only American member of the Chinese Communist Party, married a Chinese woman, and became part of Mao's inner circle. Later he was arrested by the Red Guard and imprisoned for sixteen years. Released, he returned to the United States and links China and the United States through his import and export business.[3]

Jun Wang, a native of Beijing, has made the opposite transition, from China to the United States, specifically to the South. She says of her acquaintance Sydney that he is simply Chinese—so perfect is his speech. She herself has entered American life to a striking degree. My sense of the two transitions is that both people retained their integrity and identity; I think each would still say, "I am Jun," or "I am Sydney," but each has acquired a new language, a new life, and new existence that is at once American and Chinese—in a word, global. What Sydney and Jun accomplish individually is what a culture like that of the South is beginning to accomplish collectively perhaps. It is worth reminding ourselves of the dimensions of such a synthesis of perspective.

Shifts of worldview are not merely cognitive but are also emotional, experiential, and bodily. At an Indian wedding, one dances to a different rhythm. Embodiment is part of the shift, not just in art forms such as dance or music but also in sustained, implicit experiences. I sense in my bones, still, the eighteen-hour days of living a different language, routine, worldview, and ways of friendship during the eight months I spent with Muhammadiya, the quasi-fundamentalist Muslim organization in Indonesia. Soldiers, even students and travelers, experience culture shock physically, especially when living with foreign families or traveling alone, and it sometimes manifests in serious illnesses. While illness, even death, is an acute bodily expression of dislocation, milder embodiments occur continuously as a result of global contact: think how our diets have changed owing to the influx of Asian, Latin American, and other international foods and herbal medicines. Southern Bodies may be the name of a fitness center in South Georgia, but the exercises are certainly foreign to the agrarian South where exercise traditionally meant that men cropped tobacco, picked cotton, and plowed, and women raised children, cooked, and cleaned. The machines and routines in the fitness center follow global formats, including yoga and massage, with clientele increasingly diverse in ethnicity, gender, culture, and, perhaps, class. Diseases globalize too, as traditional regional ones, such as hookworm, are replaced by malaria, which was once prevalent in the coastal South but is now brought in by southerners traveling or migrating from abroad. (The Centers for Disease Control and Prevention, the nation's major center for research and treatment of global diseases, based in Atlanta, was founded in 1946 as the Communicable Disease Center. Its mission was to eradicate malaria-carrying mosquitoes, a continuation of Malaria Control in War Areas, an agency established in 1942 to control malaria in the South and in U.S. territories.[4])

Psychology is also involved in a shift in a perspective, a shift in cognitive field, a shift, perhaps, in embodiment, and, beyond that, in the ways our emotional configurations and experiential worlds can change. Many theories explain such changes, including psychoanalysis, which interprets deep internal upheaval. While psychoanalysis has waxed and waned in influence during the century since Freud published *Die Traumdeutung* in 1900, its depth of insight stubbornly resists criticism and sustains validity and utility in explaining, especially, those emotional elements and unconscious motives out of reach of conscious cognition.[5] Despite the danger of overreaching, I shall hazard some speculative psychoanalysis of the shifts of identity entailed for the South in globalization.

Transference is the classical mechanism in which one gains a new parent, the analyst, against whom one plays out old, painful experiences. One transfers, then, these experiences to a new playing field, and the insights that the repetition of the old experiences may afford are emancipating. In the current situation in the South, there are two elements: a new playing field and, perhaps, a new parent figure. The new playing field is global, not local. In May 2004 a racist image—a figure urinating on the logo of the NAACP, with a Confederate flag nearby—on sweatshirts created in High

Point, North Carolina, aroused attention locally, but this local incident was overshadowed by the global revelation of the scandalous, sadistic treatment of Iraqi prisoners by American soldiers at Abu Ghraib prison. The High Point incident might have been seen as a southern problem, while the Iraqi prisoner affair was seen as an American problem within an international context, with little attention given to regional connections. (One exception was a *New York Times* editorial that contrasted the good and the bad West Virginians—Jessica Lynch, the hero, and Lindsay Englund, the villain.[6]) In an international context, the opposition is between the United States and elsewhere; the South is just part of the United States. Here the South gains new allies (other Americans) and new opponents (enemies from abroad, critics within America), but in either case the South is involved not alone but together with other Americans: southerners do not play a role here as southerners but as Americans. The psychology is something like "misery loves company" in that the ugly racism in the South finds commonality with the ugly quasi-racism of the nation as a whole, expressed as torture of Iraqis. Both the South and the nation can, and to an extent do, work together in acknowledging their abuse of those perceived as "other" or "enemy" and may share goals of emancipation at many levels—economic, military, political, and psychological, including liberating selves and society from abusive prejudices.

For the South or southerners as actors, the emancipating context in which old traumas and paralyzing prejudices and identities can be reevaluated is provided by the international global arena, within which one becomes a national and international actor rather than a regional one. Southerners have experienced this process repeatedly in the past by enlisting in the various American wars. Taking part in peacemaking arenas, including the Peace Corps, Rotary, the Fulbright Program, and Habitat for Humanity, can afford southerners similar insights as they join others in submerging regional identities within national and global ones. A similar process happens when ethnic minorities merge identities in national causes. (A classic literary depiction can be found in Norman Mailer's *The Naked and the Dead*, which placed a New York Jew and a Mississippi redneck together in combat.) The process is well-known, the psychology is obvious, and the effect is powerful, in that a stigmatized, particularized identity is diminished as an admired, broader identity is acquired, and even if that broader identity is decried globally, the solidarity of the newly included regional identity with the national one is intensified in opposition to a common enemy.

Consider a joke heard right after the commemoration of the sixtieth anniversary of D-day: Osama bin Laden goes to heaven, where he is met by George Washington, who slugs him; by Thomas Jefferson, who beats him with his cane; by Patrick Henry, who kicks him as he falls; and by James Madison and others, who revile him for violating principles of freedom and democracy established by the United States. Lying on the ground, Osama protests to an angel that heaven should not be like this, to which the angel replies, "I told you you'd find seventy-two Virginians." This joke, told by a nonsoutherner, sees Virginians as Americans, not southerners—in fact as the quintessential founding Americans who oppose an anti-American villain. The narrative affirms the place of the South in the United States in opposition to an international threat.

The analogy of transference is applicable in the broad sense that one moves from playing out identities and conflicts in a narrower domain (in psychoanalysis, the family; here, the region) to a broader, more emotionally open one (in psychoanalysis, the clinic; here, the nation and world). The result, at least for regional actors, is the affirmation of a broader identity and emancipation from a narrower one.

Who is the parent? The northern United States, or the nation as a whole excluding the South, has stood since the early nineteenth century as the dominant party, the parent figure, the dictator of values and points of reference, and standards, against whom the South has rebelled. Logically, if the frame of reference shifts from nation to world, the parent figure must represent not the nation but the world. In a world framework, figures or forces divide into negative and positive. Some specific person, such as Saddam Hussein, Ayatollah Khomeini, or Osama bin Laden, and some organizations, such as Al-Qaeda, become the negative, threatening parent figure against whom one plays out conflicts experienced in childhood with one's actual parents, while individuals seen as heroic, such as Mohandas Gandhi, Mother Teresa, Martin Luther King, Nelson Mandela, Bishop Tutu, Dwight Eisenhower, Winston Churchill, and Tommy Franks, and some organizations, such as the United Nations, the Red Cross, the World Council of Churches, the Marine Corps, the CIA, and the Green Berets, represent, for some, a positive, nurturing, or protecting parent. (For some, Al-Qaeda or Hamas may be the good parent.) Negative and positive entities now act on a world scale rather than on a national scale, where the conflict was once (and for some still is) between a regional champion such as Robert E. Lee and a regional villain such as General William T. Sherman and more recently between "red" and "blue" states. For southerners, adopting a global identity means joining other Americans and others around the world in a drama and struggle between global forces led by global leaders, who assume certain aspects of parental status. Whether one accepts the psychoanalytical analogy, the transformation of identity is profound. One is no longer the isolated representative of a region struggling against a nation; one is now a member of that nation joining a world struggle (or a member of a world struggle that divides the nation). At a collective level, this is analogous to Freud's grim characterization of therapy as moving the neurotic from private misery to sharing humanity's general unhappiness. By broadening the arena of struggle, one moves beyond the emotionally laden, too cozy, too traumatic, and too familial regional ground into a larger, more abstract global arena, which may have its own emotional baggage but at least is more distant from the painfully intimate roots of one's native or adopted home locale.

Southern internationalists such as Jimmy Carter, Woodrow Wilson, Andrew Young, and William Fulbright can be seen as "therapists" in this collective transference. They exemplify leaving behind regional conflict and embracing international values and perspectives, including human rights, the work of the League of Nations, or cross-cultural exchange. The philosophy of Thomas Berry further exemplifies this shift. To Berry the earth is the dominant framework, and a love-hate drama is played out with the earth. We tear the earth apart today and rejoin it, one hopes, in an Ecozoic (ecological) stage. In Berry's narrative, nation and North are present, but his account, though it acknowledges his southern background, is within a global, ecological framework, not the framework of the regional drama of defeat, occupation, and resentment of the nation. This is a much larger struggle between all humans and the earth; hence, Berry, too, is a therapist who launches a transference from vexed narrower arenas to a larger battle. Berry's Catholic perspective is also noteworthy, as is that of such southern writers as Walker Percy and Flannery O'Connor. As Catholics, they are no longer merely southerners, either in self-identity or as identified by other Catholics. They move past a regional identity to a more global or even cosmic one. A similar effect can be seen in black leaders such as Martin Luther King and Jesse Jackson (Christians) and Malcolm X (a Muslim); their religious identities transform their struggles from regional and racial to global in inspiration. Ecological movements such as the Apollo Alliance[7] and Al Gore's campaign against global warming further illustrate union of people with regional roots, white or black, in a global cause; one spokesperson for Apollo explains that it is analogous to the movement led by Martin Luther King, a bottom-up, grass-roots push, but with a goal even more global than civil rights, protecting the environment of the world. Such a dynamic—transference from regional to global identity—is a profoundly powerful one psychologically as well as philosophically or theologically, for it shifts the sources of authority and the frame for conflict while transforming perspective. This point holds true regardless of whether the specific transference model of psychoanalysis is accepted. The general logic or psychologic can be understood as an aspect—though not a defining feature or necessary condition—of the Copernican shift entailed by my first hypothesis.

Identity Matters

"Identity Matters" is the title of a manifesto that eleven scholars from eight countries formulated as part of a Fulbright project analyzing the factors behind conflict and peace. A great range of usage and definitions of "identity" are known, including academic writings and common usage in many languages. We eleven, despite our varied nationalities and disciplines, had no trouble recognizing the concept and agreeing on its importance, though we might choose to define and apply it differently. A central point was made by the social psychologist Thomas Pettigrew that identity links the personal to the collective. Unless one connects personally to a collectivity, say, a nation or region, identity remains inert, lifeless. Unless there is a collectivity to connect to, personal psychology fails to find expression. Identity is a word that recognizes such a connection.[8]

Identity can bring death. Pickett's Charge is the classic example for the South. Thousands of Confederates marched across an unprotected meadow toward enemy guns on a ridge at Gettysburg, Pennsylvania, an act that William Faulkner saw as resonating in the memory of "every Southern boy." Suicide bombers exemplify a similar commitment to death for the cause. Such death commitments, when remembered, give life to identities, whether they be regional, national, or ethnic-religious.

Vamik Volkan, in a lecture, describes how identity matters in a concrete situation, not in battle but in negotiating peace. As parties negotiate and come close to agreement, the danger of disagreement, of getting stuck on minor differences, accelerates because the parties' identities are threatened. Therefore, one must not press them to embrace a common identity, which they will stoutly resist, but instead pump up their separate identities. This may seem illogical, but it works psychologically, claims Volkan, a psychoanalyst, for it relieves anxiety about loss of identity, freeing the parties to move forward. Identity matters, then, in war and in peace. What about in other fields of action?[9]

Salman Akhtar, a Pakistani psychoanalyst who now practices in Philadelphia, describes numerous instances of ambivalence derived from a split between old and new countries. For an immigrant, for example, "one self-representation might become imbued with male and the other female attributes," and he notes historian Nina Silber's observation that around the end of the Civil War "the North constructed a feminized interpretation of the South that validated the former's superiority." He quotes

Silber further: "In emphasizing Southern helplessness, the Northerners even couched descriptions of Southern landscapes in feminine terms." While Akhtar does not explain why the southerner should resemble the immigrant, the parallel is apparent: the southerner is an outsider within the nation just as the immigrant is. The point is made clear by Tennessee Williams in *The Glass Menagerie*. The mother is a migrant from the Delta to a northern city, St. Louis. The mental illnesses suffered by her children derive in part, one surmises, from this split identity as native of some- where else and resident here, the "here" being a dominant mainstream identity, and the "somewhere else" being a dominated marginal identity. While mental illness need not result, the immigrant (or minority) identity is obviously challenged, and deeply so, as Akhtar discusses, by a split between separate and unequal identities that must be connected or tran- scended. It is this task that psychologically flows from the national frame- work within which the South is defeated, subordinate, marginal. The global framework places the South in a different position—triumphant, dominant, central—on a world stage, whether as part of a powerful na- tion or as heir to a large and rising region. The further question of the psychology of relationships between ethnic or racial groups within this region must now include not only white and black but also new immigrant groups, and their valences too are now defined within a global as well as a regional and national frame. Postcolonial readings of the South should take into account this changed global frame, which, of course, builds on the history of racial and gender relations within a regional identity.[10]

Identity matters because identity is part of a larger entity—region, na- tion, world—and because it rests deep within the individual psyche. The analogy of transference developed above illustrates the connection.

Identity to Action: Ideology

If identity matters, and if southern identity is broadening in a global direc- tion, its energies should be visible in action. One kind of action is political, driven by ideologies, of which conservative and liberal are two tendencies. Either can comfortably join globalism to direct reformism abroad rather than at home or within oneself: foreign policy can emphasize military as-sault or regime change overseas rather than domestic reform. Grounded globalism reminds us of the dangers of imbalance and excess—of un-grounded globalism on the one hand, which can correlate with unethical unaccountability, as in promiscuous outsourcing and narrow unilateral-ism, and of insularity on the other, which can correlate with oppression at home and attack abroad. Attention to local impact is part of grounded globalism, which considers viability at all levels, from local communities to states, regions, nations, and the world. Unthinking quick-fix solutions such as tax incentives (bribes) to corporations to locate locally are a kind of southern hospitality common to many colonized or poor places in the world. Although this practice brought textile plants from New England to the South, and more recently has attracted global enterprises (Mercedes to Tuscaloosa, Alabama, BMW to near Spartanburg, South Carolina, and Honda to the mountains of Tennessee), unfortunately this strategy com-petes with longer and deeper solutions, such as improving infrastructure locally, especially schools and other quality-of-life institutions. According to at least one legislator, the North Carolina senator Ellie Kinnaird, such local features rank higher in corporate priorities than tax incentives; com-munity characteristics remain a crucial concern for global corporations and projects of all kinds. Globalization requires local strength.[11]

Just as community viability, productive diversity, and other positive results do not necessarily come with globalization, neither does liberaliza-tion. The Anglicans and others demonstrate this: so-called conservative Anglicans are joining the global South. The term "liberal" bears examina-tion however. In the case of northern Episcopalians, "liberal" may imply a fairly narrow set of ideological premises—for example, that gay marriage is okay or that opposing abortion is not—and restrictive behavior codes that earn Episcopalians stereotypes as quaint or elitist. The point is not to defend (or condemn) the global Anglican condemnation of gay marriage, ordination of gay or female bishops, or of abortion, nor to celebrate (or denigrate) the liberal Episcopalian support of these positions, or to judge their liturgical differences. Nor is it to defend conservative Anglican secession from the northern liberal Episcopal community, an act eerily echoing Confederate secession a century earlier (though, one hopes, without similarly disastrous consequences.) The point is simply to think globally. So doing, we might recognize that the Anglicans of the global South affirm a broad and deep social fabric rooted in extended kinship and historic social orders and that, whatever limitations and even abuses those orders may impose, particular points of liberal ideology should be evaluated not only in the context of the societies or social circles within which they originate and resonate but also in the context of these wider, more global, but in some sense more conservative orders. In short, a broader liberalism considers specific points in context rather than necessarily adhering to them strictly without regard for context. To be sure, such a broader liberalism—a contextual ethic—is a challenging one that has vexed policy makers ranging from nineteenth-century missionaries who forbade bride-price and beer making to twenty-first-century women's rights and human rights advocates who condemn female incision; in each case, doing the "right" thing seemingly threatens a local social order. When should one consider context and when, instead, should one adhere to seemingly universal and human values?

Reversing the argument from the impact of values on social orders to the impact of social orders on values, one again comes to the question of whether globalization engenders liberalism. Chapter 8 explored permutations linking both liberalism and conservatism to globalism and globalization. One can cite examples both ways. The Anglicans suggest a way that globalism is friendly to a certain conservatism; on the other hand, in the study noted above, Pettigrew found that Germans who identified with the European Union as opposed to Germany were less inclined to violence.[12] Their greater globalism encouraged a certain liberalism. Connections can be found, but one should reject a simple assumption that those who are more global are more liberal.

Theorizing Change

Step back for a moment from experience to theory. How might we think about or theorize the process of stretching meaning and identity to embrace change? During the past century, a line of thinking about religion in social context has evolved, especially from the German scholar Max Weber, who asked so-called questions of *Sinn* (meaning). What is existence? What is meaning? How is meaning part of existence? One can distinguish many levels of, or perspectives on, existence. Three of these are the self, the society, and the culture: personality, social, and cultural systems. Personality systems contain the dynamics of the individual, such as Freud's ego, id, and superego, where superego controls id like a rider on a horse. Social systems also have a hierarchy of control, with values controlling norms, which control groups and roles. Cultural systems exert the highest control, defining the basis of existence, ethical morality, and, ultimately, grounds of being. In this conception, identity is the bridge between person and role, the personal and social systems: who am I as a person in relation to a collectivity? Meaning is given by visions of ultimacy, of what matters most, of what reality is. Who one is and what one does, as well as any of the other entities—how society operates, what are the groups, the norms, the roles—all assume meaning from this cultural configuration that frames them.

Change at any level demands reformulation at other levels and ultimately challenges meaning itself. Take sex toys. According to the *New York Times*, a Texas woman has been arrested for selling and demonstrating sex toys. This is a growing business for women around the country, and it evokes various reactions. A Seattle woman who sells sex toys reports that her husband first forbade her to bring the toys home or reveal to her children or anyone else what she was doing. But after she brought in a large income, she said, "he help[ed] me load the car."[13] In a later article on the topic, the *Times* profiled a woman in Arkansas who is the largest seller of sex toys in the business. The South is reportedly the largest sales region, followed by the West. The woman is intrepid and sensitive, a conduit for information and experience among women in a social setting that is somewhat restrictive. Respected for her integrity, she is nonetheless stigmatized for her work; once a devout churchgoer, she currently stays outside the church doors.[14] Whether it leads to arrest or greedy endorsement or ambivalence, selling sex toys in the South challenges custom, values of proper morality, behavior, and family life. The roles, norms, and meanings that frame them are potentially at stake. Sex or procreation is often the lightning rod or stimulus for such conflictual issues, as we have seen in the Anglican split over homosexuality, but so are other activities. Globalization is one. Antiglobalization protests are usually interpreted at the level of economics and social concerns, but globalization poses serious challenges for culture and meaning also.

Culture can be defined in many ways, but a succinct definition is "shared understandings," and these serve to bestow meaning (as well as define morality) for self and society. Culture can be understood to include many phenomena—language, manners, arts, style of life, codes of ethics— and it is best not to confine oneself to a list of items or to worry overmuch about naming them. Still, what we term "religion" is certainly central to human culture and demands serious discussion. At the same time, mean- ing is bestowed widely and not just by conventional religion. As Brad Weiss argues in a recent paper, hip-hop in Tanzania can bestow "on- tology," what is real, for young Tanzanians. That would without doubt be true for young people elsewhere, including here, as Riché Richardson demonstrates. This is why Michael Dyson, the African American minister and scholar, chose to deliver a commencement address in the language of rap music and why his use of this medium caused such a reaction. Some listeners walked out, and the chancellor condemned the speech; perhaps this reaction contributed to Dyson's later decision to leave the University of North Carolina at Chapel Hill. Like sex toys, rap offends and seduces, in either instance accosting cultural norms and structures of meaning.[15]

Meaning and Opening Up the South

Global citizens and locally rooted ones alike experience loss of anchors, though in different ways. Harihar Bhattarai tells the touching story of his wife Sunita, a Nepalese woman, returning to shop at the mall in Chapel Hill after moving to Raleigh. Though it was far from Nepal, that mall was familiar. While a certain nostalgia is expressed here, a more enigmatic sense is expressed by a Chinese immigrant in a dream (this is the same person who reported another dream in chapter 7). Complex, her dream involves a woman from her youth in China who sells her, in a Chinese dining hall, an Italian sandwich like one she often craves that is sold in a local North Carolina dining hall. The price is discounted, but then the sandwich turns out to lack meat. She leaves the dining hall, wishing never to see the woman again. "I eat the sandwich, thinking no meat is fine too. The taste is not bad. Then I woke up." Whatever the dream means, it does seem to express ambivalences about both her homeland and perhaps her new land: the woman selling the sandwich seems to help her but then cheats her, and the sandwich is less than expected, though not so bad. Less enigmatic but equally ambivalent, perhaps, is the repeated dream of a Japanese war bride. She experiences being pursued by the shadow of her ancestor, as though her migrating to Fayetteville and joining the Baptist church there has angered it.

While confusion and a search for meaning are part of the existential condition, arguably nothing exacerbates this condition more than changing places and, less drastically, perhaps, having one's place changed. Both conditions are apparent among students I teach, who include both "natives," immigrants, and children of recent immigrants. In a undergraduate class, for example, students were from Vietnam, India, Cyprus, Turkey, or of the Hmong community, and others were black, white, and Native Americans who were locals, "Tar Heel born and Tar Heel bred." Immigrants of course share common concerns regardless of origin, as one student of Korean background described in characterizing friends from Africa and Latin America; an obvious concern is simply to adjust to the new place. Natives, too, were experiencing change, partly because of immigrants but largely owing to globalization, which was changing the ground beneath them, reshaping their homeplace. At the extreme, one might wonder if confusion and loss of meaning coming from change is a factor in suicide among young people, which appears to be increasing and can be seen both among immigrants and natives. Durkheim's classic study targets "anomie" (normlessness, confusion about what is right and wrong and even what is) as such a factor.[16]

Fortunately, what globalization takes away, it also gives back. As globalization creates pain, it also offers relief, increasing the repertory of "therapies" and meaning-bestowing resources. Natives reach out to globalized versions of the local, and globals turn to localized versions of the global. This is evidenced among the students as they explore and participate in a spectrum of religions, from Buddhism to Greek or Russian orthodoxy to Scientology. Alice Walker's newest novel, *Now Is the Time to Open Your Heart,* depicts an African American, originally from Georgia, now living in California, who is exploring shamanism, a spiritual practice found from Siberia to South America. Veterans of the Vietnam war in a small Georgia town who met at Alcoholics Anonymous meetings now also meet in a house adapted as a temple and join a veteran who is now a priest reading and reflecting on Taoist teachings that offer advice for living. Realizing that self-seeking is not sufficient, some pursue another kind of global engagement, addressing ethical and political or economic dimensions through involvement in Habitat for Humanity, the human rights movement, and community activism; at least one of the Taoists is also an ecologist.

None of this is peculiar to the South. What is distinctive to the South is its history and culture, including its religious tradition. While that tradition may be hopelessly narrow for some, it may also offer a base for transformations of self and society, potentially resulting in synthesis and coherence and community rather than mere variety. Challenges to older tradition may be poignant, however. A Methodist woman dreams that she, in her choir robe, comes home from church with her daughter to discover many people, mostly Caucasian women, doing tai chi and yoga in her house. They do not realize it is her house. This dream can be interpreted as symbolizing the new energy coming into her life, but the poignancy of this change is expressed in the dream by the fact that the women do not realize they are in the dreamer's house.

Whatever shape the new meanings will assume, it will not be abstract— not philosophy or theology, not theory or policy only. Rather, it will be embodied meaning, grounding and framing. Pluralism, globalism, and force fields locate space and place and their associated identities with consonant actions, struggles, and experiences that at once characterize the South as a place and as an identity, changing and enduring, and connect it to the rest of the world. An example of this in action is Creighton Irons, a white southerner and college sophomore who lived in Jamaica and South Africa and joins blacks and others there and in the United States in composing and performing reggae-style music that comments on race and identity. Another is a Chinese immigrant who has a devoted coterie of tai chi practitioners. Yet another is Pentecostalism, which is at once active, global, and diverse; at a church, I see local whites and blacks, and Latino immigrants together speaking in tongues, raising their hands, running and dancing in the spirit while screens show images of world mission, and a sermon based on Joshua tells of God's promise to Israel as it applies to today's world. These examples and hundreds more that one observes embody globalism by action.

Grounded Globalism

Having explored my three hypotheses and seven-step model in conjunction with identity, ideology, and meaning, I would like to step back and view the whole in terms of our orienting concept, grounded globalism, first considering the context for this concept—the spectrum of theory and practice within which it is positioned—and then exploring implications for viewing the globalizing South.

THEORY AND PRACTICE

Various theories or perspectives debated by academics shape the way we see the world. The main question for readers of this work is what difference each of many points of view might make in understanding the South. Postcolonialism and postmodernism, structural functionalism, and multiculturalism—these are theories, or philosophies. Another set of options might be termed "practices": examples include the standard professions such as law, newer ones such as urban planning, and applications of many of the disciplines, such as anthropology or psychology or economics. We might divide the various approaches into critical, holistic, and practice types, the last of which sometimes interacts with theories.

Postcolonial, postmodern, multicultural, and feminist theorizing share the rubric "critical." All are suspicious of existing power structures because they privilege certain statuses and practices and may conceal realities to do so. Postcolonial perspectives see existing issues as a result of historical but still influential colonial structures; these are real colonial institutions or quasi ones, such as the plantation-based structures of the American South. Postmodern approaches, among other things, hold that who you are shapes what you think and, hence, that reflection about others demands self-reflection as well. Feminist theorizing especially pinpoints gendered structures, revealing how male-centered values shape everything from culture to jobs. Multiculturalism follows a similar approach but pinpoints race or ethnicity as key determinants of values and structures; its emphasis is less on overarching values, ideologies, or legal structures that purportedly define a nation, for example, than on particular ethnic or racial identities within a nation.

Holistic approaches attempt to give a balanced or broad picture, perhaps including power structures and bias but also encompassing general values and beliefs, whether ecological and economic or geographical and historical—whatever factors shape society and culture. "Structural functionalism" names one older kind of holism, the aim of which is to grasp the patterning of something (its structure) and how it works (its functioning). A certain dialectic is apparent in the history of such approaches. Critical perspectives can be traced to Marx, for example, while holistic approaches can characterize entire disciplines, such as anthropology at certain times, and individual synthesizers, such as Talcott Parsons.[17] Holistic approaches were prominent in the mid-twentieth century; critical approaches then surged in efforts to expose inequities submerged by holism. Perhaps a neoholism is emerging to restore consideration of larger patterns.

Practice approaches may combine the critical with the holistic while pointing beyond critique or synthesis to action or intervention, asking,

What can be done? Lawyers can sue, planners plan, social workers heal, policy makers make policy, and leaders lead. The question "What can be done?" exemplifies Occam's Razor in limited analysis and getting on to recommendations and action.

Each approach has its virtues and vices. Critical approaches can reveal eye-opening biases and inequities but may also yield unbalanced, tendentious analysis. Avoiding the fallacy of misplaced concreteness (essentializing, that is, treating as real what humans have constructed), critical approaches often commit what I term the "fallacy of misplaced abstraction," dissolving and reducing identities or beliefs that are real to those who engage them (even if, to critics, those identities and beliefs seem to serve nefarious purposes, such as oppressing and exploiting others). Holistic approaches may conceal questions and issues beneath an illusion of totality: the gods may see everything everywhere, but no human does. Practice cuts to the chase sometimes but can lose sight of the context and background necessary for insight and informed engagement.

My own grounded globalism approach is informed by all three perspectives. Conflicts and issues concerning oppression, whether based in gender, race, ethnicity, class, or other expressions of colonial-like histories and structures, are subsumed here under an overriding issue that is geopolitical and psychological, namely, opposition between a region and a nation and its impact on the issue of global identities. The three trends I have identified (dualism to pluralism, opposition to integration, and place to force field) attempt to sum up this pattern, drawing on multiple sources and experiences and obliquely implying practice, or ways of thinking about and perhaps shaping the region.

I follow critical approaches, accepting many of their insights and trying to incorporate these in my analysis, and I hint at implications for practice but stop short of making recommendations. One corrective is for readers to test my assertions against their own experience and action and then to work out any practice implied by what they learn. Grounded globalism, then, includes an effort at holistic summing up, touching global and local counterpoints and forces: it frames our region globally while drilling down locally, even into identities and subjectivities, space, and relationships. This perspective has guided the analyses of the South in this book.

PERSPECTIVES ON GLOBALISM

Focusing more sharply on globalization, we encounter theoretical issues similar to the general ones just noted. Ronald Niezen, in his excellent synthesis, identifies two main orientations to the question of "cultural identity in the age of globalization." One is "rational utopianism," the other, critical theory. Rational utopianism combines what I termed above "holism" and "practice." It attempts to grasp globalization by systematic thinking and then applying methodical reforms. The human rights movement is an example. Critical theory, by contrast, rebels against rational utopianism, suspicious that its systematic thinking and its methodical reforms are tools for oppression by the ruling order. Critical theory proceeds by exegesis of whatever theories or practices are followed, revealing flaws and destructive consequences but also, perhaps more fundamentally, origins: where are the theories and practices coming from, and what assumptions, statuses, and motives do those theories and practices express?[18]

As noted, analyses of oppressive power structures ranging from dominant states to capitalistic corporations to patriarchal social orders illustrate the critical approach. Antiglobalization protests are such critiques translated into activism, and, from a critical viewpoint, systematic plans for reform are often suspect, exemplifying rational utopianism or, worse, cynical tyranny. Niezen sees such critical-theory approaches, in the extreme, as nihilism, an uncritically critical dismissal of any design for living, a "leap into unfaith." Niezen also notes a dialectic, in that as many places press to sustain their distinctiveness, a global culture valuing distinctiveness emerges; particularism becomes universal. In fact, he argues that particularistic "fundamentalists" are less open to negotiation about differences than universalists—a suggestive if debatable point, suggestive because many of us favor sustaining localized identities until they assume a fundamentalist fervor followed by oppression of other differences. The

Taliban's treatment of women is a notorious instance that could illustrate Niezen's analysis, as are tribalisms that insist on female circumcision. The issue of the Confederate flag—claimed as an expression of honorable heritage by some, perceived as a symbol of oppression by others—is conceptually similar. In the end, one might favor Niezen's utopian rationalism over particularisms, since, whatever their globalist simplifications imposed on distinctiveness, the schemas are at least formulated and debated widely. Grounded globalism attempts to unite strengths of both values.

Between globalization and its seeming antithesis, place or a sense of place, one can trace themes similar to those defined by Niezen. Globalization is welcomed in different guises by different people. Capitalists welcome it as a free market process, intellectuals see it as an emancipating force to break down boundaries, and rational utopians deplore its abuses but propose their own global plans (extending human rights, for example) to correct them. All these trends would seem to override place. In cultural and literary postmodernist and postcolonialist critiques, for example, traditions of place and community are "deconstructed," shown to be constructions designed for all kinds of purposes—commercial, oppressive, public relations.[19] The so-called sense of place is shown to derive from a complex process that may result in a romanticized illusion, a sham with unsavory foundations. Less critical and more celebratory is cosmopolitanism, which urges us to be aware that everyone is creole, a mix of many global influences, and to celebrate that.

Emancipating as these critiques and celebrations may be, sober commentary finds that territory is needed for government and community; space is not so easily dismissed. This is especially true in times of conflict. Terrorists or guerilla movements retaliate when foreign armies occupy their space, as in Iraq or Palestine or, a century ago, during Reconstruction in the U.S. South. Nor is being a "traitor" taken lightly, as suggested by the cases of John Walker Lindh, the American who fought with the Taliban, or Charles Robert Jenkins, the North Carolina soldier who escaped to North Korea during the Korean War: Lindh is in prison, and although the army eventually pardoned Jenkins, when he returned to North Carolina for a visit to his ninety-year-old mother—his first visit home in half a century—a neighbor refused to shake his hand, stating that he had defiled his honor and allegiance to his country.[20]

Space becomes "place," that is, a location for identities of significance. Recognizing both the forces of globalization and the importance of place, the EU's committee on regions has worked out a middle strategy, affirming place—regions within or across nations—as a vehicle for launching economic and social development while acting as a locale for shared culture and identity.[21] In a twist on this strategy, Italy has instituted a practice that would seem at first to affirm globalism and deny attachment to place: it has declared that Italians living abroad should now elect their own representative to the national parliament. This measure recognizes globalism: some four million Italian citizens live outside Italy. But it also recognizes groundedness, in that the expatriates remain citizens, and citizenship is a requirement for representation. In fact, a leading candidate for the position lives in the United States but maintains and frequently visits his household in the village where he grew up. He tells a story about his American grandson, who picked fruit from trees the man's own grandfather had planted in their village garden in Italy; when the man explained this heritage, the grandson responded, "Awesome."[22]

Grounded globalism is a middle strategy. Accepting the insights of critical theory, of cosmopolitanism, and of globalism, grounded globalism hews to the abiding premise that despite the erasure of boundaries and the redefinition of space as an intersection of global forces described in chapter 5, certain attachments to place remain, and despite attachments to place, place, too, changes as it becomes an intersection of global forces. Grounding and globalism work together.

Perspectives on the South: Historical and Global

The South is commonly viewed in limited ways. It can be seen as a slave-based economy and society that has moved through Jim Crow and civil rights toward greater equality but still retains old hierarchies. The South can be seen as an oppositional society that moved through secession and reconstruction toward reunification with the nation. It can be seen as a patchwork of subcultures—Native American, African American, Anglo American, now Asian American and Latino American—or as a diverse society in terms of gender roles or class and occupation. The South can be seen as simply the South: here it is, just as it was, backward, conservative, hot, and humid. These aspects are the leitmotif for much commentary on the South, and they interweave with our story too, but we accentuate the global theme and its intersection with identity, which sums up much of these histories and circumstances. Who knows? Maybe the global intrusions will be swallowed up like the cars and trucks that dot the countryside and are covered with kudzu (itself a global intrusion); maybe the new South will turn out to be just an old South. But the global aspect will be at least as important as air conditioning and the resulting loss of the front porch.

The South, then, can be viewed as a prisoner to its history, a product of its "peculiar institution," slavery, and, more broadly, of its political economy, sometimes perceived as colonial, then postcolonial. Southern culture, whether literary or civic, is then seen as—and reduced to—a result of that history. Such a historical perspective may take a "critical" turn, deconstructing southern institutions and culture by tracing them to suspect motives and oppressive ruling classes, or it may take a celebratory turn, glorifying what has been achieved, or it may combine both. Whatever valence is placed on the South, positive or negative or both, a historical approach "historicizes," that it, shows that given ways of life, past or present, result from particular circumstances, and hence must be seen relative to those circumstances or contexts.

Such an approach is essential, of course, but others are also relevant. The French anthropologist and philosopher Claude Lévi-Strauss asserts, "As we say of certain careers, history may lead to anything, provided you get out of it." [23] He reminds us that the historical viewpoint is itself the product of a particular history, largely of recent modern Western history, and that a more pervasive worldview for humans in world history and around the world is a kind of totemism, conceptual schemes that classify and order our reality in terms of symbols. Without arguing for Lévi-Strauss's viewpoint in its particulars, I note his general implication: that is, the possibility of cultures being viewed in ways different from the historical. This possibility leads to a question about the South: must the South be viewed entirely in terms of its particular history, and, if not, what are alternative ways to view it? There are at least two alternatives, both of which have to do with globalism. One global view is from inside, from the South's own viewpoint, and the other from outside, viewing the South as part of a general perspective on cultures of the world. Both perspectives lead us to see the South not only in relation to its "peculiar" history but also as part of the wider world.

From inside: how can a society view itself in relation to the world? Cultures may espouse and claim authority for universal philosophies or viewpoints. The French anthropologist and philosopher Louis Dumont describes French culture as doing this.[24] India and China resemble France in their universalist ambitions. A map in Delhi shows "further India," which is most of Asia depicted as lines emanating from India as a flow of influences ranging from Hinduism to Buddhism—and properly so, since the mother civilization should enlighten the provinces. China, over its millennia of empires, including the present one, has seen itself as a central civilization subordinating minorities and regions, whether Tibetan or Uigurs and hill tribes, and has considered Chinese civilization as globally instructive. In the United States, it seems that New England and the North had similar universalist pretensions—espousing democracy, the individual, free enterprise, and freedom generally; examples range from philosophers such as Ralph Waldo Emerson to businessmen such as Henry Ford and John Rockefeller to politicians such as Theodore Roosevelt, with his bully pulpit; these were northern leaders who led in shaping a distinctive American perspective, economy, and political structure. While the North spoke as a representative of the United States, the South has been treated as the peculiar region, a product of its own history, especially of slavery, meriting at best a charming provincialism and not a universal vision or a claim to a historical and experiential ground for such a vision. In fact, if the South spoke, for itself or to others, its history would nullify its message, whereas the message of the North gains resonance from its celebrated history—the pilgrims and religious independence, the Revolution and political freedom, and winning the Civil War to initiate the end of slavery. Of course, individual southerners represented humane values: Thomas Jefferson wrote the Declaration of Independence, Jimmy Carter upheld human rights, and Martin Luther King Jr. stood for freedom. Such figures conveyed their viewpoints, however, either by transcending their histories—they were not speaking as southerners—or by struggling against them. The histories of their region were not seen as affirming these values except in a dialectical way, perhaps: despite the context, the character is admirable, as with Atticus Finch in *To Kill a Mockingbird,* the great novel by the Alabama writer Harper Lee. What is offered, then, by a global identity that is also grounded? Grounded globalism offers the opportunity to accept regional history, not to disown or discount it but to build on it through engagement with global contexts.

From the outside: what do we see when we view the South in a global framework, as one among many societies of the world? Global comparison shows that throughout its history the South has shared much with elsewhere. Many features that make the South seem odd in contrast to the North are actually commonplace globally; it is the North that is odd. Examples range from specific sayings or customs that may derive from British roots to patterns that are part of similar histories elsewhere or simply broadly human. Plantation-based societies and values are quite similar among the Junkers of East Germany, Russians, Americans of the South, and plantation dwellers elsewhere.[25] Dualisms dividing minorities and majorities in the American South are likewise paralleled globally. Alistair Sparks emphasized similarities between the southern United States and South Africa, and one can point to similar convergences from Southeast Asia to North Asia to Latin America.[26] More broadly, the struggle of women in the South is similar to those of women in many traditional societies. The Grimke sisters stood out in the South as did Kartini in Java, the sisters as southerners who opposed slavery, Kartini as a noblewoman who espoused feminism; that is, they spoke as courageous spokeswomen within patriarchal contexts. So-called "radical feminists" who inhabit cosmopolitan and urban domains have encountered resistance not only in the South but in other contexts as well, such as that of Islam, and the "steel magnolia" fusion of a certain femininity and commitment to women's rights is also common globally. Other similarities between the American South and the world include the experience of defeat, which many have noted is an experience common to most societies, but not to the northern United States. Global comparison, then, shows commonalities between the South and other societies and ways that the South is, if not exactly like other societies, part of global processes that others share. Through rethinking from within and without, the South can move toward redefining its identity in a global framework. That step can lead to assertion of a global identity, to "I am global" or to "We are global!"

The act of explicit global identification—of asserting or enacting a global identity—is part of southern identity, now emerging or reemerging as part of globalization, and this, too, it holds in common with other places. "I am a world citizen," declared Tomy, a Javanese youth, "not just an Indonesian." His statement disturbed his two aunts, who had come of age during Indonesia's struggle for national independence. They identified with Indonesia's assertion of a quasi-national–regional identity much as southerners identified with their own secession and assertion of national identity, and the resonances are similar. Tomy's statement implies, "I am not merely a part of a part, a former colony, a new nation, a particular region or culture; I am part of a whole, a world citizen."

Is a world citizen the same as a human being? Yes, in the sense that one claims identity with humanity and rejects relegation to a peculiar history and place. No, in the sense that this global identity refers to a particular wave of world forces and contexts. The global identity is, in the southern context at least, not merely global but a grounded global identity that is in dynamic relation with localized identities, regional or national. Such an identity is, therefore, not an essentialized abstraction (human) nor is it a reduced historical product, such as postcolonial. Instead it is at once grounded in a region, a locale, and engaged in a process, globalization, that is itself grounded—shaped by and shaping myriad locales while pressing in directions that transcend them.

Grounded globalism affirms and seeks embodied connectedness to locale. Globalization was greeted, joyfully or fearfully, as a disembodied connectedness—as creating markets without borders, electronic world consciousness, and cosmopolitanism. Globalization would be a magic carpet, zooming everyone everywhere in an Eden of prosperity. But as globalization has become more familiar, and as we encounter it up close, its embodied features loom negatively as job loss, immigrants' traumas, violence, pollution, and global warming. Are positives present, too, in the groundings? Yes, creative synergies join world and locale, not only economies and technologies but also new cultures, new citizens, and new identities and meanings. Old dualisms are dissolved by new pluralisms—paralyzing oppositions cured by broadening globalisms—and our sense of place is energized by new vectors and force fields. These trends challenge current frames of meaning, to be sure, but new frames emerge, expressed in myriad symbols and forms in varied cultures and communities—still inchoate, perhaps, but promising.

"Float like a butterfly, sting like a bee" was Muhammad Ali's aphoristic strategy for boxing, logically analogous to "Think globally, act locally": the floating is global, the sting local. The Goethe quotation used as an epigraph for this chapter makes a similar contrast between thought (consciousness and conscience) and action.[27] Ali's image is, however, more vivid and more synergistic, since both the floating and stinging are performed by the same person, and such synergy is the essence of grounding globalism. Grounding globalism was jokingly sloganized by an acronym, "Globgro," when we began using the notion to guide the work at our center for international studies located at the University of North Carolina at Chapel Hill; Globgro sounded like fertilizer, and we did fertilize initiatives that were grassroots as well as global. Examples included an outreach program that involved several hundred K–12 schools in the state; Carolina for Kibera, which works with a slum in Kenya; Students for Students, which enabled pupils in Zimbabwe to go to school; and our USAID-funded work that helped Eritrea develop its national university. Our center was one of two in the U.S. South to win support and recognition as a "national resource center" for international studies, largely on the basis of our work spurring international curricula and language study, yet we also connected to locales. We created, with neighboring Duke University, a Rotary-funded peace and conflict center that trains negotiators and is tied into the Rotary network grounded in community clubs and projects in some 140 countries; our graduates are working in Darfur and in other conflicted areas and with the United Nations and other agencies in Geneva, at the World Bank in Washington, and throughout the world. Within the university, we worked with academic and professional schools in areas ranging from public health to law and social work while infusing international content into liberal arts courses. To house such programs, we constructed a new building in a way that grounds our global work in a local context both physically and fiscally. This building is one of a constellation of others that complement its global focus with local ones: the Sonja Haynes Stone Center for Black Culture and History, the Love House and Hutchins Forum for southern studies, and the Coates building, built by Albert and Gladys Coates to house their institute for work with local government. A remarkable feature of the funding of our building is that most of it comes from a bond package supported by the citizens of the state. That bond, which supports a range of construction at university and community colleges, was voted in, at a ratio of seventy to thirty, in all one hundred counties. That support is a moving confirmation of grassroots commitment to education generally, and with respect to our building it symbolizes a certain grounding of globalism.

Academic programs and buildings are obviously small parts of the larger process of grounding globalism, but the examples mentioned illustrate a synergy between global and local that is rare in universities but can fruitfully energize efforts at all levels, from academic to governmental to private enterprise and community. Efforts like those mentioned suggest a few simple rules of thumb, which, as director of the Center for International Studies at the University of North Carolina, I once formalized in a memo (and implemented) as "nine steps to internationalize a university." The first step is to create and commit to a global identity—a concept and mission of a global or international university—and the ninth step is to raise money for projects. These nine steps, and the seven-step model linking regionalism to grounded and globalism, like the twelve steps of Alcoholics Anonymous, share a combination of commitment to some "higher power" or force and pragmatic action and grounding—"one day at a time." To pursue grounded globalism in any sphere—academic administration, community life, economic development, or regional culture—do such things. Envision and commit to the global vision. Embrace a global identity. Allow that identity to infuse and energize; stretch, go out on a limb, take chances. Doing these stretching moves, keep in touch with grounds. Do not be hypnotized by technologies and bureaucracies that seem magical solutions but often wrench action from context, ideal from ground. Plan but also engage. David Harvey offers similar advice for those who would build a place-based society:

1. The market model is inadequate; you can't ignore the market but society has to be more;
2. communitarianism is also inadequate; you can't build a society from local volunteers; you also need hardball politics, national, regional, global;
3. no single authoritarian solution will suffice;
4. technology alone offers no solution; and
5. urban remodeling or other architectural arrangement of just space is not enough; you must also work with social realities.[28]

These are all points that some southerners instinctively grasp, and they have resisted any single reform—urban renewal, computerizing, bottom lining, communes, big government, a great intellectual plan, including many isms—from feminism to Marxism, conservatism to liberalism—all of which disregard history, tradition, and place.

Yet simple resistance won't work; locales will be plowed under and bulldozed over. Offense provides the best defense. Float and sting. Think and act globally and locally. Make the ghost of the Confederate cavalryman Jeb Stuart ride again as a hologram merging global visions, diverse identities, and pragmatic projects.

Our "model" introduced the figure of the clown-god Semar. Semar is ground, the earth, but also global, a cosmic god. Magically, he is a catalyst for all chemistries; when he is added to a burden, his weight is subtracted instead of added, for it lightens the load by creating new energy. So it can be, and often is, with expanded horizons such as globalism, but Semar never forgets his roots. "Where does Semar come from?" goes a Javanese question. "Cowhide," is the answer, or "Old man Mangun," denoting either the material from which the puppet-figure for Semar is made or the peasant maker. Arjuna, the idealist noble warrior, cannot defeat the monster, the red-faced raksasa who personifies evil lust. Semar, Arjuna's servant, commands him, "Set me on fire." Sadly, Arjuna does so, and Semar's earthly form burns up, freeing his god form, which defeats the monster. Some such dialectical mythology must inspire and ignite our encounters with global forces, igniting energies from the ground that sustain the elevated and expansive.

Our responses to globalization polarize. Some decry the negatives; others celebrate the positives. Another polarization is less obvious but equally apparent: some "think globally," and others "act locally," to again evoke the slogan. Developers, cosmopolitans, and visionary theorists "think globally." Ecologists, preservationists, and practical organizers "act locally." The first group builds, travels, imagines, and plans; the second sustains, preserves, negotiates, and protests. The first group wants to change the world, the second to save it. Yet these seemingly polarized and conflicting tendencies can be, and often are, part of a single process, since globalization and globalism are necessarily grounded in place and experience. Obvious as this is, much thinking and acting emphasizes the one or the other but not the synergy. Either one focuses on globalization as a world process—economic, political, or cultural—or one focuses on local concerns. Some concept is needed to summarize, in a word or two, this connectivity between them: thus, "grounded globalism," a simple short-hand for a complex process. Hopefully, this notion encourages creative interplay between approaches that are often separated and polarized.

The U.S. South is classically ambivalent about abstract ethics of the kind rooted in the Puritan Protestantism that shaped New England and American ethical reformism. When Lee chose Virginia over the nation, he demonstrated that orientation, as perhaps he did also in reportedly stating, as president of Washington College, that there is only one rule of conduct: "Be a gentleman (and do your Duty)." While conservative in the implication that one should sustain the order, including the place in which it is grounded, this worldview is also organic. It refuses to give power to an abstraction, insisting on a synergy with place and ongoing existence.[29] Lee was Anglican; Jimmy Carter is Baptist. Carter is more willing to name ethics, such as human rights, and to oppose in the name of such liberalism the doctrinal conservatism of neoconservative ideologues, but he too has affirmed a strong attachment to place—specifically Plains—while work-ing globally in a vehemently mission-focused way. Lee and Carter were both trained as engineers within a military institution, and both man-ifested liberal ethics. These were tinged with conservative loyalties for Lee and with disappointment for both, Lee sacrificing for the Lost Cause, Carter for the causes of human rights, world peace, and betterment, which often seem lost. Carter's liberalism joins his globalism in a style often un-palatable to fellow southerners, especially those of conservative ilk, but it does light a lamp for those who search for a synergy among the globalizing and liberal within a context that is in part southern.

Could the South offer anything distinctive to the process of global-ization? The refusal to accept ungrounded abstraction and the quest to ground globalism in place-based context is one offering. Transcendental ethics have fostered destruction of the earth by following the pattern of defining a mission, then exploiting a place to achieve it. Grounded ethics affirm the value of place, including the earth inhabited, not merely the earth as biosphere; environmentalists themselves express a transcenden-tal ethic when they dislodge the loggers to save the owl, just as developers do when they dislodge communities to build a dam. The South is hardly a model for sustainable development or other synergies between global and ground, but it offers seeds for such flowering.

If grounded globalism summarizes an anchoring and embodiment of a global process, then the South epitomizes that grounding in its struggle to transcend regional oppositionality and dualism while retaining a regional identity and also defining its own global identity. The South captures and is captured by global forces, as are many other locales. Other souths, but also norths, face the question of how to sustain grounding in the face of globalization. To join that process is to seize a global identity in a southern context—a dangerous, promising, and perhaps emancipating endeavor.

Notes

Chapter One. A Model

1. The psychoanalyst and peace negotiator Vamik Volkan, of Charlottesville, Virginia, calls a group's "unresolved mourning," the persistent memory of a defeat and the traditions by which a group memorializes hatred for its former enemy in such a way that it reignites after generations, a "chosen trauma." See Volkan, *Blood Lines*, esp. chaps. 3 and 4. Volkan, of Cypriot Turkish origin, observes that in his psychoanalytical practice with Virginians the American Civil War lurks in the background.

2. Cash, *The Mind of the South*, 219. Obviously the extent of passion for the Lost Cause varies with time and context. One reenactor of Civil War battles told me that he kept on hand both Union and Confederate uniforms, joining whichever side needed soldiers. However, another reenactor owned a large horse on which he literally reenacted Jeb Stuart's charges and would not have considered joining the

other side. Reenactments are international, drawing soldiers, often Confederate, whose strenuous efforts to travel to the battlefields from as far away as Australia, indicate a certain passionate interest from afar.

3. Woodward, *Burden of Southern History.*

4. Davis, "World War I."

5. Dick Gordon, "Beginnings and Endings," *The Story,* heard on WUNC-FM Radio, June 20, 2006.

6. United Nations High Commission for Refugees, www.unhcr.org/basics.html.

7. Erikson, *Childhood and Society,* 326–402. Volkan carries this approach forward, applying psychoanalytical insights in actual negotiation internationally. Karina Korostelina also treats issues of regional and national identity within a social psychological framework. See her "Dynamics of Social Identities," and her chapter, "Readiness to Fight in Crimea," in Peacock, Thornton, and Inman, *Identity Matters.*

8. Freud, *Civilization and Its Discontents,* 72.

9. "To explore this model empirically" does not imply deduction of facts from theory. This model, or "theory," has grown out of experience and is now used as a rough guide to interpret those and further experiences. The point of this essay is not to verify a model or theory but to illustrate and explore ideas drawn from experience to encourage further ideas. On the distinction between verifying and generating theory, see Glaser and Strauss, *Discovery of Grounded Theory.*

Chapter Two. The South as/in the World

1. Dabbs, *Who Speaks for the South?* 3.

2. Ibid., 4.

3. Neff, "Home of the Double-Headed Eagle."

4. The following statistics are taken from MDC, "State of the South 2004," and from Guillory and Quinterno, "A Southern Snapshot" and "Notes to Southern Data." MDC and Guillory and Quinterno define the South as fourteen states, including the former Confederacy and the bordering states of Kentucky, Oklahoma, Texas, and West Virginia.

5. Despite relatively low Hispanic growth rates of 54 percent in Texas and 70 percent in Florida, the absolute increase in the Hispanic population in these two states was greater than in all other southern states combined. Removing Texas from the South reduces the proportion of Hispanics under age twenty from 17 percent to 8 percent, and increases the proportion of blacks from 25 percent to 30 percent.

6. Woodward, "Search for Southern Identity," esp. 6–7.

7. Landon Thomas Jr., "The Yin, the Yang, and the Deal," *New York Times*, June 27, 2004.

8. Knight, interview.

9. Editor's comment, *Georgia Engineer*, June/July 2004, 5.

10. Reed, *My Tears Spoiled*. Reed's "three souths" essay was included in the program for the 1996 Olympics in Atlanta. It is noteworthy that this excellent distillation of essential points about the South chooses not to emphasize global connections, even in the Olympic context. This was true also of performances and exhibits designated "southern" that were located at and sponsored by the Atlanta Olympics; these did include cultural variety, such as Tex-Mex and zydeco music, yet it was portrayed not as global (reflecting world forces) but as multicultural within a regional place, with emphasis on the South as a special place. Commentaries on the South as a special region are, of course, innumerable, and most emphasize its differences from the North rather than its relations to the wider world. Surveying a variety of perspectives on the South, Vernon Burton reported in "The South as Other," about Thomas Jefferson's 1785 comparison of the northerner and the southerner: "the northerner never eats what he can sell, while the southerner never sells what he can eat." Burton adds another perception, that southerners kill others, while northerners kill themselves: that is, the South is a homicidal culture, the North a suicidal culture. This pattern was elucidated by Sheldon Hackney, among others. See "Southern Violence." Classic and recent commentaries on the South as a region distinctive within a national context include Cash, *Mind of the South;* Daniels, *Southerner Discovers;* Wyatt-Brown, *Southern Honor*; Ayers, *Promise of the New South*; Cobb, *Away Down South*; and Crowther, *Gather at the River*.

On early periods, see Shields, *Civil Tongues*; J. Greene, *Imperatives*; and Moltke-Hansen, "Regional Frameworks" and "Southern Genesis." Moltke-Hansen depicts three individuals who personify the evolution of southern identity. The first, Wells, a Scot, came to Charleston in the eighteenth century, was a successful merchant, and then returned to Scotland. The second, Louis Remy Mignot, was the son of a Frenchman but was born in Charleston in the early nineteenth century and remained there until he went to Europe as a teenager to study painting. Returning to New York City, he was a leader in the Hudson Valley school until the Civil War, when he declared himself sympathetic to the Confederacy. Ostracized, he left New York and went to Europe, where, after finding some success as an artist, he was killed as a result of another war. The third, Trescott, was a Charlestonian who came of age at the time of the Civil War and defined a full-fledged southern identity. Wells, then, retained a global identity, Mignot developed a southern identity resulting in his death, and Trescott completed the evolution of that regional identity. See also Manthorne, *Landscapes*. Rister's "Carlota, A Confederate Colony in Mexico," and expatriate Confederate communities such as that in Brazil remind us of the earlier global expanse of southern culture.

See also Peacock, Watson, and Matthews, *The American South*, and Peacock, "South in a Global World"; Cobb and Stueck, *Globalization*; and Carlton and Coclanis, *The South, the Nation*. See also Clinton and Conway, "Mercedes and the Magnolia."

These and other works provide excellent context for my analysis, and I am indebted to them. Especially, they analyze the economic and demographic patterning of the South since its beginnings and through its history. What I add is a contemporary, cultural, and psychological exploration—how this history is unfolding in recent times as economic and demographic forces interact with cultural and psychological ones to shape identity. Different emphases among us can be noted. For example, Coclanis and Carlton emphasize that the South has always been global; I agree but simplify the history into a three-phase pattern moving from an early globalism to a regional focus to the current globalism. As another example, in his monumental work on southern identity, Cobb joins me in noting "oppositionality" as a key feature (see page 219, where he cites me and Sheldon Hackney on this point), but he does not pursue as far as I do the argument that global forces can transform this oppositionality; this is because he terminates his history at the advent of the recent global era. In his volume on globalization in the South, on the other hand, he does not focus on identity but on demographic and economic forces (as indeed do Watson, Matthews, and I in our volume that appeared in the same year Cobb and Stueck's). Cobb's work on identity and his work on globalization both appeared in 2005, each emphasizing one of the concepts; whereas this work (as well as earlier ones, such as Peacock, "South in a Global World") attempts to join them.

11. Douglas, *Natural Symbols*.

12. Chakrabarty, *Habitations of Modernity*; Appadurai, "Global Ethnoscapes"; Hannerz, "Scenarios for Peripheral Cultures," and *Transnational Connections*; Friedman, *The World Is Flat* and *Lexus and the Olive Tree*; Castells, *End of Millennium*.

13. C. Taylor, *Modern Social Imaginaries*. See Calhoun's *Critical Social Theory* and *Nationalism*; Putnam, *Bowling Alone*.

14. This Silesian representative also participated in the hundredth anniversary of the Polish Ethnological Society in Breslau (now Wroclaw), an active folklorist as well as congressperson.

15. Editorial, "UNC, the State, the World," *Charlotte Observer*, December 28, 1998; Chris O'Brien, "Grads Urged to Think Globally," *Raleigh News and Observer*, December 21, 1998.

16. To observe and then report anecdotally may seem simple and, indeed, is considered an art at which the South excels. Anecdotes are praised by Walter Benjamin as follows: "The constructions of history are comparable to military orders that discipline the true life and confine it to barracks. On the other hand: the street insurgence of the anecdote. The anecdote brings things near to us spatially, lets them enter our life . . ." (Convolute S ["Painting, Jugendstil, Novelty"], S1a, 3, 545, quoted in Matthews, "Fragments of an Anarchist Modernism"). Fundamental is the distinction between verification and generation of a theory. Anecdotes were and are demeaned ("anecdotal evidence") by old-style positivists as an inadequate basis for verification ("one swallow doesn't make a summer") but can be fruitful in generating ideas and in exploring their connection to experience. I have found this to be true in oral presentations on the topic of this book: anecdotes stimulate listeners to share their own anecdotes, to interpret or reinterpret mine and theirs and, in this way, to further the creation of a theory or develop a perspective.

The stories I tell represent a large background of documentation, fieldwork, and experience, and do not stand alone as isolated incidents. For example, I cite a monograph on the Primitive Baptists reporting on years of research; this is epitomized in the text by one anecdote. I list several dozen student reports on religious groups (and could have listed many dozens more) which are illustrated in the text with a single sketch of a spiritualist meeting I observed.

A problem is that anecdotes, precisely because they do "enter our life," evoke multiple interpretations. A partial solution to this problem is to frame anecdotes and observations with whatever argument they illustrate and evaluate that argument in light of further anecdotes and observations as well as for its logical coherence and wider context and implications. In short, see parts within wholes.

On anthropological observation and interpretation, see Peacock, "Method," and Needham, "This Is a Rose. . . ."

Chapter Three. From Oppositionality to Integration

1. Anderson, *Imagined Communities*. See also Peacock, Thornton, and Inman, *Identity Matters*.

2. According to the terms of surrender at Appomattox Court House, neither "side arms of the officers nor their private horses or baggage" were to be surrendered.

3. Steedly, conversation with author.

4. "Campus Life: Harvard; Confederate Flags Prompt Protests and Debates," *New York Times*, March 24, 1991, http://select.nytimes.com/search/restricted/article?res=F20616F93F5B0C778EDDAA0894D9494D81 (accessed 6/28/2006).

5. R. Richardson, *Black Masculinity*.

6. Schneider, "Region and Regionalism"; McKinnie, "When Regionalism Meets." Preston asked Michigan students to indicate where in the United States good and bad English is spoken; 138 of 147 indicated the South for "bad English" (Preston, "Non-standard English"). See also Preston, *Perceptual Dialectology*. An experiment by my daughter Natalie, then an eleven-year-old student in Chapel Hill, suggested the low status of southern accents even in a southern town. Asked by her teacher to conduct a telephone survey about disarmament, she decided to use her normal southern accent for half the calls and a British accent, recently acquired in England, for the other half. Respondents more frequently agreed to talk to her, talked longer, and, she felt, more seriously when she used the British accent.

7. Seymour, *A Village Voice*, 35.

8. Wilson, *Baptized in Blood*. Wilson documents a Confederate identity, which, however, is now struggling to survive. See Alan Finder, "In Desire to Grow, Colleges in the South Battle their Roots," *New York Times*, November 30, 2005. The article notes that the University of the South, at Sewanee, Tennessee, is considering removing the name "South" after a Chicago consultant advised that this name would repel students from outside the South and that the University of Texas may remove statues of Confederate leaders while students raise money for sculptures honoring Barbara Jordan and Cesar Chavez. On the other hand, another article about the difficulties of the Sons of Confederate Veterans notes a black supporter of the heritage; John Elliston, in "Sheetheads vs. Bedwetters," *Independent*, April 28, 2005, 4, depicts this twist on southern identity: African American supporters of Confederate heritage. Elliston has a photograph of H. K. Edgerton, a black Civil War reenactor, marching at a January 2000 Confederate flag rally in Columbia, South Carolina, with a sign that reads, "Heritage not hate." Also see Davis, "Southern Soldiers"; R. Richardson, "Blackness and the Global South"; Hersh, "Negotiating 'Community'"; and Conway, "Globally Competitive South." Davis shows how Confederate identity was still strong

among southerners who were, therefore, ambivalent about fighting for the Union in World War I. Richardson depicts sectionalism enduring among black rappers, and Hersh and Conway explore the impact of global forces.

9. Hassett, "Episcopal Dissidents, African Allies." Cabell King, a physician from North Carolina working in Rwanda with an Episcopalian hospital, suggests that the Anglican bishop of Rwanda and the South Carolina and other Anglicans who accepted his authority affirmed a true apostolic succession and sustained viable relationships. He felt that this was also true of their relationships to Bishop Tay of Singapore. I have heard concern about the Anglican move from liberal Episcopalians, especially clergy, and this concern is justified by instances of local churches split between liberal and conservative wings, including a Durham, North Carolina, church that is reportedly close to death after the rector and rector's wife "went conservative," thereby driving away the liberal majority in the congregation.

10. Michael Massing, "Bishop Lee's Choice," *New York Times Magazine*, January 4, 2004, 34.

11. For a more detailed account, see Peacock, Jones, and Brooks, "Gotokaca Drive," 166–74. For an Indonesian perspective, see "Amrai Targetkan Jual 500 Pesawat N-250/270" [Amrai (American Regional Aircraft Industry) Targets Sales of 500 Airplanes 250/270], *Kompas*, June 27, 1996.

12. Baker, *Columbus Celebrates the Millennium*, 178.

13. Peacock, Watson, and Matthews, *American South in a Global World*; Smith-Nonini, "Federally Sponsored Mexican Migrants"; Striffler, "We're All Mexicans Here"; Willis, "Voices of Southern Mill Workers"; and Subramanian, "North Carolina's Indians."

14. Peter Applebome states in *Dixie Rising* that the economy of the southern United States exceeds that of 94 percent of the world. John Reed has noted the South's leading role in starting new enterprises, such as Fed Ex and CNN (commencement address, "A Great Southern University," UNC–Chapel Hill, December 20, 1997).

Reportedly, Charlotte is the second largest city in bank assets in the United States after New York City. Compare this situation with that of the late nineteenth and early twentieth century centuries, when most major corporations, as in the oil and steel industries, for example, were begun in the Northeast, while the South was undergoing reconstruction. Compare also the pre–Civil War period, when more than half of U.S. exports were from the South, largely cotton. A notable post–Civil War effort at industrial development in the South is the steel industry in Birmingham, Alabama. Emiliano Corral, in "Casting Steel," analyzes how and why this regional industrialization, somewhat comparable to that in Monterrey, Mexico, was crushed by a national company, U.S. Steel.

15. Jim Brown and Donald Rollins, "It's Five O'clock Somewhere." EMI April Music Inc., Sea Gayle Music, R. Joseph Publishing, Warner-Tamerlane Publishing Corp. 2003. Performed by Alan Jackson. Featuring Jimmy Buffett. *Alan Jackson's Greatest Hits.* Vol. 2. BMG Entertainment, Arista Nashville. 2003.

16. Chakrabarty, *Habitations of Modernity*; Appadurai, "Global Ethnoscapes"; Friedman, *Lexus and the Olive Tree*; Appiah, "No to Purity." Jon Smith and Deborah Cohn richly illustrate border-crossing between the southern United States and Latin or South American culture and literature (see *Look Away*). For an argument against unanchored cosmopolitanism and for commitment to a territory, see C. Taylor, "Why Democracy Needs Patriotism," a response to Nussbaum, "Patriotism and Cosmopolitanism." Taylor is at once a distinguished philosopher and an active participant in Canadian government.

Chapter Four. Dualism to Pluralism

1. Cole, *Gender Talk*. At the 2006 King banquet, the diversity/global theme was extended by the distribution of an award to students who created a dialogue between Jews and Muslims.

2. *Raleigh News and Observer*, January 18, 2004.

3. Prince, *The Southern Part of Heaven*.

4. J. Mathews, "At the Head of the Class."

5. "AAPA Statement on Biological Aspects of Race"; Creighton Irons's musical "Soul Notes" deconstructs the concept of race musically and theatrically (see http://www.unc.edu/cirons); "American Anthropological Association Statement on 'Race,' "; Hernstein and Murray, *The Bell Curve*.

6. Chinese immigrants to the South and elsewhere in the United States interviewed by Jun Wang and Hong Zeng seemed more instrumental and less rooted here than this Indian family. One man, for example, aspired to retire, close his restaurant, return to his home village in China, live off his earnings, and play mahjong all day. On the other hand, a young woman I know who came to the United States as a young girl from Taiwan has married a local non-Chinese man and has a child. Her best friends are non-Chinese. Chinese and other Asian immigrants who have grown up in the South often speak with southern accents and melt into the culture, becoming cheerleaders and sorority sisters as well as successful professionals and community leaders. (Jun Wang and Hong Zeng interviewed

Chinese immigrants to the United States, 2003–4, as part of the author's research on the globalizing South).

7. Ray, *Highland Heritage*; Vo, "Vietnamese Experience in North Carolina."

8. Writings on southern slavery that offer useful background information include Joyner, *Down by the Riverside*, and Genovese, *Roll, Jordan, Roll*. Toni Morrison's *Beloved* probes the psychology of slavery. On civil rights, see Branch, *Parting the Water*. An important recent study is Boger and Orfield, *School Resegregation*.

9. Long was a keynote speaker at "The Multicultural South," a symposium held at the University of North Carolina–Chapel Hill, April 8, 1989, under the sponsorship of the Institute for Arts and Humanities and chaired by James Peacock and Ruel Tyson. Further comment by Long is in Barkley, "E Pluribus Unum"; Harding, "Toward a Darkly Radiant Vision." A counter-theme is not only diversity outside the black-white dichotomy but also diversity within black identity. See R. Richardson, "Gangstas and Playas." Richardson shows divisions between southern and northern black identities expressed in southern black hip-hop. Gabrielle Foreman further shows complexities of identity in African American literature in "Righteous Discontent." Foreman asserts that "the lack of an explicit racialized articulation within the novel invites the substitution of Johnson's own racial identity for her characters [Clarence and Corrine]. By using racial indeterminacy, Johnson issued a challenge to her nineteenth-century readers; for some, her use of racial simutextuality produces a stark re-corporealization of 'polluted Blackness' into white readers' own putatively pure and carefully policed notion of racial and bodily identity" (30). Thomas C. Parramore, finally, reminds us of an early multiculturalism among African Americans in "Muslim Slave Aristocrats."

10. Complexities of southern diversity are not detailed here. These include Native American, African American, and European tribes and ethnic groups, as well as Jewish, Greek, and other immigrants. Historians, archaeologists, and ethnographers provide rich documentation, as do the groups themselves. On the fusing of Jewish and southern culture, see Evans, *The Provincials*, and Ferris, *Matzoh Ball Gumbo*. On German Baptists, see Thompson, *The Old German Baptist*. At UNC–Chapel Hill, resources include the Laboratories for Archaeology, currently directed by Vincas Steponaitis; the Southern Historical Collection, currently directed by Tim West; the North Carolina Collection, directed by Robert Anthony; and the Sonja Haynes Stone Center for Black Culture and History, directed by

Joseph Jordan. See also the *Proceedings of the Southern Anthropological Society,* and M. Richardson, *Culture, Ethnicity, and Justice.* Raymond Fogelson reports in "Native American Communities" that it was predicted in 1893 that the Chero- kees would disappear by 1993; instead, we have casinos on reservations, one more instance of flourishing diversity.

Chapter Five. Southern Space

1. Blount, quoted in Cobb, "We Ain't Trash No More! Martyn Bone, in *The Postsouthern Sense of Place,* thoroughly and insightfully lays bare senses of place for the South that are much more nuanced than the sort evoked by Blount. My ar- gument focuses on the impact of global forces on whatever senses of the South are commonly experienced, and Blount captures a prominent one. The basic premise that cultural frameworks, spatial or otherwise, are constructed is fundamental.

2. Testimony of Anita S. Earls, Director of Advocacy, University of North Car- olina Law School Center for Human Rights, before the U.S. Senate Judiciary Com- mittee, May 16, 2006, pp. 1–9.

3. Anderson, *Imagined Communities,* 7, 15.

4. On the cosmopolitan world, see Chakrabarty, *Habitations of Modernity,* and *Provincializing Europe*; on the world as a global marketplace, see Friedman, *Lexus and the Olive Tree.* See also Escobar, "Culture Sits in Places," 139–74. As Terry Eagleton notes in "Culture Wars," "It is with ecological politics above all that the links between the local and the global, a Romantic pietas of place and an Enlightenment universality, have been most firmly resoldered" (16). I do not survey here the vast literature on space and place, especially as it has been treated by geographers such as David Harvey and others, though I am informed by their approaches (see Peacock, "Space into Place"): Here I illustrate through direct experience and observation.

5. Castaneda, *The Teachings of Don Juan.*

6. Tate, "Ode to the Confederate Dead."

7. Michael Jordan's paper on his experience in the 1984 Olympics is on ex- hibit at the Jordan memorabilia room at the Wilmington, North Carolina, city museum.

8. Some points noted here are elaborated in my "Olympics as Ritual" (unpub- lished paper, 1984). This paper was based in part on an anthropological study of the 1984 Olympics funded by the Wenner Gren Foundation for Anthropolog- ical Research. John MacAloon chaired the "team," which included anthropolo-

gists Bruce Kapferer from Australia, Roberto DaMatta from Brazil, and Don and Leah Handleman from Israel, as well as me. Michael Jordan, who was playing on the U.S. basketball team, also served as my research assistant and wrote a paper about his experience as part of an independent study course (Anth. 99–11) at UNC–Chapel Hill. I also attended the 1976 Olympics in Montreal and the 1996 Olympics in Atlanta.

9. On the bowl games, see Peacock, "Traditionalism and Reform," 207–16.

10. Hunter, *Unto These Hills*; Green, *The Common Glory*; Moe, Parker, and McCalmon, *Creating Historical Drama*.

11. Neville, *Kinship and Pilgrimage*, 35–39. Global trips are added to local ones, however. Marcie Sherrill claims that "road trips along Highway 78 with stops at Stuckey's are long gone" in favor of trips to explore the meaning of Mary Magdalene amidst the art of Florence ("Hit the Road," 136). On the other hand, *Dothan* magazine (September–October 2005) features the revival of downtown, and *Wiregrass Living* magazine (September–October 2005) features weddings—local themes in a less urbanized area.

12. Bone, *Postsouthern Sense of Place*, 64–74. See also Romine, *Narrative Forms*. While these works clearly inform my own, I have critical perspectives on them as well, basically that they essentialize the South in a preglobal form so that either they do not treat a postglobal situation or they term it "postsouthern," as though region dies when it changes. My thesis is that it does not; instead, it "grounds globalism."

13. See T. Berry, *The Great Work*.

14. Marks, *Southern Hunting*.

15. *Newsweek*, August 2, 2004, 21.

16. Ray, *Highland Heritage*, 19–21, 27–30, 31, 165.

17. Many of these ideas can be found in H. Greene, "Ecozoic Ideas for 2002."

18. Peacock, "Home Is Where."

19. McDonough, *The Hannover Principles*. William McDonough is the Charlottesville, Virginia, architect who composed these ecological principles to govern EXPO 2000, held in Hannover, Germany.

Chapter Six. Meaning

1. Weber, *The Protestant Ethic*, 94–154.

2. Beyer, *Religion and Globalization*; Vásquez and Marquardt, *Globalizing the Sacred*.

3. Hill, *Southern Churches in Crisis*; D. Mathews, *Religion*; Schweiger and Mathews, *Religion*; Hinson, *Fire in My Bones*; M. Richardson, *Being in Christ*; Thompson, *Old German Baptist Brethren*; White and White, *Religion*.

4. See O'Brien, *Conjectures of Order*.

5. Peacock and Tyson, *Pilgrims of Paradox*. See also Peacock, *Muslim Puritans*, and *The Muhammadijah Movement*.

6. Chappell, *A Stone of Hope*.

7. Flannery O'Connor's Haze Motes appears in the novel *Wise Blood*.

8. Hassett, "Episcopal Dissidents, African Allies." See also Hassett, *Anglican Communion in Crisis*.

9. Interview with Billy Graham, *Parade*, October 20, 1996. Missionary spirit is expressed in this prayer: "We lift up our Brazil Team as they worship this morning in Belo Horizonte and prepare for the tasks that are before them. Bless the church in Teofoli Otoni as they prepare for the coming of the team and the project that they will do together. Through this shared ministry, we are reminded of the scope of your redemptive work all over the world." The Reverend Wayne Helms, June 19, 2005, United Methodist Church, Dothan, Alabama.

The diversity of religious groups in the Triangle area of North Carolina is illustrated by the following field studies by undergraduate students in Religion and Anthropology (Anthropology 142), a course I taught during spring 2005 at UNC–Chapel Hill: Habitat (Lauren Gentry), Tibetan Buddhist group (G. Duarte), Sacred Fire, a group led by an apprentice under a Huichol shaman (Doug Blessington), Ivanwalt (Katie Gamache), YMCA—which was opened to Africans in 1853, in England, to Asians in 1875, to native Americans in 1879 (Katherine Sebastian), the Unitarian Church—which includes pagan and Buddhist groups (Gretchen Stanton), Alcoholics Anonymous (Blair Blackard), the preacher in the "pit," the university's main outdoor gathering area (Cassidy Shelley), the Society of Friends and ministry in national parks ranging from the Virgin Islands to the Blue Ridge mountains (Lauren Monroe), Sufis at Unity Church (Julian Royce), Catholic and Jewish relations (Suzanna Cavendel), Hillel activism (Anna Thompson), AME Zion Church in Carrboro, North Carolina, and the process of adopting a Guatemalan child, his new brother (Aaron Ratliffe), a local Episcopal church, polarized over the ordination of a gay bishop, and its conservative rector, who became filled with a charismatic spirit (Jennie Christian), Alpha Pi Omega, a Native American sorority apparently founded in North Carolina in 1924 (Deidre Rainwater), Occultforums.com and Campus Crusades (Matthew Shores), Hinduism (Julie Easton), SKS—Self Knowledge System, www.infidels.org, and www.raptureready.org (Chloe Plum), New Hope Presbyterian, AME Zion, and Karen immigrants from Burma (Kelly Haven), Primitive Baptists (Eddie Huffman), an Indian protestant church and a multicultural protestant church (Reena Matthew). This is only a sample of living religions that students and I have studied in the southern region, largely the Raleigh-Durham area.

Many world religions, as reported, for example, in Morris, *Religion and Anthropology*, are represented by these local groups. Religious variety in this South is more like that in a global city such as Singapore than in the historic South as depicted in Schweiger and Mathews, *Religion*, though, of course, the basic variants reported there remain the dominant ones in terms of number of adherents.

Further useful sources include Lawrence, *New Faiths, Old Fears*, and Ray, *Southern Heritage on Display*. An abiding issue is always that of studying belief, since "studying" something detaches one from engagement with it, whether that something is a distant tradition or one's own. See Peacock, "Belief Beheld."

10. Stewart, conversation with the author, August 2006. Stewart is probably quoting from Jeffery, "The Principles of Healing."

11. Rice, "Remarks at the Southern Baptist Convention."

Chapter Seven. Subjectivities

1. *The Rose*, a newsletter published in Athens, Georgia, and edited by Joyce Rockwood Hudson, connects Jungian discussions of dreams and related matters centered in Episcopal churches with other organizations around the South.

2. Quoted in Reid and Marr, *Perceptions of the Past*, 219–48.

3. Anderson, *Language and Power*, 241–70.

4. Sassen, *The Global City*.

5. Zahner-Roloff, "Dreams in Black and White." See also Peacock, "Dreams and Globalization"; Yamada, "Like My Husband's Shadow"; and Dream: Community Art Project 2005, April 7–May 27, Chapel Hill Public Arts Commission, http://www.communityartproject.org. On the question of whether dreams are nonsense or valid expressions of insight, see Mark Solms's "Freud Returns," in which he offers neurological evidence consonant with psychoanalytical clinical use; the essay also excerpts the dissident view. A forthcoming synthesis is Whitehead, "Neo-Psychoanalysis." Therapists of varying persuasions—Freudian, Jungian, transactional—continue to use dreams as deep sources of insight into unconscious themes, and students and lay people report and interpret dreams in relation to global and other themes when invited to do so.

6. The exhibits were photographed and remain displayed in a virtual gallery on

the Internet (http://www.dream.andrewross.com/). The *Chapel Hill News*, the local weekly newspaper, ran images from the project throughout its run, and the exhibit inspired at least one evening of talk radio discussion (http://www.wxyc.org/dreams/). See also http://orangepolitics.org/2005/04/dreams-on-display/.

7. This gamelan, a magnificent ensemble of percussive instruments built in Java, was purchased with expertise from the musicologist Sarah Weiss, with funding from a local donor and the center for international studies, and has been directed by Ethan, a musicology student coming from Auburn University in Alabama who is currently doing research in Java.

8. The film version of Frazier's book stars Nicole Kidman as a heroine who has moved from Charleston, South Carolina, to the mountains and from ladylike literary and musical accomplishments of that lowland city to hardscrabble farming in the highland frontier. Her character compares with Vivien Leigh's Scarlett O'Hara, who was also forced to do farm work to survive on her plantation, Tara. In *Gone with the Wind*, it is Rhett Butler who is the Charlestonian, a swashbuckling blockade runner rather than a lady. Transitions from the earlier to the later book and film suggest changes in popular images of the South in the 1940s compared with those of the early twenty-first century—preserving elements of the resourceful but ladylike heroine while moving beyond the plantation mythology to a historicized frontier-mountain hero whose poignantly romantic individualism, however, ends tragically. Vivien Leigh, who played Scarlett, was British; Nicole Kidman, who played Alba, the *Cold Mountain* heroine, is Australian (now residing in Nashville); while Rhett was played by Clark Gable, from Pennsylvania, and Inman by Jude Law, an Englishman. Julia Roberts, who is from Georgia, was reportedly coached by a dialect expert from Brooklyn on how to speak southern, and Reese Witherspoon seems to do fine with a British accent as Becky Sharp in *Vanity Fair*. Combinations and permutations of place of origin of actors and fictional characters is another facet of global culture to explore elsewhere.

9. Davis, conversation with author, Chapel Hill, N.C., June 18, 2006.

10. D. Smith, *Cuba Night*; Wright, *A Short History*.

11. See O'Brien, "Appreciation of the South"; Woodward, *Burden of Southern History*; and Smith and Cohn, *Look Away!* For a comparison of southern accounts of the Civil War, especially by women, and Indonesian reports of their analogous war and occupation, see Peacock, "Suffering, History"; a longer, unpublished, version was later written with Marilyn Grunkemyer. Faust, "Clutching the Chains." See also Peacock, "South in a Global World."

12. For information on Lomax's Global Jukebox, see Naimark, "Alan Lomax's

Multimedia Dream." A part of the Global Jukebox is published in *Wayfarer*, the CD-ROM edited by Burton, Herr, and Finnegan that accompanies Burton, *Computing in the Social Sciences*. Southern music is itself global: for example, Bobby Simmons, a black man from Montgomery, Alabama, impersonates Elvis internationally, and Japan has a bluegrass band called Rosine (for Bill Monroe's hometown), reachable via yamada@yamada-vet.com. On visual art in the South, see Cunningham and Craig, *Crowns*, and Wilder, "Seeing Eye to Eye." Jordan Matthews High School in Siler City, North Carolina, displays photographs by students from varying cultures who shared self-representations. On visual arts in the South, see Poesch, *Art of the Old South*, and Kennington, *Contemporary Mythologies*. "The Debutantes," a painting by Dale Kennington (b. 1935 in Savannah, Georgia) at the Wiregrass Museum of Art, in Dothan, Alabama, illustrates diversity as a theme in southern art. On folk art, see Patterson and Zug, *Arts in Earnest*.

13. Davis, conversation with author, June 2006, Chapel Hill, North Carolina.

14. Daniels, *Dreaming Your Way to Creative Freedom*.

15. Beyer, *Religion and Globalization*.

Chapter Eight. Politics

1. See also, Hackney, *Magnolias without Moonlight*, which includes Hackney's essay on identity and elaborates his perspective.

2. Hackney interviewed by Janet Langhart Cohen.

3. Dorothy Holland, Donald Nonini, and Catherine Lutz chaired "Local Democracy . . . An Uncertain Future?," a conference held at the Kenan Center, UNC–Chapel Hill, March 2–3, 2001. The conference explored how activists operate at the grassroots level, focusing on particular issues, often outside elite or central institutions. In his keynote address, "Activism and Private Lives," Craig Calhoun emphasized the importance of local siting for action. In "Who Will Speak for the Common Good: Local Activism in North Carolina," Holland analyzed Laurel Valley Preservation and Development, Inc., and described how localized ecology in a North Carolina community gave way to external interests such as skiing and the Heavenly Mountain Resort (a Buddhist retreat). Local people are trying to prevent the community from being overrun. They want to preserve the post office and school, both formerly in a WPA building. Lutz commented that people in Fayetteville see politics as a vehicle for wealth and power, not as an avenue for democratic participation. See also Lutz, *Homefront*, and Holland and others,

Local Democracy. A key civil rights issue is addressed by Boger and Orfield, in *School Resegregation.*

4. Chappell, *A Stone of Hope,* 140.

5. Fox, *Watching the English,* 354.

6. See Dörner, *The Logic of Failure,* for an exploration of some of the reasons why in "complex situations" prudence and an appreciation of unintended consequences outperform simple problem-solving and reliance on overarching single principles.

7. "New Strategies for Southern Progress," a conference held by the Center for American Progress (http://www.americanprogress.com) and the Center for a Better South (http://www.bettersouth.com), at UNC–Chapel Hill, February 24–25, 2005), with Ferrel Guillory, chair. Speakers included Hodding Carter III, Senator Howard Lee, Governor William Winter, Governor Roy Barnes, Senator Sam Zamarripa, Elaine Jones, Dave "Mudcat" Saunders, John Podesta, and Andrew Brack. The panel "Rethinking the Role of the Faith Community" included Representative David Price, the Reverend James Evans, the Reverend Maria Teresa Palmer, and Dr. Daphne Wiggins. See also McKibben, "The Christian Paradox." The epigraph from "Mudcat" is a comment he made during a discussion at this conference. David "Mudcat" Saunders is described as a "Democratic political operative from Virginia" and a "proud and partisan Democrat who touts the virtues of Franklin Delano Roosevelt's New Deal and Lyndon Baines Johnson's Great Society, two hallmarks of 20th century American liberalism. Just don't hang the L-word around his neck. 'It's a cuss word in the South,' said Saunders. . . ." (Jim Nesbitt, "When Did Liberal Become a Bad Word?" *Raleigh News and Observer,* May 21, 2006).

8. Chambers, "Fifty Years after Brown."

9. Lawrence, *Defenders of God,* 10; Beyer, *Religion and Globalization.*

10. Hönnighausen, Frey, Peacock, and Steiner. *Regionalism.*

11. J. Smith, *When the Hands Are Many.*

12. Conversation with Harriet Fulbright, 2003.

13. Conversation with Marion Oettinger Jr., approximately 1975.

14. A Nike seminar was taught by Richard Andrews, Nick Dido, and James Peacock at UNC–Chapel Hill in spring 1998.

15. Black, *Rise of Southern Republicans*; Black and Black, *The Vital South*; Carter, *From George Wallace*; Applebome, *Dixie Rising.*

16. A notable but failed effort to form a party between the conservative and

liberal parties was the social reform party led by the Roy Jenkins, Shirley Williams, William Rogers, and David Owens in Great Britain in 1981. The Texan Ross Perot attempted an in-between party in the United States in the next decade.

Conclusions

1. James, "A Certain Blindness."

2. http://www.universarium.net/missingLink.html (accessed 6/29/2006).

3. See Rittenberg and Bennet, *Man Who Stayed Behind*. Gary Rivlin reports on Rittenberg after his stay in China in "A Long March from Maoism to Microsoft," *New York Times*, December 5, 2004, sec. 3.

4. http://www.cdc.gov/about/ourstory.htm (accessed 6/25/2006).

5. Solms, "Freud Returns."

6. Frank Rich, "Saving Private Englund," Arts and Leisure, *New York Times*, May 16, 2004. Englund allegedly tortured Iraqi prisoners while Lynch was rescued from Iraqi captors.

7. http://www.apolloalliance.org/ (accessed 6/25/2006).

8. Pettigrew, "Social Identity Matters."

9. Volkan, "Large Group Regression." See also Volkan, *Blind Trust*, upon which the lecture was based.

10. The quotes and discussion here are from Akhtar, "A Third Individuation," 1057–58. See also Akhtar, *Immigration and Identity*.

11. Conversation with author, Chapel Hill, N.C., 2003.

12. Pettigrew, "Social Identity Matters."

13. Mireya Navarro, "Arrest Startles Saleswomen of Sex Toys," *New York Times*, January 20, 2004.

14. Senior, "Bible Belt Woman."

15. Weiss, "Hip Hop in Tanzania"; R. Richardson, "Hip-Hop"; "Some U. of N.C. Graduates Walk Out on Commencement Speech," *Chronicle of Higher Education*, 1/10/1997. http://chronicle.com/che-data/articles.dir/art-43.dir/issue-18.dir/18a00804.htm (accessed 6/25/2006). The day after the speech, I defended it in an interview conducted on the street by a TV team; I argued that its message was cogent.

16. Durkheim, *Suicide*.

17. See Parsons, *Theories of Society*. Though Parsons is stereotyped as a structural functionalist poorly adapted to understanding conflict and change, I found his overarching framework useful even in explosive circumstances. An early ex-

ample was my *Rites of Modernization*; this treated class conflict, gender ambiguity, and other social dynamics distilled by narrative symbols and apparently still addresses relevant issues in Indonesia, as suggested by a recent translation and reviews.

18. Niezen, *A World Beyond Difference*.

19. A useful example of examining the South in its colonial or postcolonial aspect was "The American South: Colony or Empire?" conference of the Southern Intellectual History Circle, Charleston, South Carolina, February 2004. Speakers and participants included Patricia Yaeger, Richard Godden, Manisha Sinha, Jonathan Smith, Deborah Cohn, Scott Romine, Steven Stowe, David Shields, Robert Bonner, Jane Dailey, Charles Joyner, and Francois Furstenberg. The keynote lecture was by John Matthews. The Southern Intellectual History Circle, begun by Michael O'Brien, the St. George Tucker Society, and other primarily history-oriented groups have provided crucial insights and scholarship on the changing South, especially for a nonhistorian and nonspecialist in the South such as me.

20. Jim Nesbitt, "Forty Years Later, Jenkins Back Home," *Raleigh News and Observer*, June 15, 2005. Other examples of the importance of territoriality are reviewed in Peacock, "Memory and Violence."

21. See Peacock, "Space into Place," which surveys much discussion by geographers on space; Harvey, *Spaces of Capital*, and *The New Imperialism*; Low and Lawrence-Zuniga, *The Anthropology of Space*; Joseph, *Against the Romance*; and Rees, "Regions, European Integration." See also, on the South, Polk, "Walker Percy's," Hönnighausen, "South and the Spirit," Goldfield, "Recasting Southern History," Hoelscher, "Memory's Region," and Norman, "A Tale of Two Regions," and, on regionalism generally, Peacock, "Retrospect and Prospect."

On the South as constructed and deconstructed, see Romine, *Narrative Forms*; Bone, *Postsouthern Sense of Place*; Kirby, *Media-Made Dixie*; Jones and Donaldson, *Haunted Bodies*; Yaeger, *Dirt and Desire*; and Fox-Genovese, *Within the Plantation Household*. These works, possibly excepting the last one, share a critique of older perspectives on the South, whether in space, race, or gender.

See also Wilson and Ferris, *Encyclopedia of Southern Culture*. Huge sales of this work attest to a certain enduring sense of place or perhaps of hope and nostalgia for it, which may be the same thing. Exports of the South abroad and imports to the South from abroad, culturally as well as commercially, also sustain a certain sense of that place. See, for example, Ward, *Britain and the American South*, and Fowler and Abadie, *Faulkner*.

22. National Public Radio interview, *All Things Considered,* January 12, 2006.

23. Lévi-Strauss, *The Savage Mind,* 262.

24. Dumont, *German Ideology.*

25. Peter Kolchin touches many themes and sources in comparative views of the U.S. South in *A Sphinx on the American Land.* Comparative analyses of aspects of the South and Java include Peacock, "Secular Ritual," various papers in proceedings of the Southern Anthropological Society, 1972–2005, and others, for example, Peacock, "Ethnographic Notes on Sacred and Profane Performances," which compares Javanese theater and Primitive Baptist ritual, and Peacock, "Fundamentalisms Narrated." With primary area training and fieldwork in Southeast Asia but residing in the southeastern United States, I have found comparison of the two geographic areas suggestive, though of course such a comparison always involves comparing oranges (or bananas) and apples. See also Mathewson, "Plantations and Dependencies"; Coclanis, *Shadow of a Dream*; Corral, "Casting Steel"; and Carlton and Coclanis, *The South, the Nation.*

26. Sparks, *Mind of South Africa.*

27. Quoted by Weber, p. 151. Goethe and Thomas Jefferson shared nearly identical life spans and a vision of grounded globalism; both were writers, administrators, and scientists localizing their visions in provinces, Weimar or Charlottesville.

28. Harvey, *Justice, Nature,* 435–38. (I condense his argument drastically to summarize it in this way.) Issues in application are discussed in Peacock, "Action Comparativism," and in Basch and others, *Transforming Academia.*

29. In this and in other allusions to Robert E. Lee, I do not presume an identity between the man and the myth. However, I attempt to characterize images of Lee and perspectives attributed to him that have come down as part of a certain kind of tradition in the South, and it is this cultural stream that I explore in suggesting global impacts. Arjuna, the aristocratic military hero of the *Mahabharata,* never existed at all, but that does not stop the myths and images about him from shaping a culture from India to Indonesia to Hari Krishna renditions throughout the world.

Bibliography

"AAPA Statement on Biological Aspects of Race." *American Journal of Physical Anthropology* 101 (1996): 569–70.

Akhtar, Salman. *Immigration and Identity: Turmoil, Treatment, and Transformation.* Northvale, N.J.: Jason Aronson, 1999.

———. "A Third Individuation: Immigration, Identity, and the Psychoanalytic Process." *Journal of the American Psychoanalytical Association* 43 (1995): 1051–84.

"American Anthropological Association Statement on 'Race.'" May 17, 1998. http://www.aaanet.org/stmts/racepp.htm (accessed 11/3/06).

Anderson, Benedict. *Imagined Communities: Reflections on the Origin and Spread of Nationalism.* London: Verso, 1983.

———. *Language and Power: Exploring Political Cultures in Indonesia.* Ithaca: Cornell University Press, 1990.

Appadurai, Arjun. "Global Ethnoscapes: Notes and Queries for a Transnational Anthropology. In *Modernity at Large: Cultural Dimensions of Globalization*, 48–65. Minneapolis: University of Minnesota Press, 1996.

Appiah, Kwame Anthony. "No to Purity. No to Tribalism. No to Cultural Protectionism: Toward a New Cosmopolitanism." *New York Times Magazine*, January 1, 2006, sec. 6.

Applebome, Peter. *Dixie Rising: How the South Is Shaping American Values, Politics, and Culture.* New York: Times Books, 1996.

Athas, Daphne. *Entering Ephesus.* New York: Viking, 1971.

Ayers, Edward L. *The Promise of the New South: Life after Reconstruction.* New York: Oxford University Press, 1992.

Baker, Pamela. *Columbus Celebrates the Millennium: An International Quest.* Montgomery, Ala.: Community Communications, 1999.

Barkley, Alice. "E Pluribus Unum: Who Are the Many? What Is the One? An Interview with Charles Long." *Touchstone* 22 (1993): 7–11.

Basch, Linda G., Lucie Wood Saunders, Jagna Wojcicka Sharff, and James Peacock, eds. Roberta Jill Craven, consulting editor. *Transforming Academia: Challenges and Opportunities for an Engaged Anthropology*, Arlington, Va.: American Anthropological Association, 1999.

Beatty, Paul. The White Boy Shuffle. Boston: Houghton Mifflin, 1996.

Benjamin, Walter. Convolute S ("Painting, Jugendstil, Novelty"). *The Arcades Project.* Cambridge, Mass.: Belknap Press, 1999. Quoted in Matthews, "Fragments of an Anarchist Modernism."

Berry, Thomas. *The Great Work: Our Way into the Future.* New York: Bell Tower, 1999.

Beyer, Peter. *Religion and Globalization.* London: Sage Publications, 1994.

Black, Earl. *The Rise of Southern Republicans.* Cambridge: Belknap Press of Harvard University Press, 2002.

Black, Earl, and Merle Black. *The Vital South: How Presidents Are Elected.* Cambridge: Harvard University Press, 1992.

Black, Merle, and John Shelton Reed, eds. *Perspectives on the American South.* New York: Gordon Breach, 1981.

Boger, John Charles, and Gary Orfield, eds. *School Resegregation: Must the South Turn Back?* Chapel Hill: University of North Carolina Press, 2005.

Bone, Martyn. *The Postsouthern Sense of Place in Contemporary Fiction.* Baton Rouge: Louisiana State University Press, 2005.

Branch, Taylor. *Parting the Water: America in the King Years, 1954–63*. New York: Simon and Schuster, 1989.

Burton, Orville Vernon, ed. *Computing in the Social Sciences and Humanities*. With a CD-ROM, *Wayfarer: Charting Advances in Social Science and Humanities Computing*, edited by Orville Vernon Burton, David Herr, and Terence Finnegan. Urbana: University of Illinois Press, 2002.

———. "The South as Other, the Southerner as Stranger." Paper presented at "The South," the fifth annual program of the Illinois Program for Research in the Humanities, University of Illinois–Urbana, April 3–5, 2003.

Calhoun. Craig J. *Critical Social Theory: Culture, History and the Challenge of Difference*. Oxford: Basil Blackwell, 1995.

———. *Nationalism*. Minneapolis: University of Minnesota Press, 1997.

Cao, Lan. *Monkey Bridge*. New York: Viking, 1997.

Carlton, David L., and Peter A. Coclanis. *The South, the Nation, and the World: Perspectives on Southern Economic Development*. Charlottesville: University of Virginia Press, 2003.

Carter, Dan. *From George Wallace to Newt Gingrich*. Baton Rouge: Louisiana State University Press, 1999.

Cash, Wilbur J. *The Mind of the South*. New York: Knopf, 1941.

Castells, Manuel. *End of Millennium*. Malden, Mass.: Blackwell, 1998.

Castaneda, Carlos. *The Teachings of Don Juan: A Yaqui Way of Knowledge*. New York: Ballantine Books, 1968.

Chakrabarty, Dipesh. *Habitations of Modernity: Essays in the Wake of Subaltern Studies*. Chicago: University of Chicago Press, 2002.

———. *Provincializing Europe: Postcolonial Thought and Historical Difference*. Princeton: Princeton University Press, 2000.

Chambers, Julius L. "Fifty Years after Brown: The Biggest Challenge Is Yet to Come." Commencement address, University of North Carolina at Chapel Hill, May 9, 2004.

Chappell, David. *A Stone of Hope: Prophetic Religion and the Death of Jim Crow*. Chapel Hill: University of North Carolina Press, 2004.

Clinton, Jim, and Carol Conway. "The Mercedes and the Magnolia: Preparing the Southern Workforce for the Next Economy." 2002 Report on the Future of the South. Southern Growth Policies Board, http://www.southern.org.

Cobb, James. *Away Down South: A History of Southern Identity*. New York: Oxford University Press, 2005.

————. "We Ain't White Trash No More!" In *The Future of the South*. National Humanities Center, American Issues Forum I, Occasional Papers 1. Research Triangle Park, N.C.: National Humanities Center, 1995. Reprinted in *The Southern State of Mind*, ed. Jan Norby Gretlund. Columbia: University of South Carolina Press, 1999.

Cobb, James, and William Stueck. *Globalization and the American South*. Athens: University of Georgia Press, 2005.

Coclanis, Peter. *The Shadow of a Dream: Economic Life and Death in the South Carolina Low Country, 1670–1920*. New York: Oxford University Press, 1989.

Cole, Johnnetta B. *Gender Talk: The Struggle for Women's Equality in African American Communities*. New York: One World/Ballantine Books, 2003.

Conway, Carol. "A Globally Competitive South: Under Construction." Paper presented at "Navigating the Globalization of the American South," a conference held at the University of North Carolina at Chapel Hill, March 3–4, 2005.

Corral, Emiliano. "Casting Steel: Region and State, Mexico and the American South, 1910–1920." PhD diss., University of Chicago, in preparation.

Crowther, Hal. *Gather at the River: Notes from the Post-Millennial South*. Baton Rouge: Louisiana State University Press, 2005.

Cunningham, Michael, and Craig Marberry. *Crowns: Portraits of Black Women in Church Hats*. New York: Doubleday, 2000.

Dabbs, James McBride. *Who Speaks for the South?* New York: Funk and Wagnalls, 1964.

Daniels, Jonathan. *A Southerner Discovers the South*. New York: Da Capo Press, 1970.

Daniels, Lucy. *Caleb, My Son*. New York: Lippincott, 1956.

————. *Dreaming Your Way to Creative Freedom*. New York: Lincoln, 2005.

Davis, David. "Southern Soldiers, American Nationalism, and Foreign Wars." Paper presented at "Navigating the Globalization of the American South," a conference held at the University of North Carolina at Chapel Hill, March 3–4, 2005.

————. "World War I, Literary Modernism, and the U.S. South." PhD diss., University of North Carolina at Chapel Hill, 2006.

Dörner, Dietrich. *The Logic of Failure: Recognizing and Avoiding Error in Complex Situations*. New York: Basic Books, 1997.

Douglas, Mary. *Natural Symbols: Explorations in Cosmology*. New York: Random House, 1970.

Dumont, Louis. *German Ideology: From France to Germany and Back*. Chicago: Chicago University Press, 1994.

Dunbar, Anthony, ed. *Where We Stand: Voices of Southern Dissent*. Montgomery, Ala.: New South Books, 2004.

Durkheim, Emile. *Suicide: A Study in Sociology*. Routledge, 2002.

Eagleton, Terry. "Culture Wars." In *The Idea of Culture*, 51–86. Oxford: Blackwell, 2000.

Erikson, Erik. *Childhood and Society*. New York: Norton, 1950.

Escobar, Arturo. "Culture Sits in Places: Reflections on Globalism and Subaltern Strategies of Localization." *Political Geography* 20 (2001): 139–74.

Evans, Eli. *The Provincials*. Chapel Hill: University of North Carolina Press, 2005.

Faulkner, William. *Absalom, Absalom!* New York: Random House, 1936.

———. *As I Lay Dying*. New York: Vintage Books, 1930.

———. *The Bear*. In *Three Famous Short Novels*. New York: Vintage Books, 1961.

Faust, Drew Gilpin. "Clutching the Chains That Bind: Margaret Mitchell and *Gone with the Wind*." *Southern Cultures* 5, no. 1 (1999): 6–20.

Ferris, Marcie Cohen. *Matzoh Ball Gumbo: Culinary Tales of the Jewish South*. Chapel Hill: University of North Carolina Press, 2005.

Foreman. Gabrielle. "Righteous Discontent, or Bobbing and Weaving: Home Protection, Literary Aggression and Religious Defense in the Life and Writings of Amelia E. Johnson." Paper presented to the Race, Nation, and Diaspora Group at the National Humanities Center in Cary, N.C., March 10, 2003.

Fogelson, Raymond. "Native American Communities in a Globalizing World." Paper presented at "Sustaining and Reimagining Community in a Globalizing World," Southern Anthropological Society Meeting, Chattanooga, Tennessee, March 10–13, 2005.

Fowler, Doreen, and Ann J. Abadie. *Faulkner: International Perspectives*. Oxford: University of Mississippi Press, 1982.

Fox, Kate. *Watching the English: The Hidden Rules of English Behavior*. London: Hodder and Stoughton, 2004.

Fox-Genovese, Elizabeth. *Within the Plantation Household: Black and White Women of the Old South*. Chapel Hill: University of North Carolina Press, 1988.

Frazier, Charles. *Cold Mountain*. New York: Atlantic Monthly Press, 1997.

Freud, Sigmund. *Civilization and Its Discontent*. New York: Norton, 1961.

————. *Die Traumdeutung*. Leipzig: F. Deuticke, 1900. Translated by A. A. Brill as *The Interpretation of Dreams* (New York: Modern Library, 1950).

Friedman, Thomas L. *The Lexus and the Olive Tree: Understanding Globalism*. New York: Farrar, Straus and Giroux, 2000.

————. *The World Is Flat*. New York: Farrar, Straus and Giroux, 2005.

Genovese, Eugene. *Roll, Jordan, Roll: The World the Slaves Made*. New York: Pantheon, 1974.

Glaser, Barney G., and Anselm L. Strauss, *The Discovery of Grounded Theory*. Chicago: Aldine, 1967.

Goldfield, David. "Recasting Southern History: Racial Reconciliation in a Multicultural Age." In Hönnighausen and others, *Regionalism in the Age of Globalism*, 2:295–312.

Gordon, Dick. "Beginnings and Endings." *The Story*, WUNC-FM Radio, June 20, 2006.

Green, Paul. *The Common Glory: A Symphonic Drama of American History, with Music, Commentary, English Folksong and Dance*. Chapel Hill: University of North Carolina Press, published for the Jamestown Corporation and Virginia Conservation Commission, 1948.

Greene, Herman F. "Ecozoic Ideas for 2002." http://www.ctr4process.org/publications/SeminarPapers/26_1ECOZOIC%20IDEAS%20FOR%202002.pdf.

Greene, Jack P. *Imperatives, Behaviors, and Identities: Essays in Early American Cultural History*. Charlottesville: University Press of Virginia, 1992.

Guillory, Ferrel, and John Quinterno. "A Southern Snapshot." Manuscript, 2005.

————. "Notes to Southern Data." Manuscript, 2006.

Hackney, Sheldon. "After Words with Sheldon Hackney." Interview. By Janet Langhart Cohen. C-SPAN, August 23, 2005.

————. *Magnolias without Moonlight: The American South from Regional Confederacy to National Integration*. New Brunswick, N.J.: Transaction, 2005.

————. "Southern Violence." In *Magnolias without Moonlight*, 1–22.

Hannerz, Ulf. "Scenarios for Peripheral Cultures." In *Culture, Globalization and the World-System: Contemporary Conditions for the Representation of Identity*, edited by Anthony King, 107–28. Binghamton: SUNY Press, 1991.

————. *Transnational Connections: Culture, People, Places*. New York: Routledge, 1996.

Harding, Vincent. "Toward a Darkly Radiant Vision of America's Truth: A Letter of Concern, an Invitation to Re-creation." In *Community in America: The Challenge of Habits of the Heart*, edited by Charles H. Reynolds, 67–84. Berkeley: University of California Press, 1988.

Harvey, David. *Justice, Nature and the Geography of Difference.* Cambridge, Mass.: Blackwell, 1996.

———. *The New Imperialism.* New York: Oxford, 2003.

———. *Spaces of Capital: Towards a Critical Geography.* New York: Routledge, 2001.

Hassett, Miranda K. "Episcopal Dissidents, African Allies: The Anglican Communion and the Globalization of Dissent." PhD diss., Department of Anthropology, University of North Carolina at Chapel Hill, 2004.

———. *Anglican Communion in Crisis: How Episcopal Dissidents and Their African Allies Are Reshaping Anglicanism.* Princeton: Princeton University Press, 2007.

Helms, Jesse. *Here's Where I Stand: A Memoir.* New York: Random House, 2005.

Hernstein, Richard J., and Charles Murray. *The Bell Curve: Intelligence and Class Structure in American Life.* New York: Free Press, 1994.

Hersh, Carie Little. "Negotiating 'Community' in the Global South." Paper presented at "Navigating the Globalization of the American South," a conference held at the University of North Carolina at Chapel Hill, March 3–4, 2005.

Hill, Samuel. *Southern Churches in Crisis.* New York: Holt, Rinehart and Winston, 1967.

Hinson, Glenn. *Fire in My Bones: Transcendence and the Holy Spirit in African American Gospel.* Philadelphia: University of Pennsylvania Press, 2000.

Hoelscher, Steven. "Memory's Region: Race and Place in the American South. In Hönnighausen and others, *Regionalism in the Age of Globalism,* 2:313–24

Holland, Dorothy, Donald Nonini, Catherine Lutz, Leslie Bartlett, Marla Frederick, Thaddeus Guldbrandsen, and Enrique Murillo. *Local Democracy Under Siege: Activisim, Public Interest, and Private Politics.* New York: New York University Press, 2006.

Hönnighausen, Lothar. "The South and the Spirit of 1968: George Garrett's *The King of Babylon Shall Not Come Against You.*" In *Regionalism in the Age of Globalism,* 2:347–54.

Hönnighausen, Lothar, Marc Frey, James Peacock, and Niklaus Steiner. *Regionalism in the Age of Globalism.* Vol. 1. *Concepts of Regionalism.* Madison: Max Kade Institute at the University of Wisconsin–Madison, 2005.

Hönnighausen, Lothar, Anke Ortlepp, James L. Peacock, and Niklaus Steiner. *Regionalism in the Age of Globalism.* Vol. 2. *Forms of Regionalism.* Madison: Center for the Study of Upper Midwestern Cultures, University of Wisconsin, 2005.

Humphreys, Josephine. *Nowhere Else on Earth.* New York: Viking, 2000.

Hunter, Kermit. *Unto These Hills: Drama of the Cherokee Indian*. Cherokee, N.C.: Cherokee Historical Association, 1966.

Huntington, Samuel. *The Clash of Civilizations and the Remaking of the World Order*. New York: Simon and Schuster, 1996.

Irons, Creighton. "Soul Notes." http://www.unc.edu/cirons.

James, William. "A Certain Blindness." *Collected Essays and Reviews*. New York: 1920.

Jeffery, H. B. *The Principles of Healing*. Cambridge, Mass.: Ruth Laighton, 1939.

Jones, Anne Goodwyn, and Susan V. Donaldson, eds. *Haunted Bodies: Gender and Southern Texts*. Charlottesville: University Press of Virginia, 1998.

Joseph, Miranda. *Against the Romance of Community*. Minneapolis: University of Minnesota Press, 2002.

Joyner, Charles. *Down by the Riverside: A South Carolina Slave Community*. Urbana: University of Illinois Press, 1984.

Kennington, Dale. *Contemporary Mythologies*. Montgomery, Ala.: Montgomery Museum of Fine Arts, 2004.

Ketchin, Susan. *The Christ-Haunted Landscape: Faith and Doubt in Southern Fiction*. Jackson: University Press of Mississippi, 1994.

Kilgo, James. *Colors of Africa*. Athens: University of Georgia Press, 2003.

Kirby, Jack. *Media-Made Dixie: The South in the American Imagination*. Athens: University of Georgia Press, 1978.

Knight, Philip. Interview by John Defterios. *In Play*, CNN, May 12, 1998.

Kolchin, Peter. *A Sphinx on the American Land: The Nineteenth-Century South in Comparative Perspective*. Baton Rouge: Louisiana State University Press, 2003.

Korostelina, Karina. "Dynamics of Social Identities." Unpublished manuscript.

———. "Readiness to Fight in Crimea: How It Interrelates with National and Ethnic Identities." In Peacock, Thornton, and Inman, *Identity Matters*, 49–72.

Kuhn, Thomas S. *The Structure of Scientific Revolutions*. 3rd ed. Chicago: University of Chicago Press, 1996.

Lawrence, Bruce. *Defenders of God: The Fundamentalist Revolt against the Modern Age*. San Francisco: Harper and Row, 1990.

———. *New Faiths, Old Fears: Muslims and Other Asian Immigrants in American Religious Life*. New York: Columbia University Press, 2002.

Lee, Harper. *To Kill a Mockingbird*. Philadelphia: Lippincott, 1960.

Lévi-Strauss, Claude. *The Savage Mind*. Chicago: University of Chicago Press, 1966.

Low, Setha M., and Denise Lawrence-Zuniga, eds. *The Anthropology of Space and Place: Locating Culture*. Oxford: Blackwell, 2003.

Lutz, Catherine. *Homefront: A Military City and the American 20th Century.* Boston: Beacon, 2001.

Mailer, Norman. *The Naked and the Dead.* New York: Rinehart, 1948.

Manthorne, Katherine. *The Landscapes of Louis Remy Mignot: Southern Painter Abroad.* With John W. Coffey. Washington, D.C.: Smithsonian Institution Press, 1996.

MDC, Inc. *The State of the South 2004.* Alison Green, Ferrel Guillory, Joan Lipsitz, and Sarah Rubin, researchers. Chapel Hill, N.C.: MDC, Inc., 2004.

Marks, Stuart. *Large Mammals and a Brave People.* New Brunswick, N.J.: Transactions, 2005.

————. *Southern Hunting in Black and White: Nature, History, and a Ritual in the Carolina Community.* Princeton: Princeton University Press, 1991.

Mathews, Jay. "At the Head of the Class." *Newsweek,* May 8, 2006, 54–59.

Mathews, Donald G. *Religion in the Old South.* Chicago: University of Chicago Press, 1977.

Mathewson, Kent. "Plantations and Dependencies: Notes on the 'Moral Geography' of Global Stimulant Production." In *Ethics and Agriculture: An Anthology on Current Issues in World Context,* edited by Charles V. Blatz, 559–67. Moscow: University of Idaho Press, 1991.

Matthews, Carrie. "Fragments of an Anarchist Modernism." PhD diss., Department of English and Comparative Literature, University of North Carolina at Chapel Hill, in preparation.

McCullers, Carson. *The Heart Is a Lonely Hunter.* Boston: Riverside Press, Houghton Mifflin, 1940.

McDermott, Alice. *Charming Billy.* New York: Farrar, Straus, Giroux, 1998.

McDonough, William. *The Hannover Principles: Design for Sustainability,* prepared for EXPO 2000, the World's Fair, Hannover, Germany. Charlottesville, Va.: Island Press, 1997.

McKibben, Bill. "The Christian Paradox: How a Faithful Nation Gets Jesus Wrong." *Harper's Magazine,* August 2005, 31–37.

McKinnie, Meghan P. L. "When Regionalism Meets Language Attitudes: Evidence from Perceptual Dialectology Studies in North America." In Hönnighausen and others, *Regionalism in the Age of Globalism,* 2:145–57.

Moe, Christian H., Scott J. Parker, and George McCalmon. *Creating Historical Drama: A Guide for Communities, Theatre Groups, and Playwrights.* Carbondale: Southern Illinois University Press, 2005.

Moltke-Hansen, David. "Regional Frameworks and Networks: Changing Identities in the Southeastern United States." In *Regional Images and Regional Real-*

ities, edited by Lothar Hönnighausen, 149–70. Tübingen, Germany: Stauffenverg Verlag, 2000.

———. "Southern Genesis: Regional Identity and the Rise of 'the Capital of Southern Civilization,' 1760–1860." PhD diss., University of South Carolina, 2000.

Morris, Brian. *Religion and Anthropology*. New York: Cambridge University Press, 2005.

Morrison, Toni. *Beloved*. New York: Knopf, 1987.

Naimark, Michael. "Alan Lomax's Multimedia Dream," http://www.alan-lomax .com/style_globaljukebox_Naimark.html.

Needham, Rodney. "This Is a Rose. . . ." Chap. 2 in *Against the Tranquility of Axioms*. Berkeley: University of California Press, 1983.

Neff, Ali Colleen. "Home of the Double-Headed Eagle: The Visionary Vernacular Architecture of Reverend H. D. Dennis and Margaret Dennis." Manuscript, 2006.

Neville, Gwen. *Kinship and Pilgrimage: Rituals of Reunion in American Protestant Culture*. New York: Oxford University Press, 1987.

Niezen, Ronald. *A World Beyond Difference: Cultural Identity in the Age of Globalization*. Oxford: Blackwell, 2004.

Norman, Ralph. "A Tale of Two Regions: Frederick Law Olmsted, Tom Wolfe, and Public Space." In Hönnighausen and others, *Regionalism in the Age of Globalism*, 2:325–36.

Nussbaum, Martha C., with respondents. *For Love of Country: Debating the Limits of Patriotism*. Edited by Joshua Cohen. Boston: Beacon Press, 1996.

———. "Patriotism and Cosmopolitanism." In Nussbaum, *For Love of Country*.

O'Brien, Michael. "The Appreciation of the South in Modern Culture." *Southern Cultures* 4, no. 4 (1998): 3–8.

———. *Conjectures of Order: Intellectual Life and the American South, 1810–1860*. 2 vols. Chapel Hill: University of North Carolina Press, 2004.

O'Connor, Flannery. *The Complete Stories*. New York: Farrar, Straus and Giroux, 1971.

———. *A Good Man Is Hard to Find*. New Brunswick: Rutgers University Press, 1993.

———. "Parker's Back." In *The Complete Stories*.

Parramore, Thomas C. "Muslim Slave Aristocrats in North Carolina." *North Carolina Historical Review* 77 (April 2000): 127–50).

Parsons, Talcott, ed. *Theories of Society*. Glencoe, Ill.: Free Press, 1961.

Patterson, Daniel W., and Charles G. Zug III. *Arts in Earnest: North Carolina Folklife*. Durham: Duke University Press, 1998.

Payne, David. *Back to Wando Passo*. New York: Morrow, 2006.

Peacock, James L. "Action Comparativism: Efforts toward a Global and Comparative Yet Local and Active Anthropology." In *By Comparison*, edited by Andre Gingrich and Richard Fox, 44–69. London: Routledge, 2002.

———. "Belief Beheld: Inside and Outside, Insider and Outsider in the Anthropology of Religion." In *Ecology and the Sacred*, edited by Michael Lambek and Ellen Messer, 207–25. Ann Arbor: University of Michigan Press, 2001.

———. "Dreams and Globalization: Far Away and Deep Within." *Forum* 48:2 (Fall 2004).

———. "Ethnographic Notes on Sacred and Profane Performances." In *By Means of Performance*, edited by Richard Schechner and Willa Appel, 208–20. Cambridge: Cambridge University Press, 1990.

———. "Fundamentalisms Narrated: Muslim, Christian, and Mystical." With Tim Pettyjohn. In *Fundamentalisms Comprehended*, edited by Martin Marty and Scott Appleby, 115–34. Chicago: University of Chicago Press, 1995.

———. "Home Is Where the Heartless Aren't: Sense of Place in the Global South." Paper delivered at "Sustaining and Reimagining Community in a Globalizing World," Southern Anthropological Society conference, Chattanooga, Tennessee, March 10–13, 2005

———. "Memory and Violence." *American Anthropologist* 104 (September 2002): 4–7.

———. "Method." Chap. 2 in *The Anthropological Lens: Harsh Light, Soft Focus*. Rev. ed. Cambridge: Cambridge University Press, 2001.

———. *The Muhammadijah Movement in Indonesian Islam*. Palo Alto: Cummings, 1978.

———. *Muslim Puritans*. Berkeley: University of California Press, 1978.

———. "Retrospect and Prospect: Region in Global and Comparative Perspective." In Hönnighausen and others, *Regionalism in the Age of Globalism*, 2:355–69.

———. *Rites of Modernization: Symbolic and Social Aspects of Indonesian Proletarian Drama*. Chicago: University of Chicago Press, 1968.

———. "Secular Ritual and Archaic but Changing Society: Java and the American South." Paper presented at "Secular Rituals Reconsidered," a conference held at Wenner Gren Foundation, Burg Wartenstein, Austria, August 24–September 1, 1974. Published in a shortened version as "Traditionalism and Reform."

————. "The South in a Global World." *Virginia Quarterly Review* 78 (Fall 2002): 581–94.

————. "Space into Place." In *Space 2000*, edited by Lothar Hönighaussen, 88–100. Tubingen, Germany: Staufferverlag, 2002.

————. "Suffering, History, and Life Stories." Paper presented at the Symposium on Narrative, Suffering, and Its Transformations, annual meeting of the American Anthropological Association, New Orleans, November 27–December 2, 1990.

————. "Traditionalism and Reform: Constancy and Climax in Java and the South." In Black and Reed, *Perspectives on the American South*, 207–16.

Peacock, James L., Carla Jones, and Catherine Brooks. "Gotokaca Drive: Global Relations between Souths in Mobile, Alabama." In Peacock, Watson, and Matthews, *The American South in a Global World*, 166–74.

Peacock, James L., Patricia Thornton, and Patrick Inman, eds. *Identity Matters: Ethnic and Sectarian Conflict*. Oxford: Berghahn, 2007.

Peacock, James L., and Ruel W. Tyson Jr. *Pilgrims of Paradox: Calvinism and Experience among the Primitive Baptists of the Blue Ridge*. Washington, D.C.: Smithsonian Institution Press, 1989.

Peacock, James L., Harry L. Watson, and Carrie R. Matthews, eds. *The American South in a Global World*. Chapel Hill: University of North Carolina Press, 2005.

Percy, Walker. *The Last Gentleman*. New York: Farrar, Straus and Giroux, 1966.

————. *The Moviegoer*. New York: Knopf, 1961.

Pettigrew, Thomas. "Social Identity Matters: Predicting Prejudice and Violence in Western Europe." In Peacock, Thornton, and Inman, *Identity Matters*, 34–48.

Poesch, Jessie. *The Art of the Old South: Painting, Sculpture, Architecture and the Products of Craftsmen, 1560–1860*. New York: Knopf, 1983.

Polk, Noel. "Walker Percy's Sense of Place." In Hönnighausen and others, *Regionalism in the Age of Globalism*, 2:337–46.

Preston, Dennis. "Non-standard English." Paper presented at "The South," the fifth annual program of the Illinois Program for Research in the Humanities, University of Illinois, Urbana, April 3–5, 2003.

————. *Perceptual Dialectology: Nonlinguists' Views of Areal Linguistics*. Dordrecht, Holland: Forix Publications, 1989.

Prince, William Meade. *The Southern Part of Heaven*. New York: Rinehart, 1950.

Putnam, Robert. *Bowling Alone*. Washington, D.C.: National Endowment for Democracy, 1995.

Ray, R. Celeste. *Highland Heritage: Scottish Americans in the American South.* Chapel Hill: University of North Carolina Press, 2001.

————. *Southern Heritage on Display: Public Ritual and Ethnic Diversity within Southern Regionalism.* Tuscaloosa: University of Alabama Press, 2003.

Reed, John Shelton. *My Tears Spoiled My Aim, and Other Reflections on Southern Culture.* Columbia: University of Missouri Press, 1993.

Rees, Nicholas. "Regions, European Integration, and the Global Context: Assessing the Role of the European Commission in EU Regional Development." In Hönighaussen and others, *Regionalism in the Age of Globalism*, 2:4–22.

Reid, Anthony, and David Marr, eds. *Perceptions of the Past in Southeast Asia.* Hong Kong: Heinemann, 1979.

Rice, Condoleezza. "Remarks at the Southern Baptist Convention Annual Meeting," Greensboro Coliseum, Greensboro, N.C., June 14, 2006. http://www .state.gov/secretary/rm/2006/67896.htm (accessed 6/29/2006).

Richardson, Miles. *Being in Christ and Putting Death in Its Place: An Anthropologist's Account of Christian Performance in Spanish America and the American South.* Baton Rouge: Louisiana State University Press, 2003.

————., ed. *Culture, Ethnicity, and Justice in the South: The Southern Athropological Society, 1968–1971.* Tuscaloosa: University of Alabama Press, 2005.

Richardson, Riché. *Black Masculinity and the U.S. South: From Uncle Tom to Gangsta.* Athens: University of Georgia Press, 2007.

————. "Blackness and the Global South." Paper presented at "Navigating the Globalization of the American South," a conference held at the University of North Carolina at Chapel Hill, March 3–4, 2005.

————. "Gangstas and Playas in the Dirty South." Chapter 5 in "Black Masculinity and the U.S. South: From Uncle Tom to Gangsta." Manuscript.

————. "Hip-Hop." Paper presented at "Navigating the Global South," a conference held at Chapel Hill, North Carolina, University Center for International Studies, March 2005.

Rister, Carl Coke. "Carlota, A Confederate Colony in Mexico." *Journal of Southern History* 11, no. 1 (1945).

Rittenberg, Sydney, and Amanda Bennet. *The Man Who Stayed Behind.* New York: Simon and Schuster, 1993.

Romine, Scott. *The Narrative Forms of Southern Community.* Baton Rouge: Louisiana State University Press, 1999.

Sassen, Saskia. *The Global City: New York, London, Tokyo.* Princeton: Princeton University Press, 2001.

Schneider, Klaus. "Region and Regionalism in Linguistics: A Brief Survey of Concepts and Methods." In Hönnighausen and others, *Regionalism in the Age of Globalism,* 1:139–58.

Schweiger, Beth, and Donald G. Mathews. *Religion in the American South: Protestants and Others in History and Culture.* Chapel Hill: University of North Carolina Press, 2004.

Senior, Jennifer. "Everything a Happily Married Bible Belt Woman Always Wanted to Know about Sex but Was Afraid to Ask." *New York Times Magazine,* July 4, 2004, 32–37.

Seymour, Robert E. *A Village Voice: Collected Columns from the Chapel Hill News.* Chapel Hill, N.C.: Chapel Hill Press, 2003.

Sherrill, Marcie. "Hit the Road." *Atlanta Homes and Lifestyles,* August 2004.

Shields, David S. *Civil Tongues and Polite Letters in British America.* Chapel Hill: University of North Carolina Press, 1997.

Smith, Dave. *Cuba Night: Poems.* New York: Morrow, 1990.

Smith, Jennie M. "The Latinization of Rome, Georgia: Undergraduate Research and Community Activism." In Peacock, Watson, and Matthews, *The American South in a Global World,* 223–34.

———. *Where the Hands Are Many: Community Organization and Social Change in Rural Haiti.* Ithaca: Cornell University Press, 2001.

Smith, Jon, and Deborah Cohn. *Look Away!* Durham: Duke University Press, 2004.

Smith-Nonini, Sandy. "Federally Sponsored Mexican Migrants in the Transnational South." In Peacock, Watson, and Matthews, *The American South in a Global World,* 59–82.

Solms, Mark. "Freud Returns." *Scientific American,* May 2004, 82–88.

Southern Anthropological Society Proceedings. Athens: University of Georgia Press, 1968–.

Sparks, Alistair. *The Mind of South Africa.* New York: Knopf, 1990.

Spencer, Elizabeth. *The Light in the Piazza.* New York: McGraw-Hill, 1960.

Striffler, Steve. "We're All Mexicans Here: Poultry Processing, Latino Migration, and the Transformation of Class in the South." In Peacock, Watson, and Matthews, *The American South in a Global World,* 152–65.

Subramanian, Ajantha. "North Carolina's Indians: Erasing Race to Make the Citizen." In Peacock, Watson, and Matthews, *The American South in a Global World,* 192–204.

Tate, Allen. "Ode to the Confederate Dead" In *Selected Poems,* 21–25. New York: Charles Scribner's Sons, 1937.

Taylor, Charles. *Modern Social Imaginaries.* Durham: Duke University Press, 2004.

———. "Why Democracy Needs Patriotism." A response to Martha Nussbaum, "Patriotism and Cosmopolitanism." In Nussbaum, *For Love of Country,* 119–21.

Taylor, Peter. "A Long Fourth." In *A Long Fourth and Other Stories,* 130–66. New York: Harcourt, Brace, 1948.

Thigpen, Corbett. *The Three Faces of Eve.* Kingsport, Tenn.: Kingsport Press, 1957.

Thompson, Charles D., Jr. *The Old German Baptist Brethren: Faith, Farming and Change in the Virginia Blue Ridge.* Urbana: University of Illinois Press, 2006.

Twelve Southerners. *I'll Take My Stand: The South and the Agrarian Tradition.* Introduction by Louis D. Rubin Jr. Biographical essays by Virginia Rock. Baton Rouge: Louisiana State University Press, 1977.

Vásquez, Manuel A., and Marie Friedmann Marquardt. *Globalizing the Sacred: Religion across the Americas.* New Brunswick, N.J.: Rutgers University Press, 2003.

Vo, Long. "The Vietnamese Experience in North Carolina." Honors essay, Department of Anthropology, University of North Carolina at Chapel Hill, 2003.

Volkan, Vamik. *Blind Trust: Large Groups and Their Leaders in Times of Crisis and Terror.* Charlottesville, Va.: Pitchstone, 2004.

———. *Blood Lines: From Ethnic Pride to Ethnic Terrorism.* Boulder: Westview Press, 1998.

———. "Large Group Regression and September 11." Lecture delivered at the National Humanities Center, May 13, 2004.

Ward, Joseph P., ed. *Britain and the American South: From Colonialism to Rock and Roll.* Oxford, Miss: University Press of Mississippi, 2003.

Weber, Max. *The Protestant Ethic and the Spirit of Capitalism.* Translated by Talcott Parsons. New York: Scribner, 1930.

Walker, Alice. *Now Is the Time to Open Your Heart.* New York: Random House, 2004.

Weiss, Brad. "Hip Hop in Tanzania." Symposium, Department of Anthropology, University of North Carolina at Chapel Hill, September 2003.

White, O. Kendall, Jr., and Daryl White, eds., *Religion in the Contemporary South.* Athens: University of Georgia Press, 1995.

Whitehead, Clay C. "Neo-Psychoanalysis: A Paradigm for the 21st Century." *Journal of the American Academy of Psychoanalysis and Dynamic Psychiatry.* Forthcoming.

Wilder, Laena. "Seeing Eye to Eye: A Cultural Exchange." Lecture delivered at the University Center for International Studies at the University of North Carolina at Chapel Hill, April 3, 2003.

Willis, Rachel A. "Voices of Southern Mill Workers: Responses to Border Crossers in American Factories and Job Crossing Borders." In Peacock, Watson, and Matthews, *The American South in a Global World*, 138–51.

Wilson, Charles Reagan. *Baptized in Blood: The Religion of the Lost Cause, 1865–1920*. Athens: University of Georgia Press, 1980.

Wilson, Charles Reagan, and William Ferris, eds. *Encyclopedia of Southern Culture*. Chapel Hill: University of North Carolina Press, 1989.

Wolfe, Tom. "The Last American Hero." In *The Kandy-Kolored Tangerine-Flake Streamline Baby*, 121–66. New York: Farrar, Straus, Giroux, 1965.

Woodward, C Vann. *The Burden of Southern History*. New York: Vintage, 1960; rev. ed, Baton Rouge: Louisiana State University Press, 1968.

———. "The Search for Southern Identity." In *The Burden of Southern History*, 3–24. Rev. ed. Baton Rouge: Louisiana State University Press, 1968.

Wright, Charles. *A Short History of the Shadow*. New York: Farrar, Straus, and Giroux, 2002.

Wyatt-Brown, Bertram. *Southern Honor: Ethics and Behavior in the Old South*. New York: Oxford University Press, 1982.

Yaeger, Patricia. *Dirt and Desire: Reconstructing Southern Women's Writing, 1930–1990*. Chicago: University of Chicago Press, 2000.

Yamada, Yutaka. "Like My Husband's Shadow: Patterns of Language and Action in a Southern Church." In *Diversities of Gifts: Field Studies in Southern Religion*, edited by James L. Peacock, Ruel W. Tyson, and Daniel W. Patterson, 177–91. Urbana: University of Illinois Press, 1988.

Zahner-Roloff, Lee. "Dreams in Black and White." In *Modern South Africa in Search of a Soul*, edited by Graham S. Saayman, 19–45. Boston: Sigo, 1990.

Index